A Saddlebag Doctor of the Mahantongo Valley of Pennsylvania

The Life and Practice of Reuben Harris Muth, M.D., 1826–1899

Lawrence K. Knorr, Ph.D.

an imprint of Sunbury Press, Inc.
Mechanicsburg, PA USA

an imprint of Sunbury Press, Inc.
Mechanicsburg, PA USA

For information about special discounts for bulk purchases, please contact Sunbury Press Orders Dept. at (855) 338-8359 or orders@sunburypress.com.

To request one of our authors for speaking engagements or book signings, please contact Sunbury Press Publicity Dept. at publicity@sunburypress.com.

FIRST DISTELFINK PRESS EDITION: May 2025

Set in Adobe Garamond Pro | Interior design by Crystal Devine | Cover by Lawrence Knorr | Edited by Lawrence Knorr.

Publisher's Cataloging-in-Publication Data
Names: Knorr, Lawrence K., author.
Title: A saddlebag doctor of the Mahantongo Valley of Pennsylvania : the life and practice of Reuben Harris Muth, M.D., 1826–1899 / Lawrence K. Knorr, Ph.D.
Description: First trade paperback edition. | Mechanicsburg, PA : Distelfink Press, 2025.
Summary: The life and career of Reuben H. Muth (1826–1899), a medical doctor who graduated from the University of Pennsylvania and served a rural Pennsylvania Dutch community in the Mahantongo Valley, is presented based on an extant set of his daybooks and many other sources.
Identifiers: ISBN : 979-8-88819-314-3 (softcover).
Subjects: HISTORY / United States / State & Local / Middle Atlantic | BUSINESS & ECONOMICS / Economic History | HISTORY / United States / 19th Century | HISTORY / Social History.

Designed in the USA
0 1 1 2 3 5 8 13 21 34 55

For the Love of Books!

Cover: Based on the painting *The Doctor* (1891) by Luke Fildes at the Tate Gallery in London.

Contents

Contents

Acknowledgments

A sincere thank you to Mrs. Knorr for listening to all the "trivial" discoveries unearthed about a rural Pennsylvania Dutch doctor who lived long ago in a valley not so far away.

1

Introduction

As Robert E. Lee's Army of Northern Virginia retreated into Maryland following the Battle of Gettysburg, they engaged with Union forces at Monterey Pass, Pennsylvania, on July 4 and 5, 1863. Meanwhile, over one hundred miles northeast, across the Susquehanna River, near the village of Dornsife, Northumberland County, Pennsylvania,[1] a young wife, Sarah Wynn, was experiencing contractions warning of the pending birth of the baby she had been expecting.[2] Sarah, nee Witmer, was twenty-five and the mother of two surviving young children: Emma, aged five, and William, aged 4.[3] Sadly, Sarah had lost her third child, daughter Mary, soon after her birth in 1861.[4] Thus, the tension and worry in the household between her and her twenty-nine-year-old husband, Jacob Wynn, must have been heightened. Jacob, a laborer,[5] had just been drafted a few weeks earlier[6] and was likely waiting to report to duty pending the birth of this child. The couple were at Jacob's parents' farm,[7] perhaps seeking a

---

1. Griffith Morgan Hopkins Jr, J. A. J Cummings, and Kimber Cleaver. *Map of Northumberland County, Pennsylvania*: from actual surveys by G.M. Hopkins, Jr., Civil Engineer. Chillisquaque, PA: J.A.J. Cummings, 1858. Map, accessed January 5, 2025, https://www.loc.gov/item/2006629792/.

2. Reuben H. Muth, *Physician's Daybooks*, vol. 5, entry for July 6, 1863 (1858–1898, in possession of Lawrence Knorr, Mechanicsburg, Pennsylvania).

3. "Jacob Samuel Wynn," *Family Search*, Record ID KLXF-D1B, accessed January 5, 2025, https://ancestors.familysearch.org/en/KLXF-D1B/jacob-samuel-wynn-1834-1911.

4. Ibid.

5. National Archives and Records Administration (NARA); Washington, D.C.; *Consolidated Lists of Civil War Draft Registration Records* (Provost Marshal General's Bureau; Consolidated Enrollment Lists, 1863–1865); Record Group: 110, Records of the Provost Marshal General's Bureau (Civil War); Collection Name: Consolidated Enrollment Lists, 1863–1865 (Civil War Union Draft Records); NAI: 4213514; Archive Volume Number: 2 of 7.

6. Ibid.

7. "Charles Clinton Wynn," *Family Search*, Record ID LHFV-GD8, accessed January 5, 2025, https://ancestors.familysearch.org/en/LHFV-GD8/charles-clinton-wynn-1863-1945.

safer location than their home further south in the Lykens Valley, closer to Harrisburg. The recent emergency had chased many of the citizens from their homes to more secure regions. It appears the Wynns, with the children, headed to the grandparents to weather whatever may come. It is for this reason that Dr. Reuben Harris Muth was summoned from his home in nearby Mahanoy (now Red Cross), nine miles to the south.

July 6, 1863, was a Monday. That morning, Dr. Muth saddled his horse and headed north to the Wynn farm. It was early summer, and the wooded hills he traversed were surely lush with green as he traveled along the Mahanoy Creek, heading upstream. Perhaps cicadas buzzed in the trees, and a light mist rose from the nearby brook as his horse cantered along the single-lane dirt road. Thoughts of the news of the recent battle and Union victory likely entered his mind. At age thirty-seven, while he had not volunteered to disrupt his family life and service to the community to join in the conflict, he had been drafted at the same time as Jacob Wynn.[8] It is quite possible the two met as they registered in the same book before the same provost marshal.

Dr. Muth had not seen any patients the prior week, his ledger being blank.[9] Perhaps he had headed south to assist with one of the field hospitals. Or, perhaps, he had taken his pregnant wife away for a few days. Now, he was back in practice, and Sarah Wynn would be his first stop of the day.[10] Perhaps he was contemplating the pending birth of a newborn so soon after the thousands of dead to the south. He likely also knew his assistance was being requested because the birth may be difficult. Usually, these things were handled by midwives,[11] and certainly Sarah's mother-in-law, Rachel Wynn, aged 58,[12] had plenty of experience. However, Dr. Muth had assisted Sarah with a birth nearly two years prior,[13] and that child had apparently not survived.

8. National Archives and Records Administration (NARA); Washington, D.C.; *Consolidated Lists of Civil War Draft Registration Records* (Provost Marshal General's Bureau; Consolidated Enrollment Lists, 1863–1865); Record Group: 110, Records of the Provost Marshal General's Bureau (Civil War); Collection Name: Consolidated Enrollment Lists, 1863–1865 (Civil War Union Draft Records); NAI: 4213514; Archive Volume Number: 3 of 7.

9. Reuben H. Muth, *Physician's Daybooks*, vol. 5, entries for June 28 through July 4, 1863 (1858–1898, in possession of Lawrence Knorr, Mechanicsburg, Pennsylvania.

10. Ibid.

11. Emily Adams Korff, "The Widow Was a Midwife," *The Historical Review of Berks County* 92, no. 1 (Winter 2025): 8–11.

12. "Rachel Elizabeth Shipman," *Family Search*, Record ID KDMQ-W5D, accessed January 5, 2025, https://ancestors.familysearch.org/en/KDMQ-W5D/rachel-elizabeth-shipman-1805-1890.

13. Reuben H. Muth, *Physician's Daybooks*, vol. 3, entry for October 12, 1861 (1858–1898, in possession of Lawrence Knorr, Mechanicsburg, Pennsylvania).

Figure 1. Jacob and Sarah Wynn later in life.

As Dr. Muth continued his estimated ninety-minute ride to the Wynn farm, he may have passed other families returning in their wagons from points north and east. Certainly, there was a sense of relief throughout the valley as he stopped at the Wynn home, grabbed his bag, and entered. Fortunately, there was good news this day, as Sarah gave birth to baby Charles Clinton Wynn, born July 6, 1863.[14] Jacob Wynn paid the doctor that day a fee of two dollars.[15] At some point, perhaps after returning to his horse, Dr. Muth retrieved his daybook from his coat pocket and the fountain pen from its case and made an entry, noting the obstetric visit and the fact it was paid. Besides this "O" in his log, there was only one other entry for the week, several check-ins on the home of Emanuel Stempel.[16] The following week would be much busier.[17] But his

14. "Charles Clinton Wynn," *Family Search*, Record ID LHFV-GD8, accessed January 5, 2025, https://ancestors.familysearch.org/en/LHFV-GD8/charles-clinton-wynn-1863-1945.

15. Reuben H. Muth, *Physician's Daybooks*, vol. 5, entries for July 6, 1863 (1858–1898, in possession of Lawrence Knorr, Mechanicsburg, Pennsylvania).

16. Ibid.

17. Ibid.

total income for the week following the Gettysburg emergency was five dollars (approximately $122 in current money).[18]

Much has been written in recent times about the cost of healthcare and its explosive growth, often outpacing the rate of inflation.[19] However, little is known about the cost of healthcare in the nineteenth century, especially in rural areas.[20] Granted, the science and related services delivered to patients have changed incredibly over the years and have been the focus of nearly all medical historians. But what about the business side of the equation? What did it cost to see a doctor who was traveling around the countryside on his horse, bag with instruments behind his saddle? How many patients did the doctor see in a day? How far could he range? How much money did his practice generate? How did his income compare to other professions and his peers? How much did rural patients spend on healthcare as a proportion of their incomes? These questions and many others remain largely unanswered in the literature.[21] The reason for this opacity is that the data required to provide the answers to these questions is locked away in the daybooks and ledgers of the practitioners, the vast majority lost or discarded over the years.

Additionally, transcribing the daybooks and journals that remain is a time-consuming exercise. Researchers focused on the history and development of therapies, and procedures were less interested in this data as it was mostly economic and financial. Thus, an economic study of a 19th-century doctor's career is unprecedented due to the lack of primary sources, the difficulty of transcribing, and the cross-discipline nature of the analysis.

It is likely a country doctor was not building a massive fortune like the entrepreneurs of the Gilded Age but rather subsisting as a middle-class member of society. It is also likely he had to rely on other endeavors to cover his expenses, especially if he had a large family. As for the patients, there were not many procedures, devices, or advanced medicines in the 1800s, so the cost of healthcare per patient was probably much lower

18. Ian Webster, "CPI Inflation Calculator," accessed January 5, 2025, https://www.in2013dollars.com/us/inflation/1863?amount=1.

19. Diane Alexander, "The Recent Rise in Health Care Inflation." *Chicago Fed Letter*, no. 407, 2018, accessed January 5, 2025, https://www.chicagofed.org/publications/chicago-fed-letter/2018/407.

20. Paul Starr, "Medicine, Economy and Society in Nineteenth-Century America." *Journal of Social History* 10, no. 4 (Jun 01, 1977): 588.

21. Ibid.

in proportion to other expenses, especially in rural areas. Likewise, the utilization of health services was probably less than in modern times. And, in the Pennsylvania Dutch community, especially in rural areas, there was superstition, self-reliance, and a general mistrust of outsiders.[22] Could a formally trained physician's practice thrive in a community of uneducated farmers and artisans? Certainly, the more successful doctor among them would be the one who could speak the local Pennsylvania Dutch dialect and appreciate the culture of his neighbors.

Fortunately, there is a previously unknown primary source that can be used to discern some of these answers. Reuben Harris Muth, M.D., who lived from 1826 until 1899,[23] was born into a Pennsylvania Dutch community in rural Berks County, Pennsylvania. Muth, educated at Marshall College and the University of Pennsylvania's medical school, was a prominent physician and church member in rural Mahanoy, Northumberland County, Pennsylvania, during the latter half of the nineteenth century. These important primary sources were acquired at auction, including a box of thirty-four traveling physician's daybooks[24] and additional papers and ephemera[25] comprising a fascinating time capsule of the rural Pennsylvania Dutch community in which Muth worked as well as the daily practice of a country doctor during the Victorian era.

The daybooks and ledgers were key to this research. They are a time capsule into the personal care of patients during the antebellum and postbellum periods in rural Pennsylvania. Muth's thirty-four pocket-sized leather-bound volumes contained records for forty-one years of service. Each page contained one week's worth of visits. Depending on the publisher, there were one or two pages per week available for notations. The books were pre-printed with the dates, Sunday through Saturday. Typically, there were twenty-five rows per page, representing the likely limit for patient visits in a given week. Dr. Muth typically marked only the fee charged and rarely made notes about a specific procedure, the exceptions being the setting of broken bones and childbirths. He then tallied the

22. Richard M. Dorson, *Buying the Wind: Regional Folklore in the United States* (Chicago: University of Chicago Press, 1964), 118.

23. Reuben H. Muth tombstone, 1899. Inscription carving. Saint Peters Lutheran Church Cemetery, Red Cross, Pennsylvania. Viewed July 22, 2020.

24. Reuben H. Muth, *Physician's Daybooks*, 34 volumes (1858–1898, in possession of Lawrence Knorr, Mechanicsburg, Pennsylvania).

25. Reuben H. Muth, and Henry L. Muth, papers and records (1876–1924, in possession of Lawrence Knorr, Mechanicsburg, Pennsylvania).

amounts charged for the week for one or more visits per patient. The day-books form the backbone of Dr. Muth's daily activities, including who he saw, when he saw them, in what order, and how much he charged. These records were then transcribed into computer spreadsheets and tabulated chronologically and by household. Cross-referencing other sources such as cemetery records, mortality records, local newspapers, maps, census records, and other ephemera was necessary to highlight several of his patients and to derive economic comparisons.

A tallying of the logbooks summed by year and month the patients seen and the total amounts charged. Accumulating this by year provided an annual view of the fees charged by this rural doctor. Did they increase, decrease, or remain stable? Did his practice increase, reach a peak, or decline? Did it appear he was limited by his ability to see patients, considering he had no partners or assistance? How did a rural doctor's income compare to national norms of the time? How did it compare, adjusted for inflation, to the cost of care in the present?

Another angle was to review the census records for Dr. Muth versus his income. Did his estate valuation align with his income? According to the 1870 census, Dr. Muth had a personal estate valued at one thousand dollars and real estate valued at two thousand dollars.[26] Compared to his immediate neighbors, he appears to be in the middle.

Likewise, some of the ephemera hinted at other economic activities for Dr. Muth. For instance, he also appeared to have raised livestock. This made sense from a veterinary perspective. Was it possible he treated animals in addition to human patients?

Dr. Muth likely traveled about the countryside first on horseback and then in a carriage, bringing his bag and instruments with him. From the logbooks, the household names were aligned with period maps of the area and census records to plot the travels of the physician each day and to discern the relative proximity of patients. What was the daily range of the traveling doctor? Did he travel through different areas on certain days of the week? Did he always return home at night? Roughly, how many miles did he travel in a day, week, month, or year? Was there a time when he saw patients at his home or office in Mahanoy? How many other doctors also served this region?

26. US Census Bureau. 1870 United States Federal Census. Census Place: Jackson, Northumberland, Pennsylvania; Roll: M593_1384; 202A.

Cross-referencing primary records from different sources provided a more concise and richer view of the patients Dr. Muth served. For example, in 1858, from August 15 to 21, Dr. Muth saw Mary Petre four times for a total of $4.00.[27] Was this a maternity visit or perhaps dealing with the end of a life?

That same week, he saw Isaac Bordner five times for a charge of $5.50.[28] Was Isaac dealing with a serious health issue? He also saw Joseph Kreider once for fifteen cents.[29] All three of these people were seen while Muth lived in the Fredericksburg, Lebanon County, area. Local records were aligned with Muth's to determine possible outcomes.

Another example was from January 1 to 7, 1893. Dr. Muth saw John Bahner every day that week.[30] A John Bahner was buried in Snydertown, Northumberland County, Pennsylvania. His tombstone stated he lived from 1826 to 1914.[31] Was this Dr. Muth's patient?

Likewise, that same week, he saw Elias Kobel's wife daily.[32] Elias Kobel (1865–1958) was buried in Mahanoy, the town in which Muth lived. Elias's wife was named Sarah.[33] They lost an infant, according to cemetery records, in 1894.[34] Was this the same situation?

There was so much potential to cross-reference various mortality records and news accounts. A narrative was constructed of several families over the history of his career. But this was not without its difficulties. While the patient logs were a very detailed resource, they did not contain information about specific diagnoses or treatments. We also did not always know which household member was being seen. We knew the doctor called or the patient came to see the doctor.

Likewise, aligning specific people to these records was challenging. There were often many people with the same name, even in a finite region of a few miles. Families tended to reuse names from one generation to

27. Reuben H. Muth, *Physician's Daybooks*, vol. 1, entries for August 15 to 21, 1858 (1858–1898, in possession of Lawrence Knorr, Mechanicsburg, Pennsylvania).

28. Ibid.

29. Ibid.

30. Ibid., vol. 29, entries for January 1 to 7, 1893.

31. "John Bahner," *Find a Grave*, Memorial ID 51082257, accessed January 5, 2025, January 5, 2025, https://www.findagrave.com/memorial/51082257/john-banher.

32. Reuben H. Muth, *Physician's Daybooks*, vol. 29, entries for January 1 to 7, 1893 (1858–1898, in possession of Lawrence Knorr, Mechanicsburg, Pennsylvania).

33. "Elias K Kobel," *Find a Grave*, Memorial ID 38975635, accessed January 5, 2025, https://www.findagrave.com/memorial/38975635/elias-k-kobel.

34. Ibid.

the next. Thus, the alignment of a specific mortality record, tombstone, or newspaper article was based on probabilities derived from numerous factors.

Regardless, this was a very useful resource for data about doctor/patient interactions in the mid to late nineteenth century. By connecting this extensive primary source with other available sources, previously hidden details about this doctor's practice and the patients he served were assembled forensically, providing a view into the history of this Pennsylvania Dutch community.

The study of the life, medical practice, and the surrounding community of Reuben Harris Muth, M.D. was, at first, a biographical effort. This was essential in fleshing out the primary actor in this medical practice and understanding the context of his career and the time in which he lived.

There has been a shift in more recent decades to focus less on the biographies of great men and more on persons of the middle and lower classes. Long gone are the days of Thomas Carlyle and his impression that "The history of the world is but the biography of great men."[35] One famous oft-cited book in this regard is Alfred F. Young's *The Shoemaker and the Tea Party* (1999). Young (1925–2012), who earned his Ph.D. at Northwestern University in 1948, was a social historian of the American Revolution. He wrote about the exploits of a commoner in Boston, George Robert Twelves Hughes, who participated in the Boston Tea Party and as a militiaman during the war. Rather than writing about more famous revolutionaries such as Joseph Warren, Samuel Adams, John Hancock, Paul Revere, and other Bostonian leaders, Young focused on the participation in historic events of this mere shoemaker, not "discovered" until he was in his nineties at the time of the fiftieth anniversary of our nation.

Of course, this study was not about the Revolutionary War but about a middle-class doctor who practiced during the mid to late 1800s. There are biographies of many great men of medicine, a few of whom lived in Pennsylvania. Benjamin Rush of Philadelphia certainly comes to mind from an earlier period. Stephen Fried, who has been a journalism professor in the Ivy League, wrote a biography about Rush that delves into his

---

35. Thomas Carlyle, "The Hero is Divinity" in *On Heroes, Hero-Worship, & the Heroic in History* (London: James Fraser, 1841).

accomplishments with mental illness, in addition to being a Founding Father.[36] Likewise, James E. Gibson's book about Dr. Bodo Otto (1937) of Berks County was about a doctor from the American Revolution who practiced in the same county in which Dr. Muth was later born. Gibson (1875–1953) was an amateur historian who was a graduate of the Wharton School of Finance at the University of Pennsylvania. He wrote about his wife's ancestor (Otto) and other early Pennsylvania physicians. He was a member of the Pennsylvania Historical Society. This book is typical of many biographies or histories of local interest, focused on a family connection. Gibson does not focus on the community of Otto's day-to-day practice. Rather, he focuses on the great accomplishments of Otto and his interactions with the Revolutionary leadership, typical of the romantic period of history.[37] Another Revolutionary-era doctor was General Edward Hand from Lancaster, Pennsylvania. Michel Williams Craig, a descendant of Hand, also wrote about his ancestor's accomplishments, barely covering his medical contributions despite the subtitle *Winter's Doctor*.[38] Craig focused more on Hand's military movements and assignments. Perhaps the most widely read book of biographies about early doctors was James Thomas Flexner's *Doctors on Horseback*, first published in 1937.[39] Though the title hinted at a broader scope of coverage, again, the physicians are the famous ones, mostly from one or two generations before Dr. Muth.

Switching to an overall perspective of the history of medicine, William Frederick Norwood was an early scholar in this field in the United States. He received his Ph.D. from the Universit of Southern California and spent many years at the Loma Linda School of Medicine.[40] Norwood focused on the history of medical institutions, especially the development of medical education before the Civil War.[41]

---

36. Stephen Fried, *Rush* (New York, N.Y.: Crown, 2018).

37. James E. Gibson, *Dr. Bodo Otto and the Medical Background of the American Revolution* (Springfield, Ill.: C.C. Thomas, 1937).

38. Michel Williams Craig, *General Edward Hand: Winter's Doctor* (Lancaster, PA: Rock Ford Foundation, 1984).

39. James Thomas Flexner, *Doctors on Horseback: Pioneers of American Medicine* (New York, N.Y.: Dover, 1937).

40. "Dr. Norwood Fills Loma Linda School of Medicine Post," *The San Bernardino County Sun*, October 6, 1961, 16.

41. William Frederick Norwood, *Medical Education in the United States Before the Civil War* (Philadelphia, PA: University of Pennsylvania Press, 1944).

Richard Harrison Shyrock (1893–1972) was a professor of medical history at Johns Hopkins School of Medicine for many years.[42] A veteran of World War I, Shyrock earned his Ph.D. in American History at The University of Pennsylvania and was a member of the American Philosophical Society.[43] Shyrock wrote about the transformation of medicine and medical technology and training in the years before it was formalized.[44]

Nearly mirroring Shyrock's work, Joseph Francis Kett also wrote about the rise of the medical profession prior to the Civil War.[45] Kett taught American Intellectual & Cultural History at the University of Virginia for 47 years.[46] He earned his Ph.D. from Harvard University and focused on the cultural impacts of institutions. All three scholars, Norwood, Shyrock, and Kett, noted the rise of the University of Pennsylvania as the first medical school in the United States based on European science, admitting its role in advancing the profession during its formative years.

A more recent work of physician biography related to institutions was by historian Irwin Richman (b. 1937), who is presently Professor Emeritus of American Studies and History at Penn State's School of Humanities. Richman wrote *The Brightest Ornament: A Biography of Nathaniel Chapman, M.D.* (1967). His subject, Dr. Chapman, was well-connected in Philadelphia and founded the American Medical Association in 1847. Chapman lived two generations before Dr. Muth, and his career was ending as Muth's was beginning. However, they both had connections to the University of Pennsylvania's School of Medicine. Richman's work is more scholarly than Gibson's work but focuses on the impactful accomplishments and famous connections of the subject.[47]

Notably, all three biographies of Pennsylvania physicians mentioned previously, Rush, Otto, and Chapman, dealt with physicians living in urban areas. Medical historian Jan Gregoire Coombs (b. 1933) was

42. Owsei Temkin, "Richard Harrison Shyrock: 1893–1972," *Journal of the History of Medicine and Allied Sciences* 27, no. 2 (1972): 131–32.

43. Ibid.

44. Richard Harrison Shyrock, *Medicine and Society in America, 1660–1860* (New York, N.Y.: New York University Press, 1960).

45. Joseph F. Kett, *The Formation of the American Medical Profession: The Role of Institutions, 1780–1860* (New Haven, Ct.: Yale University Press, 1968).

46. Richard Gard, "In Memoriam: Joseph Francis Kett," *Virginia* 113, 23 (Summer 2024): 68.

47. Irwin Richman, *The Brightest Ornament: A Biography of Nathaniel Chapman, M.D.* (Bellefonte, PA: Pennsylvania Heritage, 1967).

educated at the University of Rochester School of Nursing and a member
of the Wisconsin Historical Society. In her 1990 journal article in the
Bulletin of the History of Medicine, Coombs expounded on the realization
that most of the medical writings about the 19th century deal with the
elite doctors in urban centers and ignore the vast number of rural physicians, noting "two-thirds of all Americans lived in rural areas, farms, or in
communities of less than 4,000 residents."[48] Coombs sought to quantify
how many doctors were practicing in rural Wisconsin, finding that local
histories could only account for roughly ten percent of them.[49] She had
to dig into advertisements, newspapers, census, and mortality records to
identify the entire population to determine the ratio of the number of
residents to physicians. She also noted the lack of journals or daybooks
for most of these physicians, assuming they had not been saved.[50] Her
methods bridged from biography to sociology and ethnography.

Based on Coombs's observations about rural doctors in Wisconsin
during the latter period of Dr. Muth's career in Pennsylvania, it would
indicate a complete set of doctor's daybooks from the career of a rural
physician would be of great value to historians. Likewise, there is currently little research available about the lives and careers of rural physicians of the Pennsylvania Dutch country where Muth practiced, or for
any region, for that matter.

Barnes Riznik, for a time, was a researcher at the Old Sturbridge
Museum in Massachusetts after earning his Ph.D. in History from Stan-
ford and teaching at Stanislaus College in Turlock, California.[51] Among
his many writings was an article about New England doctors in the
nineteenth century that appeared in the *Journal of the History of Medicine
and Allied Sciences* in 1964.[52] While Riznik was anchored in rural New
England, hundreds of miles from Dr. Muth, Riznik wrote about many
issues and problems that Muth likely faced. At the root of Riznik's analysis were the daybooks and account books of the doctors. Though not a
detailed dive into a single physician's career, Riznik's methods and general

48. Jan Coombs, "Rural Medical Practice in the 1880s: A View from Central Wisconsin," *Bulletin of the History of Medicine* 64, no. 1 (1990): 35–62.
49. Ibid.
50. Ibid.
51. "Riznik Resigns At SSC, Takes Post At Museum," *Turlock Journal,* July 9, 1962, 2.
52. Barnes Riznik, "The Professional Lives of Early Nineteenth-Century New England Doctors." *Journal of the History of Medicine and Allied Sciences* 19, no. 1 (January 1964): 1–16.

observations about physicians' performance and motivations were very useful.

Steven M. Stowe's interest is in the history of the antebellum South and not the area considered in this study. However, some of his methods and findings were very useful, regardless. Stowe (b. 1946) earned his Ph.D. in history from the State University of New York at Stony Brook (1979). He is currently an Emeritus Professor in the Department of History at Indiana University-Bloomington. One aspect he has researched extensively is concerning rural physicians in southern communities in his 2004 book *Doctoring the South*.[53] Stowe utilized census records to determine the number of persons claiming to be physicians and then detailed their practices via daybooks, diaries, and other contemporary sources. Stowe's focus concerned the medicines and therapies utilized and the outcomes of the patients. In other words, this is more so a scientific history rather than an economic or business history.

Jacalyn Mary Duffin's work shares more similarities with this study. Duffin is currently a Professor Emerita at Queen's University (Canada) and the former Hannah Chair of the History of Medicine. She earned her M.D. from the University of Toronto (1974) and Ph.D. in the History and Philosophy of Science from the Sorbonne (Paris). She published *Langstaff: A 19th-Century Medical Life* (1993) based on the forty years of daybooks[54] of one physician, James Miles Langstaff (1825–1889), who was a rural physician in Ontario contemporary to Dr. Muth. Duffin also utilized doctor's daybooks in her 1997 article in the journal *Continuity and Change*.[55] She corroborated government census records from Canada to daybooks containing doctor-patient interactions to understand patient mortality better. Duffin was able to use this near-complete set of daybooks to compile the number of patients seen and the outcomes recorded therein. While her analysis was quantitative regarding the causes of death and the ages of the patients, she did not focus on economic data. Again, it seems medical historians are most interested in the history of the use of medicines and therapies, bypassing the cost of medical care and doctors'

53. Steven M. Stowe, *Doctoring the South: Southern Physicians and Everyday Medicine in the Mid-Nineteenth Century* (Chapel Hill: The University of North Carolina Press, 2004).

54. Jacalyn Duffin, *Langstaff: A Nineteenth-Century Medical Life* (Toronto: University of Toronto Press, 1993).

55. Jacalyn Duffin, "Census versus Medical Daybooks: a Comparison of Two Sources on Mortality in Nineteenth-Century Ontario," *Continuity and Change* 12, no. 2 (1997): 199–219.

incomes. However, while not of a Pennsylvania Dutch community, the methods used in this work guided the study of Dr. Muth's daybooks.

Another scholar who utilized doctor's daybooks was Anú King Dudley (b. 1948). He earned his Ph.D. in history from the University of Maine (2007). Dudley has researched and written about medical history topics, focused on the use or performance of specific medicines or therapies. King's 2010 article in the *Journal of the History of Medicine and Allied Sciences* mentions the use of doctors' daybooks in pursuit of the proliferation of Eastern medicine in Antebellum times.[56] Of course, the daybooks useful for this purpose contained notes about medicines and therapies.

Regarding doctor's daybooks and their potential research value, Jonathan S. Jones, who recently earned his Ph.D. in history at Binghamton University and specializes in the history of medicine during the Civil War period, wrote in a 2017 blog article for The Historical Medical Library of The College of Physicians of Philadelphia about this topic.[57] Jones was seeking data on opiate use during the Civil War era and found useful quantitative data in the doctor's daybooks and ledgers. He also noted that while not perfect, these underutilized sources are "without parallel in narrative sources."[58] Jones has two books currently under contract with the University of North Carolina Press, including *Opium Slavery: The Civil War, Veterans, and America's First Opioid Crisis* and *A Great American Fraud: The Civil War and the Development of Medical Capitalism, 1861–1914*. Jones appears to use economic and business history methods in his work, combining economic data with historical narratives.

Given the more recent interest in the business and economics of medicine of the 19th century and the lack of treatment or therapy notations in Dr. Muth's journals, a more quantitative business-focused research approach was necessary for this study. The research questions shifted from the how and what of medical care to the who, how much,

---

56. Anú King Dudley, "Moxa in Nineteenth-century Medical Practice," *Journal of the History of Medicine and Allied Sciences* 65, no. 2 (2010): 187–206. muse.jhu.edu/article/379270.

57. Jonathan S. Jones, "What Can (and Can't) We Learn From 19th Century Physicians' Account Books?" *Fugitive Leaves: a blog from The Historical Medical Library of The College of Physicians of Philadelphia*, accessed December 30, 2024, https://histmed.collegeofphysicians.org/19th-century-physicians-account-books/.

58. Ibid.

and when questions. In other words, who were the patients, when and how often they were seen, and how much were they charged? From this, the doctor's income was also derived and compared to others.

Paul Starr (b. 1949) is best known for his book *The Social Transformation of American Medicine* (1983). Starr earned his Ph.D. in sociology from Harvard (1979). He is a professor of sociology and public affairs at Princeton University. In an article in the *Journal of Social History* (1977), he wrote, "The economic history of medicine, especially before the twentieth century, remains almost entirely to be written."[59] He attributed this to a lack of cross-sectional interest between medical historians and economics historians. Starr recounted the cost of attending medical school and the gradual movement to standardized fees among doctors.

Todd L. Savitt also specializes in medical history. He earned his Ph.D. from the University of Virginia (1975). He is especially interested in nineteenth-century medicine in the South and West, especially with slave populations. He contributed to an exhibit at the University of Virginia titled "Physician Price Fixing in 19th Century Virginia."[60] The scheme discussed in the exhibit was conceived in 1848 and includes numerous images of period ephemera and documents, including a pricelist of doctor fees. While these might not align exactly with the fees recorded by Dr. Muth, the relative differences between charges, especially for visitations versus procedures, were very helpful. Other ephemera that were more local to Dr. Muth were analyzed to understand better the amounts recorded in his daybooks.

Lastly, any study of medicine in the United States of America would likely draw upon the work of the late William G. Rothstein (1937–2020), a Professor of Sociology who taught for many years at the University of Maryland, Baltimore County.[61] Rothstein earned his Ph.D. in Sociology from Cornell University in 1965. His book *American Physicians in the Nineteenth Century* provided a high-level framework for the history of medical practice and medical societies prior to the twentieth century.[62]

59. Paul Starr, "Medicine, Economy and Society in Nineteenth-Century America." *Journal of Social History* 10, no. 4 (Jun 01, 1977): 588.

60. Todd L. Savitt, "Physician Price Fixing in 19th Century Virginia," exhibit at The Claude Moore Health Sciences Library, University of Virginia, accessed December 30, 2024, http://blog.hsl.virginia.edu/feebill/credits/.

61. "Rothstein, William 'Bill' G.," *Baltimore Sun*, December 8, 2020, A8.

62. William G. Rothstein, *American Physicians in the Nineteenth Century* (Baltimore, MD: Johns Hopkins University Press, 1972).

His follow-up, *American Medical Schools and the Practice of Medicine*, detailed the development of medical schools in America and the transition of the profession from reliance on apprenticeships to formalized instruction at institutions of higher learning.[63]

In summary, there was agreement that doctor daybooks were excellent resources for quantitative data. While some researchers used them to discern the frequency or effectiveness of medicines and treatments, little has been done to analyze the economics of physician care during this period. Thus, this study of Dr. Muth's extant daybooks was similar to the work by Jaclyn Duffin but more quantitative, similar to the recent work of Joseph Jones or the earlier work of Jan Coombs. Paul Starr noted in 1977 about the lack of economic history of medicine. This has not changed much in the intervening years and is thus still fertile ground for research. However, the methods used by others provided models for forensically constructing and evaluating the business career of our rural physician. Claire Prechtel-Kluskens suggested a framework for such research in her 2004 article in the National Archives' journal *Prologue Magazine*.[64] An archivist in the Research Support Branch of the National Archives, Prechtel-Kluskens posited that a biography of an otherwise unknown physician could be crafted "from federal records, local government records, newspaper articles, and other sources."

Following this introduction is an overview of the life of Dr. Reuben Harris Muth from the time of his birth near Rehrersburg, Berks County, Pennsylvania, until he died in Mahanoy (now Red Cross), Northumberland County, Pennsylvania. Included are details of his family life; his affiliation with the Lutheran Church; his training in medical school at the University of Pennsylvania; his first marriage and first practice in Fredericksburg, Lebanon County, Pennsylvania; and his subsequent move to Northumberland County, second marriage, and his second practice in the greater Mahanoy area. This first topic is about critical aspects of Muth's life that can be discerned from primary and secondary sources, some of which were in the researcher's possession or were available at local historical societies, church records, or online resources. Fortunately,

63. William G. Rothstein, *American Medical Schools and the Practice of Medicine: A History* (New York: Oxford University Press, 1987).

64. Clair Prechtel-Kluskens, "Researching the Career of a 19th-Century Physician." *Prologue Magazine* 36, no. 2 (Summer 2004). Accessed online at: https://www.archives.gov/publications/prologue/2004/summer/genea-doctor.html.

Dr. Muth was not invisible to us, having appeared in several historical references. After he completed his medical training, Dr. Muth settled first in Fredericksburg, Lebanon County, also known as Old Stumpstown. A book about the area referred to his appearance and manner, "He was a small man and wore a red beard, closely cropped. His quiet and unassuming manners and his lack of aggressiveness prevented him from getting more than a limited amount of business at Fredericksburg."[65] After his wife passed away from consumption, he remarried and moved to Northumberland County.

Regarding his genealogy, the baptism record for Muth confirmed his lineage and birth location as well as his religious denomination. Maps from the period provided the geographic locations of the family as they moved over the years. Census records provided corroboration of the family members and their locations. Tombstones of the family confirmed vital information and language use (from the inscriptions).

The third chapter covers the communities in which Muth grew up and then practiced and their suspicion of outsiders. He was of deep Pennsylvania Dutch roots and lived and worked among the Pennsylvania Dutch in several counties. While the Anabaptist "plain people" of Lancaster County are modern-day tourist attractions, the Pennsylvania Dutch of Muth's experiences were dominated by the "fancy" culture of the Lutheran and Reformed.[66] These people interacted more with outsiders but continued to speak their Pennsylvania Dutch dialect among themselves. The collection of physician's daybooks and ephemera provided examples of the subject's language skills and clues concerning the ethnic makeup of his patients. Secondary sources such as books and journal articles were used to tie in aspects of the Pennsylvania Dutch culture regarding resistance to language assimilation throughout their history, the role of doctors in society, and details concerning immigrant assimilation in other cultures.

How can we be sure Dr. Muth was of Pennsylvania Dutch roots? Despite most of the surnames of his clients being of Germanic origin, Muth's journals are all written in English, showing that professionally,

65. Ezra Grumbine. *Stories of Old Stumpstown: A History of Interesting Events, Traditions, and Anecdotes of Early Fredericksburg Known for Many Years as Stumpstown* (Lebanon, PA: Lebanon County Historical Society, 1910), 229–230.

66. Walter E. Boyer, Albert F. Buffington, and Don Yoder, *Songs Along the Mahantongo: Pennsylvania Dutch Folksongs* (Hatboro, PA: Folklore Associates, 1951).

at least, he used the English language for his records. However, Muth left several clues hinting at his Pennsylvania-Dutch ties. His 1861 journal includes a newspaper clipping announcing his marriage to Louisa Deppen. It also lists him as being from Rehrersburg. The clipping is in German and likely from a local German-language newspaper.[67] His 1862 journal contains his name inscribed in Germanic script on a piece of newspaper. It is glued to one of the first pages.[68] Also interesting is his 1886 journal. It includes a Pennsylvania Dutch poem on newsprint that was clipped and glued to the back. The poem is "Ich Wot Ich Ware Ein Bauer."[69] This translates to "I Wish I Were a Farmer." According to Boyer, Buffington, and Yoder, this Pennsylvania Dutch song was very popular in the region. Professor Abraham Reeser Horne published it in his pioneer volume of the Pennsylvania Dutch language.[70] These seemingly trivial details hint at Muth's knowledge of not only English but also German and Pennsylvania Dutch.

Regarding resources about the Pennsylvania Dutch culture, from its genesis during the colonial period through the 19th century, Dr. Arthur Graeff produced, as his dissertation in 1939 at Temple University, the book *The Relations Between the Pennsylvania Germans and the British Authorities, 1750–1776*. Graeff's work emphasized the cultural roots and differences of the German-speaking Pennsylvanians from their Scots-Irish and English counterparts.

Three scholars contemporary to Graeff include Don Yoder, Albert Buffington, and Walter Boyer. Yoder, a Ph.D. from the University of Pennsylvania, pioneered the concept of the academic study of the Pennsylvania Dutch culture. Their book *Songs Along the Mahantongo* highlights the region's culture immediately around Dr. Muth when he was alive.

Consequently, the journal started by these three scholars, *Pennsylvania Folklife*, produced excellent research during the latter half of the

---

67. Reuben H. Muth, *Physician's Daybooks*, vol. 3, attached to inside cover (1858–1898, in possession of Lawrence Knorr, Mechanicsburg, Pennsylvania). German: "*Um 13ten Juni, durch benselben, bei Port Trevorton, Doktor Ruben H. Muth, fruher von Rehrersburg, Berks Co., mit Miss Louisa Deppin, von ersterem Drt.*" Translation: "On the 13th of June, through the same, at Port Trevorton, Dr. Reuben H. Muth, previously of Rehrersburg, Berks County, with Miss Louisa Deppen, from the former place."

68. Ibid., vol. 4.

69. Ibid., vol 23.

70. Walter E. Boyer, Albert F. Buffington, and Don Yoder, *Songs Along the Mahantongo: Pennsylvania Dutch Folksongs* (Hatboro, PA: Folklore Associates, 1951), 103.

20th century. Many articles from those archives remain relevant to the research on Dr. Muth.

One example was the work of Lisa Colbert, who wrote about the attitudes of the Amish toward doctors and their treatments. At the time, Colbert was a student at Millersville University. Of most interest to this study are the home remedies commonly used by these rural farmers, including the ingredients and instructions for their use.[71]

Another related article by Holly Cutting Baker expanded upon the various patent medicines available to Pennsylvanians in the nineteenth century. Baker, a doctoral student of folklore at the University of Pennsylvania, included lists of products and various advertisements and ephemera from the period.[72]

Ned Heindel co-authored an article with Natalie Foster about the Allentown Academy, the first German medical school in America.[73] While Muth did not attend this institution, the article provides background regarding medical training in Pennsylvania during the period in focus. Both Heindel and Foster were chemistry professors at Lehigh University. Heindel was also affiliated as a professor of nuclear medicine at Hahnemann Medical College in Philadelphia.

Finally, David Rausch contributed an article to *Pennsylvania Folklife* about medicine during the Civil War period, but from the patient's perspective. Rausch earned his Ph.D. from Kent State in American History. His article included excerpts from letters of a soldier who was a long-term patient following his injuries near Atlanta in 1864.[74] While Muth did not serve during the war, he likely had veterans among his many patients.

Contemporary writings provided an interesting view of life in Pennsylvania Dutch communities during the post-Civil War period. Among the best is the work by Phoebe Gibbons, who gained the confidence of the communities and wrote about them in national magazines. She accessed Amish and Mennonite events and observed Lutheran and Reformed German culture. In her book *Pennsylvania Dutch and Other*

---

71. Lisa Colbert, "Amish Attitudes and Treatment of Illness." *Pennsylvania Folklife* 30, no. 1 (Autumn 1980): 9–15.

72. Holly Cutting Baker, "Patent Medicine in Pennsylvania Before 1906." *Pennsylvania Folklife* 27, no. 2 (Winter 1977–78): 20–33.

73. Ned D. Heindel & Natalie I. Foster, "The Allentown Academy: America's First German Medical School." *Pennsylvania Folklife* 30, no. 1 (Autumn 1980): 2–8.

74. David A. Rausch. "Civil War Medicine: A Patient's Account." *Pennsylvania Folklife* 26, no. 5 (Summer 1977): 46–48.

Essays, first published in 1872, one nugget related how the Dutch locals resisted English speakers who knocked on the doors selling their wares. These salesmen resorted to trickery and charming the Dutch with stories to sell their wares.[75] Perhaps Dr. Muth used the Pennsylvania Dutch language when interacting with his rural patients to gain their confidence and trust. Gibbons' book remains a key resource to the present.

Though a professor of literature at Swarthmore College, Fredric Spang Klees (1901–1985) wrote the most comprehensive and bestselling book about the Pennsylvania Dutch culture in 1950.[76] Klees captured the gamut of cultural aspects, from food to religion and emphasized the regional and denominational differences.

Richard M. Dorson (1916–1981) also wrote about Pennsylvania Dutch folklore and superstitions as part of his work on the topic of regional folklore in the United States.[77] Referred to as the "father of American folklore,"[78] Dorson was Harvard-educated and worked at Indiana University for many years.

Of course, there is also a need to understand a bit about Dr. Muth's medical practice during this time before antibiotics. Chapter four delves into the medical practice of the period from an economic perspective. While about a physician practicing during the latter years of Dr. Muth's tenure, Beatrice Fox Griffith's biography *Pennsylvania Doctor* captures the attitudes and interactions of her ancestor, a physician who practiced after the Civil War.[79] Given the proximity to Muth's practice, this resource is helpful in understanding the daily practice of nineteenth-century physicians in the region. What services did a doctor offer in these rural communities? How many doctors were competing for services in the same locale? Were there local associations or collaboration among them? How much did they charge their customers?

Data from Dr. Muth's daybooks was used to forensically reconstruct his practice in terms of patients seen and amounts earned throughout his

---

75. Phoebe Earle Gibbons, *Pennsylvania Dutch and Other Essays* (Philadelphia: J. B. Lippincott & Co., 1872), 10.

76. Fredric Klees, *The Pennsylvania Dutch* (New York: Macmillan Publishing, 1950).

77. Richard M. Dorson, *Buying the Wind: Regional Folklore in the United States* (Chicago: University of Chicago Press, 1964).

78. Nikolai Burlakoff, "Richard Mercer Dorson (1916–1981): A Memorate." *Journal of American Folklore* 131, no. 519 (2018): 91+.

79. Beatrice Fox Griffith, *Pennsylvania Doctor* (Harrisburg, PA: Stackpole, 1957).

career. These summations were compared to what is known about the medical profession of the time and also to other professions.

Regarding the physician's logs, every patient seen between 1858 and 1898 is recorded. The only gap in the record is eleven months from February through December 1876. Day by day, the patients are listed in the order they were seen. Amounts charged and other notes are also evident. These unique primary resources provided the data for the foundation of this research. While it was a monumental task to transcribe every detail of all 34 volumes into one database, other methods were used to summarize the data in various ways to develop meaningful information.

Chapter five further analyzes the practice of Dr. Muth, including a deeper look at some of the patients whom Dr. Muth serviced and the peers around him. There were other resources beyond the daybooks that were helpful in this analysis. The Cummings maps of 1858 and 1874 provided snapshots of the geography of Northumberland County, Pennsylvania, and its prominent residents. The residence of R. H. Muth was marked near the village of Mahanoy. Also, when corroborating the physician's logs with names on the map, it was evident the logs recorded residents within about twenty miles of Muth's home. Many of these patient households appeared on period maps. From this, many questions could be answered. What was his travel range in a day? What routes did he travel? What do we know about the families seen at each documented stop? Of interest are any anecdotal evidence of their lives. Several patients whom Muth visited frequently are analyzed in detail, including the frequency of service. Comparisons are also made to other practicing doctors in the region with whom Dr. Muth interacted.

The concluding chapter summarizes Dr. Muth's life in terms of his family, faith, and finances. Was Reuben Harris Muth a successful physician? Was he an important member of his community? Did he leave any lasting impacts beyond his box of daybooks and his tombstone at Mahanoy? Perhaps most importantly, what can we make of the life and career of Dr. Muth from the perspective of the economic dimensions of medical history? Is the story of Reuben Harris Muth instructive to other potential researchers?

Ultimately, this study of a rural physician during the nineteenth century does not recount a robber baron of the medical field or a doctor who serviced the rich and famous. Rather, it is a study of a middle-class doctor who served his community in more ways than one. Without the box of daybooks and other ephemera, Dr. Reuben Harris Muth would have been lost to time. Thankfully, with these primary sources in hand, we not only get a sense of the work of the doctor, but also the community he served.

2

Rehrersburg Roots

The summer of 1826 was a momentous one for the young American republic as it celebrated its 50th anniversary since the Declaration of Independence in the midst of the presidency of John Quincy Adams. The *Lancaster Intelligencer Journal* of July 4, 1826, reproduced the Declaration on its second page, following a first page of mostly advertisements.[1] Page three included a pronouncement of the planned activities of the day to include orations and celebrations throughout the nation.[2] The town of Lancaster was no exception. Unknown to all except those close to Thomas Jefferson and John Adams, the father of the president, those founding fathers passed on this day, bookending the first fifty years of the nation. This young United States was still mostly a rural three-mile-an-hour world connected by horses, stagecoaches, and the mail. If not communicated in person, news came via letter or newspaper or on Sundays at church. The telegraph and telephone were decades away from introduction. It was a time before the railroads and great industries would burst forth on the landscape.

Thirty miles almost due north, near the rural village of Millersburg (now Bethel), Bethel Township, Berks County, Pennsylvania,[3] in the household of Frederick Muth, Esquire, he and his wife, Elisabeth Schaffer Muth, awaited the birth of their grandchild.[4] Frederick Muth's youngest son, Frederick Junior, had recently married Anna Maria Schneider,

1. "Declaration of Independence," *Lancaster Intelligencer Journal*, July 4, 1826, 2.
2. Ibid., 3.
3. "The Physician's Register," *The Sunbury Weekly News*, Aug 26, 1881, 2.
4. US Census Bureau. 1830 United States Federal Census. Census Place: Tulpehocken Township, Berks County, Pennsylvania, 15.

and the couple was expecting. Frederick Junior had taken to tending the family farm between Millersburg and Rehrersburg. Frederick Senior's home was situated near the Altalaha Lutheran Church, across the road that became Gottfried Street in the village.[5] This home was the former "Inn at Tolheo," "the last outpost" on the Tulpehocken Path to Shamokin and points west.[6] For many years, the town's founder, Gottfried Rehrer, operated the inn and laid out the village.[7] Frederick Senior continued to operate the rustic inn and a store. In the rear or the property was a lumber yard described as "the greatest lumber yard in eastern Pennsylvania."[8] The eldest son, John, lived on a nearby farm on the other side of the village.[9] Also in Rehrersburg was Dr. Michael Tryon,[10] whose son Jacob had recently completed medical training at the University of Pennsylvania.[11]

Johann Frederick Muth, aka Frederick Senior, had married Elizabeth Zerbe on November 21, 1797, at the Trinity Tulpehocken Reformed Church,[12] situated in Jackson Township, Lebanon County, Pennsylvania, about ten miles south of Rehrersburg on the road to Lancaster. Frederick Senior and Elizabeth had two boys, John, born 1799,[13] and Frederick Junior, born November 25, 1802.[14] This region, in western Berks County and eastern Lebanon County, was the former stomping grounds of the Indian Agent Conrad Weiser earlier in the 18th century. The nearby Tulpehocken Path was often traversed by Weiser and his friend, the Iroquois vice-regent Shikellamy, and many others on their

5. Ibid.

6. Dolores Hill, Sandra Kauffman, Barbara Loose, Carol Mehler, Barry Miller, and Jodie Ziegler, *History of Rehrersburg* (Rehrersburg, PA: Andulhea Heritage Center, 2019), 28.

7. Ibid.

8. Ibid., 211.

9. US Census Bureau. 1830 United States Federal Census. Census Place: Tulpehocken Township, Berks County, Pennsylvania, 15.

10. US Census Bureau. 1820 United States Federal Census. Census Place: Tulpehocken Township, Berks County, Pennsylvania, 1.

11. Dolores Hill, Sandra Kauffman, Barbara Loose, Carol Mehler, Barry Miller, and Jodie Ziegler, *History of Rehrersburg* (Rehrersburg, PA: Andulhea Heritage Center, 2019), 55.

12. *Trinity Tulpehocken Reformed Church, Lebanon County, Pennsylvania, Marriage Records, 1769–1844* (Philadelphia, PA: Genealogical Society of Pennsylvania, 2001), 9. Accessed January 13, 2025, https://genpa.org/wp-content/uploads/member-collections/Trinity_Tulpehocken_Reformed_Church_Marriages_pages_1-38.pdf

13. "John Muth," *Find a Grave*, Memorial ID 35875897, accessed December 30, 2024, https://www.findagrave.com/memorial/35875897/john-muth.

14. "Old Tombstones in Cemetery of the Altalaha Evangelical Lutheran Church, Rehrersburg, Tulpehocken Twp.

Berks County, Penna.," *Genealogical Society of Pennsylvania*, pg. 7, no. 214, accessed December 30, 2024, https://genpa.org/wp-content/uploads/member-collections/fritz-berryman/OldTombstone_Altalaha Evangelical-Berks.pdf.

way to and from treaty negotiations in Philadelphia and Lancaster. This was also the area at which the Moravian Count von Zinzendorf began his trek into the wilderness, traveling from Weiser's near Womelsdorf, up the Tulpehocken Path, past the future Rehrersburg and Millersburg, into what would later become Northumberland County, Pennsylvania, and beyond. This was also the region caught up in the Tulpehocken Confusion, a lapse in church governance among the Pennsylvania Germans caused by a lack of trained ministers in the recently settled rural sections of the area in the 1740s. The Confusion ended with the arrival of Henry Muhlenberg, who preached at Trinity Tulpehocken Church and many others in the region, spreading the Lutheran denomination throughout, Altalaha being one of the benefitting institutions. Unfortunately, this was also the region, in 1757, during the French and Indian War, which witnessed the Native attack on Pennsylvania German settlers just east of Rehrersburg, near Shartlesville. There, Jacob Hochstetler, an avowed pacifist, did not permit his sons to defend themselves against the attacking Natives, resulting in his capture and two of his sons and the deaths of several other family members.[15] Thus, when the Muths settled in Rehrersburg in western Berks County, there had only been a few decades of relative calm. One can only imagine the tales told by the hearth in the evening at what was previously the last stopping point on the edge of the wilderness. How many notable people slept on the floor of that inn on their may to and from Philadelphia and Shamokin or points west?

By the summer of 1826, the United States was mostly east of the Mississippi River, except for Louisiana and the recently formed state of Missouri. The regions in the west and northwest were governed by Arkansas, Michigan, Northwest, and Missouri Territories. The Oregon Territory was yet to be, and most of what would become the American Southwest belonged to Mexico. Thus, the great westward movement had yet to occur.

On September 11, 1826, the 53rd birthday of Frederick Muth Senior, Anna Maria Muth, age 20, gave birth to a baby boy, the first child of Frederick Muth Junior.[16] He was named Reuben Harris Muth. It is very

---

15. The author is a descendant of Jacob Hochstetler.
16. Hebert C. Bell, *History of Northumberland County, Pennsylvania* (Brown, Runk & Co, Chicago, 1891), 1235.

possible that the mother-in-law, Elisabeth Muth, now 51 years of age, attended the birth. It is also likely that one or both of the Tryons from Rehrersburg came to the Muth farm and assisted with medical services.

Three weeks later, on the east side of Rehrersburg, John Muth and his wife had their second son, Jefferson, on October 4, 1826. This was the couple's third child after Richard in 1822 and Amanda in 1825. Mary Ann followed in 1829, and then Amelia in 1831, Cyrus in 1833, Harriett in 1837, Catharine in 1840, and Edmund in 1842.

The Frederick Muth family also enlarged rapidly over the years. Henriette followed in 1828, Eliza in 1831, Anna Maria in 1833, John in 1836, William in 1839, George in 1847, and Clementine in 1850. Thus, young Reuben was exposed to a brood of siblings and first cousins in his vicinity. In summary, as the oldest son of the second son, he was the third grandchild.

Young Reuben Muth's first experience with the frailty of life was the death of his younger sister, Henriethe, on September 6, 1832.[17] Henriethe was not yet four years old, and Reuben was five days shy of his sixth birthday. Most likely, the little girl succumbed to one of several childhood diseases that often took the lives of children before bacteria and viruses were understood and ample antibiotics and vaccinations were available. Perhaps after this experience, the bedtime prayers of the surviving Muth siblings were said with more gravity, knowing what happened to little Henriethe.

Sometime when Reuben Muth was very young, perhaps approaching school age in the early 1830s, Frederick Junior's family moved from Millersburg to the old inn at Rehrersburg.[18] Frederick Senior moved to a house in the town built from old logs that had been part of the original church.[19] John Muth and his family moved out of the area to Myerstown, Jackson Township, Lebanon County.[20]

---

17. "Old Tombstones in Cemetery of the Altalaha Evangelical Lutheran Church, Rehrersburg, Tulpehocken Twp.

Berks County, Penna.," *Genealogical Society of Pennsylvania*, accessed December 30, 2024, https://genpa.org/wp-content/uploads/member-collections/fritz-berryman/OldTombstone_AltalahaEvangelical-Berks.pdf.

18. US Census Bureau. 1840 United States Federal Census. Census Place: Tulpehocken Township, Berks County, Pennsylvania, 3.

19. Dolores Hill, Sandra Kauffman, Barbara Loose, Carol Mehler, Barry Miller, and Jodie Ziegler, *History of Rehrersburg* (Rehrersburg, PA: Andulhea Heritage Center, 2019), 29.

20. US Census Bureau. 1840 United States Federal Census. Census Place: Tulpehocken Township, Berks County, Pennsylvania, 4.

While there are no records of the childhood of Reuben Harris Muth, there were nine members of the Frederick Muth household in 1840,[21] including one male, ten to fourteen, matching Reuben's age. Without family journals, diaries, or letters, we can only assume they participated in the common traditions of the time. One tradition particular to the Pennsylvania Dutch was the visitation two weeks before Christmas by the *Belsnickel*, a scrubby character with a switch who would check on the children to be sure they were behaving. Those who misbehaved received a switch in their stockings, while the well-behaved children received treats.[22] Many other traditions in the Muth household at that time would have been different from our present time. In the days before Christmas, it was typical for a rural farmer to butcher a pig. While processing the animal, the fat would be made into a stew with some sausage, known as Metzel Soup. This was shared with less fortunate neighbors. Prior to the invention of Santa Claus, the Lutheran and Reformed among the Pennsylvania Dutch honored the *Christkind* or *Christkindl*[23], as the gift giver. The day after Christmas, referred to as *Zweite Weihnachten* or Second Christmas, was a time for shooting matches and games of chance at the tavern, fox hunts, and dances. If there were snow, sleigh rides were very popular, especially with young couples. On New Year's Eve, it was common for men to make their rounds with their muskets and fire them off in succession in front of a farmer's house or tavern. In exchange, the farmer or tavernkeeper would provide a drink. There was a tradition of poking fun at the local militia at these times, and the "captain" of the shoot would say, "When I say 'Fire,' all of you with muskets must shoot. Those with only sticks and cornstalks must aim and cry 'Boo!'"[24] Prior to Lent, Shrove Tuesday was a time for dancing and courting. On Ash Wednesday, the last one out of bed was responsible for the *eschapuddel* (the ash pile) and was required to apply the ash to everyone's foreheads.[25] There were some subtle similarities to more recent traditions, including a modest Christmas tree decorated with gingerbread cookies, ribbons, and wood carvings, and, at Easter, painted eggs.[26]

21. US Census Bureau. 1840 United States Federal Census. Census Place: Tulpehocken Township, Berks County, Pennsylvania, 3.

22. Alfred L. Shoemaker, *Christmas in Pennsylvania* (Mechanicsburg, PA: Stackpole, 1999), 75–90.

23. English: Christ Child.

24. Mildred Jordan, *The Distelfink Country of the Pennsylvania Dutch* (New York.: Crown Publishers, 1978), 130.

25. Ibid., 131.

26. Alfred L. Shoemaker, *Christmas in Pennsylvania* (Mechanicsburg, PA: Stackpole, 1999), 75.

Growing up at the inn on the edge of the village, Reuben Muth was only a few steps from the nearest school. In 1795, Gottfried Rehrer built a two-room school on his property across the road from the church. This school was used until 1882 when a larger, more modern facility was built in town.[27] While we do not know the teacher, Daniel Ulrich was pastor of the congregation from 1811 until 1851.[28] During this time, the famous Dieffenbach organ built in Millersburg was installed in the church.[29] Most likely this was a sound heard often by young Reuben Muth.

27. Dolores Hill, Sandra Kauffman, Barbara Loose, Carol Mehler, Barry Miller, and Jodie Ziegler, *History of Rehrersburg* (Rehrersburg, PA: Andulhea Heritage Center, 2019), 437.

28. George E. Hein, Jr. and Schuyler C. Brossman, *A History of Altalaha Evangelical Lutheran Church, Rehrersburg, Berks County, Pennsylvania* (Rehrersburg, PA: Altalaha Church Council, 1982), 12.

29. Ibid., 24.

3

Marshall College Days

Perhaps the biggest event of Reuben's youth was the passing of his grandfather, Frederick Senior, on September 11, 1846,[1] Reuben's twentieth birthday. According to the grandfather's will, the grandchildren were each to receive money upon their 22nd birthdays.[2] By the time the will was probated on August 6, 1847, only Richard and Amanda, the son and daughter of John Muth, received their funds. John Muth, as executor, took over the other brick home in Rehrersburg, the farm he was living on near Rehrersburg in Bethel Township, Berks County. The land given to John was officially transacted via an indenture to which Reuben was a witness and affixed his signature.[3] The will glowingly recounted how John fetched apple trees for the house and built the barn. All personal goods, books, and livestock were left to this older son. The will was less kind to Frederick Junior, the second son, permitting him to keep the farm on which he was living and a horse and wagon. He was also required to settle with his brother on expenses previously paid by their father. John, as executor, also settled expenses owed to Jacob Trion, the doctor, and John Housenet, the merchant, on behalf of his widowed mother. Thus, on his 22nd birthday, on September 11, 1848, Reuben would have received over $100 allotted to each grandchild that had been held in escrow by his uncle.

During this time, Reuben Muth had begun attending Marshall College in Mercersburg, Pennsylvania. Unfortunately, the academic records

1. "Friederick Muth," *Find a Grave*, Memorial ID 61620552, accessed December 30, 2024, https://www.findagrave.com/memorial/61620552/friederick-muth.
2. "Frederick Muth," Berks County Wills, 1847 TU, 21.
3. "Muth, Frederick" Berks County Indentures, Book 53, 685.

of Reuben H. Muth's attendance at that institution are now lost. A dev-
astating fire at the Old Main building in 1927 destroyed most of the
institution's archives.[4] Fortunately, some ephemera from the era survived
that mentioned our student. In 1848, Reuben H. Muth was mentioned
in the 1847/1848 catalog for the school as attending from Berks County,
who was in Mr. Hassler's rooms.[5] While we cannot know for sure what
classes he took, at what time, with whom, or how he performed, we can
surmise quite a bit from the catalog. The college started as an offshoot
of the German Reformed Church and was initially focused on training
ministers for that denomination.[6] There were fourteen faculty members
at the time, including the President, Rev. John W. Nevin, D.D., who was
also a Professor of Intellectual and Moral Philosophy. Hon. Alexander
Thompson, LL.D., was the Professor of Law. William M. Nevin, Esq.,
A.M., was the Professor of Ancient Languages and Belles Lettres. Traill
Green, M.D., was a Professor of Natural Science. Rev. Philip Schaff,
Ph.D., was a Professor of Aesthetics and German Literature. Thomas
D. Baird, Esq., A.M., was a Professor of Mathematics, Mechanical
Philosophy, and Political Economy. E. W. Reinecke, A.M.; David A.
Wilson, A.B.; and Franklin D. Stem, A.B., were Tutors. Reinecke and J.
S. Ermentrout, A.B., were the Instructors in German. Rev. A. J. M. Hud-
son, A.M., was the Rector of the Preparatory Department. Ermentrout,
Aaron S. Leinbach, A.B., and J. Bossard, Ph.D., were Assistants.[7]

According to the catalog, the institution began graduating students
in 1837; the first was Rev. John A. Bomberger, A.M.[8] Then five or six
per year followed until 1842 when nine graduated. One of the 1841
graduates was James Lefevre Reyolds, the younger brother of John Ful-
ton Reynolds.[9] James Reynolds later became an attorney but earned his
A.M. degree at Marshall and then became the Quartermaster General for
Pennsylvania during the Civil War. Older brother John became a Major
General in the Union Army and was killed on the first day of the Battle

---

4. Richard D. Altick, "Pranks and Punishment in an Old Pennsylvania College," *Pennsylvania History: A Journal of Mid-Atlantic Studies* 4, no. 4 (1937): 241.

5. *Catalogue of the Officers and Students of Marshall College for 1847 – '48* (Mercersburg, PA: H. A. Mish, 1848), 14.

6. Ibid., 19.

7. Ibid., 4.

8. Ibid., 5.

9. Ibid.

of Gettysburg. Faculty members Schaff, Reinecke, Wilson, Ermentrout, Hudson, and Leinbach were also all recent Marshall graduates.[10]

Reuben H. Muth was listed as being in the Preparatory Department with 68 other classmates.[11] The assigned rooms appear to be either dormitory rooms on campus, which were likely few, and accommodations at private homes in the Mercersburg community. Sharing accommodations in Mr. Hassler's rooms were students named Michael Ruby from Cumberland County, Pennsylvania,[12] also in the Preparatory Department, and George W. Ruby, a senior in the law school, listed as from Wrightsville, York County, Pennsylvania.[13] Jacob Hassler Jr. had graduated in 1845 and is likely not the same Mr. Hassler who rented rooms to students.[14] Rather, it is likely Jacob's father, Jacob Hassler Sr., who was a well-known local architect and builder and an early investor in the formation of Marshall College.[15] He passed away on July 29, 1848, and was buried at Fairview Cemetery in Mercersburg, Pennsylvania.[16] Also of note was the prominent home of the Buchanan family, converted to a hotel. James Buchanan was the Secretary of State under President James K. Polk at this time.

The catalog delineated the expectations of a Preparatory student over two years. There were two semesters per year. For Reuben Muth, during his first semester, he was exposed to Latin Grammar in the Classical section, Arithmetic in the Mathematical and Physical section, and English Grammar, Geography, Penmanship, Reading and Elocution, and Declamation and Composition in the English section. During the second term of the first year, the student continued Latin Grammar and added reading Caesar and Greek Grammar and Exercises in the Classical section. He completed his course of Arithmetic in the Mathematical and Physical section. He completed Geography and continued with the other aspects of the English section.

According to the catalog, Preparatory students were expected to attend Bible Class in the Preparatory Department on the Sabbath and

10. Ibid., 6.
11. Ibid., 13–14.
12. Ibid., 14.
13. Ibid., 9.
14. Ibid., 6.
15. Woman's Club of Mercersburg, *Old Mercersburg* (New York, NY; Journal of American History, 1913), 49.
16. "Hassler, Jacob," Genealogical Card File. Lancaster Mennonite Historical Society, Lancaster, Pennsylvania. Hassler burial location is noted as 60-2-11, in the N.E. Section.

attend the service at the College Chapel afterward. Students paid $13.50 for the full course per semester for the Winter Session and $11.50 for the full course per semester for the Summer Session.[17] Room and board was $1.50 to $2.00 per week, and students who preferred to stay in private homes versus dormitories were permitted to do so.[18] The Winter Session lasted 22 weeks versus 18 for the Summer Session, which is why the price was different. The sessions were separated by six weeks of vacation.[19]

Muth's roommates at Hassler's were an interesting duo. George Washington Ruby lived from 1824 to 1890 and, according to his obituary, graduated from Marshall College in 1848. He was the Principal and Professor at the York County Academy for many years.[20] He was the son of Heinrich Ruby. Michael Gordon Ruby was born in Silver Spring, Cumberland County, Maryland, in 1826. He later moved to Missouri and died in Bethany.[21] He was the son of Samuel Gordon Ruby. It seems plausible that the two Rubys were cousins. It seems highly unlikely two young men with the same surname would end up rooming together in a small country college and not be related. It was also likely they did not know Muth when they arrived to share the rooms at Hassler's. Of course, there is no record that roommate Reuben Muth kept in touch with these gentlemen afterward.

On Saturday, September 4, 1847, during the Summer Session, there was a great commotion in Mercersburg. Apparently, there had been tension between "town mechanics" and Marshall faculty and students over the last decade due to the school's stance against slavery. A Marshall student, Alfred Dubbs, was walking through town when one of the town fellows walked up and blew smoke in his face. Many students rushed to his aid, and a rumble occurred between them and the "town fellows."[22] While no one was permanently injured, the school administration threatened to expel the students until a law professor came to their defense. While it is not known if Dr. Muth was involved in the scrape, at

17. *Catalogue of the Officers and Students of Marshall College for 1847 – '48* (Mercersburg, PA: H. A. Mish, 1848), 26.

18. Ibid.

19. Ibid., 18.

20. "George Washington Ruby," Find *a Grave*, Memorial ID 207413571, accessed December 30, 2024, https://www.findagrave.com/memorial/207413571/george-washington-ruby.

21. "Michael Gordon Ruby," Sons of the American Revolution Membership Applications, 1889–1970.

22. Joseph Henry Dubbs, *History of Franklin and Marshall College; Franklin College, 1787–1853* (Lancaster, PA: Franklin & Marshall College Almuni Association, 1903), 226–227.

a minimum, it would likely have been viewable from the Hassler home and certainly discussed for days after.

The following year, Reuben Muth was back at Marshall College. Gold had been discovered in California in January 1848, but rather than heading West, Muth continued his studies, now staying with Mrs. Hassler.[23] Former roommate George W. Ruby graduated in 1848 with his A.B.[24] Attendance in the Preparatory School had dropped to only 39,[25] perhaps due to the impact of the Gold Rush. The faculty was also greatly reduced to only eight individuals, down from fourteen. Dr. Traill Green, M.D., had moved on, and there were no more tutors and only one assistant. "C. Zwingli Weiser" was a new roommate at Mrs. Hassler's.[26] He was attending from Pottstown, Pennsylvania. Weiser was a great-great-grandson of Conrad Weiser and graduated from Marshall in 1850. He then became a Reformed minister.[27] "Samuel G. Wagner" was also a new roommate from Lebanon, Pennsylvania.[28] Samuel Gross Wagner (1831–1909) was a longtime Reformed minister in Allentown, Pennsylvania.[29] Another new roommate was John O. Ogle from New Dublin, Maryland.[30] He appears to be the same John Oliver Ogle who was born in Maryland in 1827 and settled in the Russian River Valley in California by the 1860s.[31] Perhaps he was lured away by the Gold Rush at some point. Henry Wissler from Lancaster County, Pennsylvania, was the final new roommate at Mrs. Hassler's.[32] He was the only other Preparatory student with Reuben. He was likely Rev. Henry Wissler (1831–1889), who was a longtime minister in Thurmont, Maryland.[33]

23. *Catalogue of the Officers and Students of Marshall College for 1848 – '49* (Chambersburg, PA: The German Reformed Messenger Office, 1849), 13.

24. Ibid., 7.

25. Ibid., 14.

26. Ibid., 10.

27. "Rev. Clement Z. Weiser Dead," *Lancaster Intelligencer Journal*, March 2, 1898, 4.

28. *Catalogue of the Officers and Students of Marshall College for 1848 – '49* (Chambersburg, PA: The German Reformed Messenger Office, 1849), 10.

29. "Samuel Gross Wagner," *Find a Grave*, Memorial ID 87369979, accessed December 30, 2024, https://www.findagrave.com/memorial/87369979/samuel-gross-wagner.

30. *Catalogue of the Officers and Students of Marshall College for 1848 – '49* (Chambersburg, PA: The German Reformed Messenger Office, 1849), 12.

31. "John Oliver Ogle" *Great Register Sonoma County (California)*, pg. 107 no. 4264, accessed January 13, 2025 at: https://www.ancestry.com/search/collections/2221/records/4281632?tid=&pid=&queryId=3a0 ab065-0d28-4b0b-9ab3-c6da8c286175&_phsrc=GLB373&_phstart=successSource.

32. *Catalogue of the Officers and Students of Marshall College for 1848 – '49* (Chambersburg, PA: The German Reformed Messenger Office, 1849), 14.

33. "Middletown Matters," *The News* (Frederick, MD), April 20, 1889, 4.

Given the number of ministers in his midst, it is possible Reuben H. Muth was contemplating the ministry while attending Marshall College. At a minimum, he was exposed to "true Christian Philosophy" with "no sympathy with the school of Paley and Locke."[34]

During this second and final year at Marshall, assuming Muth did not have to repeat any courses, during his first semester in the Classical section, he continued Latin and Greek Grammar, completed his reading of Caesar, and started reading Virgil and Xenophon's *Anabasis*; started Algebra

Figure 2. Dr. Traill Green.

and Natural Philosophy in the Mathematical and Physical section; and History and Declamation and Composition in the English section. During the second term of the second year, the student continued Latin and Greek Grammar, completed Virgil and Xenophon's *Anabasis*, and started Sallust in the Classical section. He completed his courses in Algebra and Natural Philosophy in the Mathematical and Physical sections. He completed History and Declamation and Composition in the English section.[35]

Soon after he started the semester at Marshall College in 1848, his grandmother, Elisabeth Muth, passed away in Rehrersburg on October 26.[36] It is unlikely that Reuben heard about this in time to return for her funeral. Instead, he would have paid his respects during the break between semesters.

Unfortunately for Muth, subsequent catalogs do not list him as a graduate of Marshall College. Thus, we do not know why or when Muth returned home to Rehrersburg. Perhaps the loss of Dr. Traill Green, whom

34. *Catalogue of the Officers and Students of Marshall College for 1848 – '49* (Chambersburg, PA: The German Reformed Messenger Office, 1849), 23.

35. Ibid., 25.

36. "Old Tombstones in Cemetery of the Altalaha Evangelical Lutheran Church, Rehrersburg, Tulpehocken Twp.

Berks County, Penna.," *Genealogical Society of Pennsylvania*, accessed December 30, 2024, https://genpa.org/wp-content/uploads/member-collections/fritz-berryman/OldTombstone_AltalahaEvangelical-Berks.pdf.

Muth was exposed to in his first year but not the second, discouraged Muth from continuing at Marshall. Dr. Green was a well-known medical professor who was highly regarded. He was also an 1835 graduate of the University of Pennsylvania and a longtime professor at Lafayette College who was the first president of the American Academy of Medicine.[37]

Another explanation for the lack of a diploma could have something to do with disciplinary action. According to Richard Altick's research into student behavior at Marshall College in the early days, "a few months previous [to 1850]," an incident had occurred at the house of Mrs. Hassler. Apparently, there was a "riotous party who showed off their orgies around the boarding house . . . last night." The offending students were deprived of their degrees, though some "expressed penitence before the professors and were awarded their diplomas."[38] Marshall graduate Reverend Theodore Appel, D.D. discussed the problems with some of the students and alcohol in his memoir.[39] According to Appel, there was tension between some of the faculty, who promoted temperance, and many of the students who preferred to partake in alcohol, some of them to excess.[40] Reuben H. Muth was certainly present at Mrs. Hasslers during the timeframe of the trouble and was without a diploma. It is hard to imagine future reverends Weiser, Wagner, and Wissler involved in the shenanigans. They later graduated and may have been able to recover their diplomas despite any misbehavior. Interestingly, John Oliver Ogle never received a degree at Marshall. Perhaps he was involved. While we can never know, there is enough circumstantial evidence to be concerned.

Another consideration for Reuben Muth's return from Mercersburg may have to do with him running out of funds. Given his inheritance of between one hundred and two hundred dollars, it would not have been enough for more than two years of school. Tuition alone would have totaled fifty dollars, and with room and board at least one hundred and twenty dollars,[41] young Reuben may have been tapped out.

---

37. "Dr. Traill Green Dead," *The Times Leader* (Wilkes-Barre, Pennsylvania), May 4, 1897, 3.

38. Richard D. Altick, "Pranks and Punishment in an Old Pennsylvania College," *Pennsylvania History* 4, no. 4 (October 1937), 241.

39. Rev. Theodore Appel, D.D., *Recollections of College Life at Marshall College, Mercersburg, Pennsylvania, from 1839 to 1845* (Reading, PA: Daniel Miller, 1886), 126–27.

40. Ibid.

41. Tuition was $25 per year. Room and board was at least $1.50 a week for 40 weeks. Thus, one year of tuition, room and board was at least $85. Two years would be $170.

4

University of Pennsylvania

By the time the 1850 census was taken at the Muth household on August 27, 1850, Reuben was in his 24th year and had dropped out of college. The census taker logged the "Mood" family, a misspelling of Muth based on its phonetics. Frederick, age 50, a farmer, was the head of the household, including wife, Mary, age 43; son Reuben H., age 23; daughter Eliza, age 16; daughter Mary, age 14; son John S., age 12; son William M., age 10; son George W., age 2; and Isaac Long, age 18, a farmhand. Reuben was noted as having attended school within the last year.[1] This aligns with the record of him at Marshall college the previous two years.

Down *Gottfried Strasse* (Godfrey Street), the main street in Rehrersburg, a young man named Samuel K. Treichler, age 17, appeared in the 1850 census in Tulpehocken Township, Berks County. He was a store clerk in the household of Jonathan Housnet.[2] A few doors away, on the same census sheet, was the residence of Dr. Jacob Tryon, all captured on August 26, 1850. Dr. Tryon, across the street from the Muth residence, was likely the Muth family's physician.

It is not known exactly how or when Reuben Muth and Samuel Treichler became acquainted, but they would soon be attending the University of Pennsylvania Medical School. Young Samuel, six years Muth's junior, headed off to the University of Pennsylvania in 1852.[3]

---

1. US Census Bureau. 1850 United States Federal Census. Census Place: Tulpehocken Township, Berks County, Pennsylvania, 49 (House 240, Family 281).

2. US Census Bureau. 1850 United States Federal Census. Census Place: Tulpehocken Township, Berks County, Pennsylvania, 46 (House 194, Family 229).

3. *Catalogue of the Trustees, Officers, and Students of the University of Pennsylvania, Session 1852–53* (Philadelphia, PA: T. K. and P. G. Collins, Printers, 1853), 24.

Treichler listed as his preceptor, the physician overseeing his internship, as "J. & P. J. Tryon." This would be Dr. Jacob Tryon of Rehrersburg and his son Percival J. Tryon, who had become a medical doctor very recently in 1851 and was also listed as practicing in Rehrersburg.[4] Thus, young Samuel was traveling back and forth from Philadelphia and interning at the Tryon office. Given the rules at the University of Pennsylvania, Treichler's internship with Dr. Tryon may have started in 1851, allowing for a year of training before attending classes. This aligns with the arrival of the newly minted Dr. Percival Tryon. Reuben Muth would also have known of Percival Tryon's success at the University of Pennsylvania but was lagging a year behind. Perhaps Reuben needed to save some funds before starting his training.

Circa 1852, it appears Reuben Muth began an apprenticeship with Dr. Lewis Royer in Schuylkill Haven, Schuylkill County, Pennsylvania.[5] Lewis Royer, a graduate of the University of Pennsylvania,[6] was also the husband of Isabella Tryon, the daughter of Jacob Tryon of Rehrersburg.[7] The couple had been married in 1841 at the church in Rehrersburg,[8] across the street from the Muth residence. Perhaps young Reuben, at age 15, had witnessed the wedding and met the groom at that time. Regardless, it appears that Dr. Jacob Tryon, via his son-in-law, Lewis Royer, was intimately involved in furthering Muth's career.[9]

According to the 1850 census, Lewis Royer, a physician aged 29, was living with his wife, Isabella, aged 28, in Schuylkill Haven, Schuylkill County, Pennsylvania, with their three daughters: Emma, 8; Isabella, 5; and Henrietta, 2.[10] Also in the household were Susanna Goldson, aged 11, and George Loucks, aged 42. The Royer home was on Main Street, and the doctor also engaged in a general store in partnership with J. M. Shoemaker

4. *Catalogue of the Trustees, Officers, and Students of the University of Pennsylvania, Session 1851–52* (Philadelphia, PA: L. R. Bailey, Printer, 1852), 25.

5. US Census Bureau. 1850 United States Federal Census. Census Place: Schuylkill Haven, Schuylkill County, Pennsylvania, family 229, household 245.

6. "Dr. Lewis Royer Dead," *The Philadelphia Inquirer*, October 28, 1904, 4.

7. "Lewis Royer," *(Pennsylvania) Senate Library*, Biography ID: 4358, accessed January 13, 2025, at https://library.pasen.gov/people/member-biography?id=4358.

8. "Lewis Royer and Isabella Tryon, 27 July 1841," *Historical Society of Pennsylvania, Marriage Records, 1512–1989*, Historical Society of Pennsylvania, Philadelphia, Pennsylvania, accessed January 13, 2025, at https://www.familysearch.org/ark:/61903/1:1:6CYF-2HTZ.

9. *Catalogue of the Trustees, Officers, and Students of the University of Pennsylvania, Session 1853–54* (Philadelphia, PA: T. K. and P. G. Collins, Printers, 1853), 24.

10. US Census Bureau. 1850 United States Federal Census. Census Place: Schuylkill Haven, Schuylkill County, Pennsylvania, family 229, household 245.

on the same block.[11] Dr. Royer was one
of only two physicians in Schuylkill
Haven at the time.[12] As of 1846, three
years after he graduated from the University of Pennsylvania, Dr. Royer was
positioned in a booming town of 1640
people living in 258 houses.[13] He was
also doubling as Schuylkill County's
coroner, having handled the sensational Peifer murder case.[14]

It is likely Reuben Muth spent
most of his time in Schuylkill Haven,
about fifteen miles northeast of Rehrersburg, assisting Dr. Royer. The
apprenticeship typically lasted three
years, costing about one hundred dollars per year and coincided with two

Figure 3. Dr. Lewis Royer later in life.

years of formal classroom training.[15] At the time Muth began his training, the population of the United States was in the midst of rapid growth,
exploding from over five million people in 1800 to over thirty million in
1860.[16] To meet the demand for trained physicians during the transition
from heroic medicine to educated professionalism, the nation went from
only nine medical schools in 1800 to sixty-three by 1860, accounting
for the forty-four that opened and closed in the period.[17] Also, at this
time, there were very few hospitals, so students were trained by following
their preceptors during their daily visitation rounds.[18] So, Reuben H.
Muth, medical apprentice, probably acted as Dr. Lewis Royer's assistant,
preparing his horse, packing his bag, and tagging along to observe. This
would be especially interesting to assist a county coroner. However, it was
unlikely as an apprentice that he performed any services himself prior to

11. "Reminiscences of Sch. Haven And Vicinity By One Of Its Early Citizens." *The Call* (Schuylkill Haven, Pennsylvania), December 16, 1910, 1.
12. "Schuylkill Haven No. 4," *The Miners' Journal*, January 10, 1846, 2.
13. Ibid. Note: That is 6.35 persons per household and 129 households per doctor if split evenly.
14. "Local Affairs," *The Miners' Journal*, March 22, 1851, 2.
15. R.G. Slawson, "Medical Training in the United States Prior to the Civil War," *Journal of Evidence-Based Complementary & Alternative Medicine.* 2012;17(1): 14.
16. Ibid., 14.
17. Ibid., 12–16.
18. Ibid., 17.

his final year of schooling. To pay his preceptor, it is possible that young Reuben assisted in Royer's general store.

October 13, 1853, was an exciting day for both Reuben Muth and Samuel Treichler. The pair arrived and signed in at the University of Pennsylvania, Treichler first followed by Muth. They both listed 174 Arch Street (Philadelphia) as their boarding location.[19] Treichler was beginning his second year at the institution, while Muth was beginning his first. The distance from Rehrersburg to Philadelphia is about eighty miles, and the young men likely traveled by stagecoach to Reading, Pennsylvania, and then via rail to the big city. The conversation along the way was likely very lively as the younger Treichler shared his experiences and expectations with the older Muth. This simultaneous arrival was the first documented record of their friendship and collaboration as young medical doctors.

At the time, the University of Pennsylvania was located at Ninth and Market Streets, near what is now Independence Mall. The young doctors had a brief walk of about seven city blocks from their boarding house, past Christ Church and the grave of Benjamin Franklin, past Independence Hall, and up Market Street to the university. At the time, the address for the boarding house was also the location of Mrs. E. Roberts's millinery,[20] a place where young ladies would be perusing the latest fashionable headwear. Clearly, the bustle of Philadelphia, the second-largest city in the nation, was a sight to behold for Muth, who had spent his youth in rural Berks County and two years in remote Mercersburg.

When signing in on October 13, Treichler again listed "J. & P. J. Tryon" as his preceptors. Muth listed Lewis Royer.[21] To attend the school, all candidates must have been at least 21 years of age.[22] They must have committed to the study of medicine for three years, with two years as a "private pupil" of a respectable practitioner.[23] Regarding Treichler, who was 17 in 1850, he would have just turned 21 upon his graduation in

19. *Inscription Book of the University of Pennsylvania Medical Department*, School of Medicine, Student Records, call number UPC 2.7#16, entries for October 13, 1853 (University of Pennsylvania Archives and Records Center, Philadelphia, Pennsylvania).

20. "Mrs. E. Roberts" *Public Ledger* (Philadelphia), March 3, 1853, 2.

21. "Reuben H. Muth," *Inscription Book of the University of Pennsylvania Medical Department*, School of Medicine, Student Records, call number UPC 2.7#16, entry for October 13, 1853 (University of Pennsylvania Archives and Records Center, Philadelphia, Pennsylvania).

22. *Catalogue of the Trustees, Officers, and Students of the University of Pennsylvania, Session 1854–55* (Philadelphia, PA: T. K. and P. G. Collins, Printers, 1855), 28–29.

23. Ibid., 29.

Figure 4. View of the University of Pennsylvania Medical School circa 1850.

1854. The medical students had to complete two years of study at the university, including Theory and Practice of Medicine, Chemistry, Surgery, Obstetrics and the Diseases of Women and Children, and Institutes of Medicine.[24] Prior to graduation, the candidate must complete a thesis and defend it in front of a faculty member.

When Reuben Muth returned to the university in the fall of 1854, Samuel Treichler had graduated, and Muth arrived alone. He signed in a week earlier, on October 6, 1854, and listed his boarding house as 110 Filbert Street.[25] Filbert Street was little more than an alley and Muth's arrangements appeared to be more spartan than the apartment above the millinery shop. His route to school was roughly the same but closer to Market Street. These factors seemed to indicate a seriousness on the part of Muth to complete his degree. His thesis, approved on February 20,

24. *Catalogue of the Trustees, Officers, and Students of the University of Pennsylvania, Session 1854–55* (Philadelphia, PA: T. K. and P. G. Collins, Printers, 1855), 29.

25. "Samuel Treichler," *Inscription Book of the University of Pennsylvania Medical Department*, School of Medicine, Student Records, call number UPC 2.7#16, entry for October 6, 1854 (University of Pennsylvania Archives and Records Center, Philadelphia, Pennsylvania).

Figure 5. View of a Classroom at the University of Pennsylvania circa 1845.

1855, was 21 pages in length and discussed a variety of situations and treatments regarding wounds from snakes, rabid animals, insects, and plants.[26] Muth's writing style was deliberate and informative, without much flair. However, the description of a person afflicted with rabies was unsettling. This incurable condition merited heavy doses of sedatives like opiates to settle the patient.[27]

Thus, on March 31, 1855, Reuben Harris Muth, in his 29th year, graduated from medical school[28] and returned home from Philadelphia. Muth was now one of 17,213 newly minted physicians who had graduated from universities in the 1850s.[29] This was just slightly less than the number of graduates from the prior two decades combined.[30] Thus, Dr. Muth was stepping into an environment teeming with new doctors seeking to carve out a livelihood. Muth was still unmarried, and since being away, his former home was the domain of his parents and younger siblings.

26. Reuben H. Muth, Thesis: "Poisoned Wounds, 1855," University of Pennsylvania Libraries Special Collections, call number 378.748 POM 1855.2.33 Pt. 2. Catalog ID 992878763503681.

27. Ibid.

28. "The Physician's Register" *The Sunbury Weekly News*, Aug 26, 1881, 2.

29. William G. Rothstein, *American Physicians in the Nineteenth Century* (Baltimore, MD: Johns Hopkins University Press, 1972), 98.

30. Ibid.

5

A Brief Stay in Old Stumpstown

It appears Reuben may have only made a short stop at home on his way to Fredericksburg, also known as Stumpstown, in Lebanon County, about ten miles to the west. He was likely drawn there through some collaboration with Dr. Samuel K. Treichler, his former roommate at the university. Perhaps Treichler was doing well and could use some assistance with his practice, now in Jonestown, just west of Stumpstown. Perhaps Treichler realized there was room for another doctor if they stayed in the vicinity of Stumpstown, or perhaps Muth was simply indebted to Treichler for assisting him financially at the university.

Dr. Ezra Grumbine, M.D., mentioned that Dr. Muth began his practice in Fredericksburg, Lebanon County, in 1855.[1] Grumbine (1845–1923)[2] was born and raised in Fredericksburg and was an 1868 graduate of the University of Pennsylvania Medical School. He was the son of John Grumbine, who happened to be a stop on Dr. Muth's rounds on several occasions in 1859 and 1860. He was an astute observer of the people in the town at the time. He described Dr. Muth as having arrived in 1855 from Berks County, a graduate of the University of Pennsylvania.[3] According to Grumbine, Muth had an office at the "sharp corner of Market Street and the Jonestown Road."[4] He later moved his office to "the brick dwelling on the east end of Market Street." Grumbine

---

1. Ezra Grumbine, *Stories of Old Stumpstown: A History of Interesting Events, Traditions, and Anecdotes of Early Fredericksburg* (Lebanon, PA: Lebanon County Historical Society, 1909), 79.
2. "Dr. Grumbine Passed Away This Morning," *The Daily News* (Lebanon, Pennsylvania), February 16, 1923, 6.
3. Ezra Grumbine, *Stories of Old Stumpstown: A History of Interesting Events, Traditions, and Anecdotes of Early Fredericksburg* (Lebanon, PA: Lebanon County Historical Society, 1909), 79.
4. Ibid., 80.

described Muth as "a small man" with "a red beard, closely cropped." He surmised Muth's quiet demeanor prevented him from gaining a larger practice before he moved to Northumberland County.[5]

There is no record of Muth buying or selling the building on the corner described by Grumbine, but it may have been rented, and perhaps Samuel K. Treichler, practicing medicine in nearby Jonestown, about four miles to the west, may have used this as an extension of his practice. If Muth had daybooks for the years 1855 through 1857, they are lost. Perhaps he was in the employ of Dr. Treichler for that period.

During this time, James Buchanan, formerly of Mercersburg, was elected the President of the United States as a Democrat. Ezra Grumbine included an anecdote about that election night in old Stumpstown. Some of the Fremont Republicans and Buchanan Democrats were at a local tavern, drinking merrily and carousing. Among the Republicans was Isaac Bordner, who was with a group of men who were bouncing back and forth in the barroom, deliberately bumping the Democrats on the bench at the bar. Among the Democrats was a stonemason, Jacob Hauer, who was irritated by the harassment and reached for his pocket-knife. After another collision with the Fremonters, Bordner shouted he had been stabbed. Hauer slipped out of the bar and left. Soon, Bordner realized he was bleeding severely and was taken to Dr. Beaver, where a boot full of blood was discovered. The doctor tended to Bordner, whose life was threatened by the wound. Fortunately, he survived.[6] While we cannot know if Dr. Muth was present at the tavern, both men, Bordner and Hauer, would later play a part in Dr. Muth's life.

According to Grumbine, Dr. Daniel H. Beaver, a University of Pennsylvania graduate from 1846, had arrived in the village that year and started a practice on Market Square in the heart of Fredericksburg. He married Anna Barbara Grove and grew a successful practice in town, which lasted until he died in 1884.[7] By 1856, this practice would have been well-established, so it is puzzling that Dr. Muth set up his practice so close, though two other doctors had attempted practices prior to Muth along the Jonestown Road area.

5. Ibid.
6. Ibid., 35–36.
7. Ibid., 79.

In 1857 and early 1858, Muth logged sixteen days of service for which he tallied $24.50 for the settlement of a debt.[8] Perhaps Muth had been indebted to Treichler for other school-related expenses in the past. In 1857, Muth purchased many of Treichler's books by working for him in the Jonestown area.[9]

It is not known how the young Dr. Muth met the teenage Margaret Hauer, fourteen years his junior. Margaret Hauer/Hower, Dr. Muth's first wife, was listed in the 1850 Census, recorded on October 2, as the daughter of Isaac (age 40) and Nancy "Hower" (age 40), residing in Fredericksburg, Lebanon County. Isaac Hauer was likely a brother or cousin of Jacob Hauer, involved in the election day incident of 1856. Margaret was nine years old at the time of the 1850 census.[10] Sisters Louisa, 15, and Lucinda, 13, were listed along with younger brothers William, 8; John Henry, 7; and Washington, age 4. Isaac was a tailor living in a modest home. According to Dr. Muth's records, Margaret was born January 7, 1840,[11] which would make her ten years old in 1850 rather than nine.

Perhaps Muth, the 31-year-old recent medical school graduate, was assisting his friend, Dr. Treichler when he called upon the Hauer residence. According to Dr. Muth's notes, Margaret had been suffering from consumption since June 20, 1857. Regardless, the courtship was likely very brief, and the couple wed on October 18, 1857,[12] at a time when Muth was still in the service of Dr. Treichler.[13] At the time, the pale, thin appearance of a consumptive sufferer was seen as attractive.[14] So, Dr. Muth may have found Margaret's appearance alluring and perhaps hoped he could successfully treat her.

The move of office described by Ezra Grumbine may have occurred around the time of Muth's wedding to Margaret. Given her illness, it may have been desirable for them to rent a home near her family in

8. Reuben H. Muth, *Physician's Daybooks*, vol. 1, "General Memoranda [1858]" (1858–1898, in possession of Lawrence Knorr, Mechanicsburg, Pennsylvania).

9. Ibid.

10. US Census Bureau. 1850 United States Federal Census. Census Place: Fredericksburg, Bethel Township, Lebanon County, Pennsylvania. Household 55, family 55.

11. Reuben H. Muth, *Physician's Daybooks*, vol. 1, "Memoranda for November [1858]" (1858–1898, in possession of Lawrence Knorr, Mechanicsburg, Pennsylvania).

12. Ibid.

13. Ibid.

14. Emily Mullin, "How Tuberculosis Shaped Victorian Fashion," *Smithsonian*, May 10, 2016, accessed November 28, 2024, https://www.smithsonianmag.com/science-nature/how-tuberculosis-shaped-victorian-fashion-180959029/.

the town. Curiously, Dr. Muth's first patient mentioned in his daybook was Isaac Bordner,[15] most likely the survivor of the stabbing by Muth's future in-law back in 1856. He saw Bordner several times during the first week of the year prior to assisting with the birth of John Lutz's child on January 7.[16]

For the next few weeks, Dr. Muth had a few appointments, struggling to exceed one dollar in proceeds per week. On February 11, 1858, he attended the birth of Mary Wolf, the daughter of Daniel B. Wolf.[17] Dr. Muth collected three dollars for these services.

As the spring months arrived, Dr. Muth's practice picked up. That summer, Dr. Muth called on the home of young Ezra Grumbine's father.[18] On this day, Lee Light Grumbine was born for the fee of three dollars. He went on to become a well-known attorney and popular spokesperson nationwide on behalf of prohibition.[19]

Dr. Muth noted the first snow of the year on October 26.[20] Perhaps, as a visiting physician, he was concerned about his ability to travel around the community. Or, perhaps, if he was meeting patients in his office, he was concerned about their ability to arrive. Regardless, this weather event may be related to the subsequent service for Betsy Sarge.

On October 29, 1858, Dr. Muth was called to set a fracture for "Betsy Sarge." The charge was five dollars.[21] Elizabeth Sarge (1829–1884) was living with her uncle Melchior Behny.[22] By 1870, forty-one-year-old Elizabeth cohabited with her mother and uncle. She was noted as "insane" and unable to read or write.[23] Perhaps Elizabeth was mentally disabled and subject to seizures, explaining her broken bones. Regardless, this was an unusual patient for Dr. Muth.

15. Reuben H. Muth, *Physician's Daybooks*, vol. 1, entry for January 2, 1858 (1858–1898, in possession of Lawrence Knorr, Mechanicsburg, Pennsylvania).

16. Ibid., entries for January 3 through 9, 1858.

17. Ibid., entry for February 11, 1858. Also, "Mary Fisher Wolf Klick," *Find a Grave*, Memorial ID 26823234, accessed December 30, 2024, https://www.findagrave.com/memorial/26823234/mary_fisher_klick.

18. Reuben H. Muth, *Physician's Daybooks*, vol. 1, entry for July 25, 1858. (1858–1898, in possession of Lawrence Knorr, Mechanicsburg, Pennsylvania).

19. "Death of Lee L. Grumbine," *Lebanon Courier*, August 24, 1904.

20. Reuben H. Muth, *Physician's Daybooks*, vol. 1, entry for October 26, 1858. (1858–1898, in possession of Lawrence Knorr, Mechanicsburg, Pennsylvania).

21. Reuben H. Muth, *Physician's Daybooks*, vol. 1, entry for October 29, 1858. (1858–1898, in possession of Lawrence Knorr, Mechanicsburg, Pennsylvania).

22. US Census Bureau. 1860 United States Federal Census. Census Place: Fredericksburg, Bethel Township, Lebanon County, Pennsylvania, 29.

23. US Census Bureau. 1870 United States Federal Census. Census Place: Fredericksburg, Bethel Township, Lebanon County, Pennsylvania, 1.

Figure 6. Lee Light Grumbine.

Dr. Muth saw four patients on November 23, including Catharine Feis, whom he had treated twice the day before.[24] The following day, Wednesday, November 24, 1858, he only saw Catharine Feis and then must have headed home.[25] Perhaps he realized that Margaret's health was failing and had reached a critical stage. Unfortunately, Margaret Muth's consumption was too severe. She died on November 25, 1858, at 4 AM.[26] Doctor Muth did not see patients for the next two days as he prepared for Margaret's burial on Saturday, November 27.

As a young widower, Dr. Muth recorded the funeral expenses in his memoranda.[27] The biggest expense was $12 for a coffin purchased from "E. Heffelfinger." Muth did not hire "Yuck" Wagner, described by Dr. Ezra Grumbine in his *Stories of Old Stumpstown*. Mr. and Mrs. Wagner

24. Reuben H. Muth, *Physician's Daybooks*, vol. 1, entries for November 22 and 23, 1858. (1858–1898, in possession of Lawrence Knorr, Mechanicsburg, Pennsylvania).

25. Ibid., *entry* for November 24, 1858.

26. Reuben H. Muth, *Physician's Daybooks*, vol. 1, "General Memoranda [1858]" (1858–1898, in possession of Lawrence Knorr, Mechanicsburg, Pennsylvania).

27. Ibid.

were hired by many families to "lay out the dead" in the 1840s and 1850s. They were a peculiar couple, "she was tall and bony; he, short gray and unshaven."[28] Grumbine and the other children thought them a pair of "frightful ogres, merciless and cruel who bore away old and young to a dark grave."[29]

Regarding the Wagners, "Yuck" would measure for the coffin by using two sticks. One would measure the deceased from head to foot. The other would measure across the widest point of the breast and arms. He would then tie the sticks together as a cross and use the bound result to guide the dimensions of his carpentry.[30] Dr. Muth's coffin maker may have been the "Ed Heffelfinger" he saw as a patient in late December 1858.[31] Heffelfinger likely used the same methods as described for Wagner. Perhaps Muth preferred Heffelfinger to the creepy couple described by Grumbine.

Another funeral expense recorded by Dr. Muth was fifty cents for "Mrs. Walborn."[32] While it does not appear that the Walborns were patients while Muth was in the area, Grumbine provided an interesting anecdote about the role of Mrs. Walborn and local funerals. According to Grumbine, Mrs. Maria Walborn was a "sweet and lovely lady who smoked cigars and made the clothes for the dead."[33] She was the wife of John Walborn, a veteran of the War of 1812. She ran a millinery business on Market Street in Stumpstown for many years. She and her daughter Caroline sewed. One son, John, had headed West for the Gold Rush.[34] Given the gravity of the situation, it is difficult to make light of an elderly woman chomping on a stogie while she stitched the white funeral shroud that was customary for the times. Hopefully, none were ever ruined by hot ashes dropping off the tip!

Besides the $6.95 for "store expenses," the next most expensive item was "$6.50 for Rev Stine and Gring."[35] Grumbine pictures Reverend

28. Ezra Grumbine, *Stories of Old Stumpstown: A History of Interesting Events, Traditions, and Anecdotes of Early Fredericksburg* (Lebanon, PA: Lebanon County Historical Society, 1909), 96.

29. Ibid.

30. Ibid., 96.

31. Reuben H. Muth, *Physician's Daybooks*, vol. 1, entries for December 30 and 31, 1858 (1858–1898), in possession of Lawrence Knorr, Mechanicsburg, Pennsylvania).

32. Reuben H. Muth, *Physician's Daybooks*, vol. 1, "General Memoranda [1858]" (1858–1898, in possession of Lawrence Knorr, Mechanicsburg, Pennsylvania).

33. Ezra Grumbine, *Stories of Old Stumpstown: A History of Interesting Events, Traditions, and Anecdotes of Early Fredericksburg* (Lebanon, PA: Lebanon County Historical Society, 1909), 97.

34. Ibid., 97–98.

35. Reuben H. Muth, *Physician's Daybooks*, vol. 1, "General Memoranda [1858]" (1858–1898, in possession of Lawrence Knorr, Mechanicsburg, Pennsylvania).

John Stein in his book.[36] Likewise, Reverend John Gring (1801–1885) was buried at Cedar Hill Cemetery in Fredericksburg, Pennsylvania.[37] It appears both men officiated at the funeral in one way or another. Dr. Muth notes Reverend Gring as reading Psalms 39:5, acknowledging her short life, and Reverend Stein reading Proverbs 8:7, about seeking the love of God.[38]

Figure 7. Rev. John Gring.

Besides the coffin, officiants, and shroud, totaling $19, an additional $14.14 was spent on a variety of items and services, for a total sum of $33.14.[39] Dr. Muth lists ten line items, some food-oriented and the others named individuals. According to Grumbine, it was customary for the widower or widow to provide a meal for the townsfolk. This explains the beef mentioned in Muth's journal, as well as the store expenses. Together, this was $9.27 for food. Grumbine also described the funerary customs of the time. The church bell would be rung for each year of the deceased's life. Several individuals would be tasked with informing various family and friends of the demise of their loved ones and the funeral plans. The people of the town then graciously organized the post-funeral dinner gathering, cooking and baking as needed. Typically, the deceased was moved to the family's parlor in her coffin. It was customary for someone to watch over the deceased at all times, and there were often vigils and the quiet singing of hymns as various friends and family arrived to pay their respects. Four men of the town were designated to be gravediggers and pallbearers. On the day of the funeral, the hearse, most likely an open farm wagon, tailed the reverend's carriage in which also rode the fore-singer, who would lead the hymn singing. The hearse would stop by the church and the coffin opened to display the upper portion of the deceased. The coffin would then be lifted to the graveside, and the service held. The entourage then

---

36. Ezra Grumbine, *Stories of Old Stumpstown: A History of Interesting Events, Traditions, and Anecdotes of Early Fredericksburg* (Lebanon, PA: Lebanon County Historical Society, 1909), 95.

37. "Rev John Gring," *Find a Grave*, Memorial ID 31313675, accessed December 30, 2024, https://www.findagrave.com/memorial/31313675/john-gring.

38. Reuben H. Muth, *Physician's Daybooks*, vol. 1, "Memoranda November [1858]" (1858–1898, in possession of Lawrence Knorr, Mechanicsburg, Pennsylvania).

39. Reuben H. Muth, *Physician's Daybooks*, vol. 1, "General Memoranda [1858]" (1858–1898, in possession of Lawrence Knorr, Mechanicsburg, Pennsylvania).

headed into the church for a sermon while the gravediggers closed and lowered the coffin into the ground and covered it. They would then join the congregants.[40]

Of course, this was likely a difficult time for Dr. Muth emotionally. Ezra Grumbine, who was a lad of thirteen at the time, was a keen observer. But when later describing Dr. Muth as "quiet and unassuming"[41] and faulting his "lack of aggressiveness"[42] for his lack of success at Fredericksburg, Grumbine fails to connect the loss of Dr. Muth's wife with his mood.

While Dr. Muth continued to live and work in Fredericksburg, he had lost his young wife, and his attachments to the town and prospects for the future may have been waning. On Friday, September 17, 1859, Dr. Muth noted attending the Womelsdorf Battalion.[43] According to the *Reading Times*, this spectacle drew a large crowd and included military units from Womelsdorf, Jonestown, Myerstown, and Rehrersburg.[44] This was an opportunity for Dr. Muth to socialize with friends. "Marion" also reported speeches by several Democratic candidates for office and a brawl that ensued at the local hotel.

On September 21, 1859, word came that his younger brother, William M. Muth, had passed away at age 20. Dr. Muth's daybook contains a blank slate for this day, indicating he saw no patients.[45] Perhaps while home, he conversed with one of his mentors, Dr. Jacob Tryon, who likely cared for the late William. Dr. Tryon may have informed Dr. Muth that his cousin, Dr. Michael Trion, who lived in Northumberland County, now in his late sixties, was planning to retire. Dr. Michael Trion (1790–1871) is now buried at Himmel Church in Rebuck, Northumberland County, Pennsylvania. He was the son of Dr. Frederick Trion Sr. (1762 – 1840), who was also buried at Himmel Church. Frederick Trion was a brother of Dr. Michael Trion (1761 – 1828), who was buried at Altalaha Church in Rehrersburg. This Michael Trion was the father of Dr. Jacob

40. Ezra Grumbine, *Stories of Old Stumpstown: A History of Interesting Events, Traditions, and Anecdotes of Early Fredericksburg* (Lebanon, PA: Lebanon County Historical Society, 1909), 94–98.
41. Ibid., 80.
42. Ibid.
43. Reuben H. Muth, *Physician's Daybooks*, vol. 1, Memoranda for September 1859 (1858–1898, in possession of Lawrence Knorr, Mechanicsburg, Pennsylvania).
44. "Marion, Sept. 27, 1859" *Reading Times*, September 29, 1859, 2.
45. Reuben H. Muth, *Physician's Daybooks*, vol. 1, entry for September 21, 1858 (1858–1898, in possession of Lawrence Knorr, Mechanicsburg, Pennsylvania).

Tryon (1800–1887) of Rehrersburg. Thus, the Trion/Tryon family connections likely paid dividends once again for Dr. Muth, now 33 and still a widower.

Throughout his tenure in the Fredericksburg area, Dr. Muth appeared to be a visiting physician, given the hay and shoeing expenses he incurred regularly. He also noted in his journal weather that was out of the ordinary, tracking the Indian Summer of September 1859 and counting the snowfalls. He noted numerous weddings, perhaps of friends or potential suitors now lost. On the final page of his first daybook, he noted a recipe of one pint of flaxseed oil (warm), sheep tallow (one pound), beeswax (six oz.), rosin (4 oz.), and lavender oil (one oz.).[46] This appears to be a balm or liniment, perhaps to treat minor burns.[47]

Dr. Muth's move to Northumberland County most likely occurred the following spring, during the weeks of March 23 to April 6, 1860. During those days, Dr. Muth had no activity logged in his daybook.[48] His last patients in Lebanon County were John Grumbine and Jacob Buchmoyer on March 22, 1860.[49] According to the 1860 Census, John Grumbine, age 27, was living with his elderly parents, Michael, age 64, and Eve, age 58, in Bethel Township, Lebanon County.[50] The family were farmers. Jacob Buchmoyer, age 57, was the shoemaker in Fredericksburg.[51] Most likely, it was the Buchmoyer family to whom he said his last farewell.

---

46. Ibid., "General Memoranda."

47. R. Eglesfeld Griffith, M.D., *Medical Botany: or Descriptions of the More Important Plants Used in Medicine, with Their History, Properties, and Mode of Administration* (Philadelphia, PA: Lea and Blanchard, 1847), 207.

48. Reuben H. Muth, *Physician's Daybooks*, vol. 2, entries for March 23 through April 6, 1860 (1858–1898, in possession of Lawrence Knorr, Mechanicsburg, Pennsylvania).

49. Ibid., entry for March 22, 1860.

50. US Census Bureau. 1860 United States Federal Census. Census Place: Bethel Township, Lebanon County, Pennsylvania, house 255, family 260.

51. Ibid., house 222, family 224.

6

The Move to Mahanoy

As Dr. Muth traversed the 45 miles from Fredericksburg, Lebanon County, to Mahanoy, Northumberland County, we do not know if he packed everything on his horse and rode the distance, up and down hill and vale on windy muddy roads, or if he utilized the Pennsylvania and Reading Railroad. The latter seems more likely, given the number of books and instruments, a professional wardrobe, and the personal effects of a mature thirty-three-year-old widower. Regardless, he was entering a less settled region. At the time, neighboring Schuylkill County was known to have numerous druggists who acted as physicians. Many were "quacks."[1] Surely, the well-educated Dr. Muth, who recently graduated from the finest medical school in America, could find more opportunities here.

The first patient Dr. Muth encountered in Northumberland County was Casper Sowers, whom he saw on Saturday, April 7, 1860.[2] Dr. Muth saw Casper Sowers several times over the next two years. Someone named Casper Sowers, aged 70 years, 10 months, and 3 days, died on May 14, 1882, at Chapman Township, Snyder County, Pennsylvania, near Port Trevorton.[3] Casper Sowers was then buried at Grubbs Cemetery near Mount Pleasant Mills, Snyder County.[4] Given the bridge over the Susquehanna River between Port Trevorton and Herndon, it appears Dr. Muth was focusing on this area for his next enterprise.

---

1. Ella Zerbey Elliott, *Old Schuylkill Tales* (Pottsville, PA: Ella Zerbey Elliott, 1906), 284.
2. Reuben H. Muth, *Physician's Daybooks*, vol. 2, entry for April 7, 1860 (1858–1898, in possession of Lawrence Knorr, Mechanicsburg, Pennsylvania).
3. "Died," *Snyder County Tribune*, May 25, 1882, 2.
4. "Casper Sowers," *Find a Grave*, Memorial ID 133848803, accessed December 30, 2024, https://www.findagrave.com/memorial/133848803/casper_sowers.

Philip Gruber was Muth's next patient on April 10, 1860.[5] Gruber was visited over the next few weeks. The next day, April 11, 1860, Muth again visited with Gruber and then "W. H. Lamb."[6] Gruber was charged the customary one-dollar fee for a visit, but Lamb was only charged 15 cents. This was likely for medication. William H. Lamb, age 33, was a storekeeper in Jackson Township, Northumberland County, Pennsylvania.[7] The medication could have been for him, his wife Susan, age 20, their infant son William, 1, or Lamb's mother, Lorain, who was 71 years old and living with them. Jackson Township included the village of Mahanoy, where Dr. Muth ultimately settled as well as the bridge to the west shore of the Susquehanna. Curiously, in Bell's *History of Northumberland County*, William H. Lamb immediately follows Reuben H. Muth in the biographical section. According to Bell, Lamb was the lead engineer for the bridge and then the bridge tender, express agent, and postmaster.[8] Clearly, this bridge across the river was in focus for Dr. Muth, and helping the local postmaster was certainly beneficial.

Two weeks later, on April 26, 1860, Dr. Muth assisted John Deppen, charging him only 12 cents, likely for medication. Perhaps the two were connected via Mr. Lamb. "John Deppin," age 44, was a resident of Jackson Township, Northumberland County, with a farm of significant value.[9] This was Dr. Muth's first interaction with the Deppen family into which he would later marry. John Deppen was the brother of Abraham Deppen, who was the father of Louisa Deppen, who lived on White's Island below the expansive bridge.[10]

It appears Dr. Muth may have begun attending the newly built St. Peter's Church in Mahanoy. He recorded its consecration on May 6, 1860.[11] Five days later, the high water noted by Dr. Muth in his

5. Reuben H. Muth, *Physician's Daybooks*, vol. 2, entry for April 10, 1860 (1858–1898, in possession of Lawrence Knorr, Mechanicsburg, Pennsylvania).

6. Ibid., April 11, 1860.

7. US Census Bureau. 1860 United States Federal Census. Census Place: Jackson Township, Northumberland County, Pennsylvania, house 320, family 320.

8. Herbert C. Bell, *History of Northumberland County, Pennsylvania* (Chicago, IL: Brown, Runk & Co., 1891), 1234–1235.

9. US Census Bureau. 1860 United States Federal Census. Census Place: Jackson Township, Northumberland County, Pennsylvania, house 413, family 413.

10. E. E. Deppen, M. L. Deppen, *Counting Kindred of Christian Deppen* (Myerstown, PA: Church Center Press, 1940) 71.

11. Ibid.

Memoranda for May 11, 1860, may have been a concern for the Deppens on White's Island.[12]

As his practice began to build, Muth assisted Isaac Deppen, a brother of John Deppen, on several occasions and returned to John's home on July 24, 1860, to tend to the birth of his daughter, Susan.[13] Dr. Muth charged three dollars for the service.

According to Dr. Muth's December Memoranda (1860), he started keeping two horses on December 8,[14] indicating his practice was likely building. He closed out December by noting he had acquired "eight shirts and twelve collars."[15] He also noted, on the last page, the address for the *Medical and Surgical Reporter,* whose publication office was at 108 South Eight Street, Below Chestnut St.[16] This was a weekly medical journal published in Philadelphia. Sadly, Dr. Muth's daybook for 1860 contained none of the social events of the prior years. He did not note the weddings and meetings of the various Battalions. He also did not note the weather. This year of relocation appeared to be all business.

The previous month, Abraham Lincoln won the presidency, triggering turmoil across the South. South Carolina seceded from the Union on December 20, 1860. Mississippi, Florida, and Alabama followed on successive days from January 9 through 11. With the Buchanan presidency in turmoil, on January 13, 1861, Dr. Muth called upon William Deppen, the teenage son of Abraham Deppen, and charged one dollar.[17] The next day, on January 14, 1861, Dr. Muth called upon Abraham Deppen, charging him 25 cents, likely for some medication or for tending a child.[18] The prior census listed Abraham as 48 years old, living with his wife, Mary, 49; sons George, 23; Joseph, 20; Alexander, 18; and William, 16; and daughter Louisa, 24. Mary McCormack, 13, was also listed.[19] Interestingly, the Deppens were listed only two stops away from William H. Lamb on the census. While it cannot be ascertained exactly

12. Reuben H. Muth, *Physician's Daybooks*, vol. 2, Memoranda for May 1860 (1858–1898, in possession of Lawrence Knorr, Mechanicsburg, Pennsylvania).

13. Ibid., entry for July 24, 1860.

14. Ibid., Memoranda for December 1860.

15. Ibid.

16. Ibid.

17. Reuben H. Muth, *Physician's Daybooks*, vol. 3, entry for January 13, 1861 (1858–1898, in possession of Lawrence Knorr, Mechanicsburg, Pennsylvania).

18. Ibid., entry for January 14, 1861.

19. US Census Bureau. 1860 United States Federal Census. Census Place: Jackson Township, Northumberland County, Pennsylvania, house 322, family 322.

which person in the household Dr. Muth saw on the 14th, it very well could have been Mary McCormack, given the amount charged. Regardless, except for opportunities to meet at church, this might have been the first encounter with Louisa Deppen.

Unfortunately, Dr. Muth returned from January 17 to the 28th and then twice each day on January 29 and 30.[20] The additional charges totaled sixteen dollars and may have been for naught. William Deppen passed away despite what must have been Dr. Muth's best efforts.

For three weeks in February 1861, Dr. Muth was back at the Deppen household to tend to Louisa Deppen,[21] the daughter of Abraham Deppen, who was living on their plantation on White's Island in the Susquehanna River between Herndon and Port Trevorton. At the time, an impressive railroad bridge spanned the river at this point, connecting the east and west shores, run by the Trevorton and Susquehanna Railroad. Curiously, Dr. Muth listed her name rather than her father's. Muth's journals rarely listed the names of the women in the household, so naming the unmarried twenty-six-year-old daughter of Abraham Deppen was not his typical *modus operandi*. While we cannot know what ailment afflicted the young woman, Dr. Muth visited daily for five days from February 4 through February 8, charging one dollar per visit.[22] This rate of visitation was eerily similar to Louisa's late brother William, who had just passed. Perhaps there was a virus going through the household and now Louisa was infected.

Meanwhile, the recently seceded states, South Carolina, Mississippi, Florida, Alabama, Georgia, Louisiana, and Texas, met in Montgomery, Alabama, to organize the Confederate States of America. Jefferson Davis was elected the first president on February 9.

The following week, on Sunday, February 10, Louisa was the only patient on the docket.[23] The next day, Monday, he visited again before attending to the birth of William L. Deppen, the son of Isaac and Priscilla Deppen.[24] He saw Louisa again on February 13 and 15, despite the

20. Reuben H. Muth, *Physician's Daybooks*, vol. 3, entries for January 17 to 30, 1861 (1858–1898, in possession of Lawrence Knorr, Mechanicsburg, Pennsylvania).

21. Ibid., entries for February 4 through February 23, 1861.

22. Reuben H. Muth, *Physician's Daybooks*, vol. 3, entries for February 4 through February 8, 1861 (1858–1898, in possession of Lawrence Knorr, Mechanicsburg, Pennsylvania).

23. Ibid., entry for February 10, 1861.

24. E. E. Deppen, M. L. Deppen, *Counting Kindred of Christian Deppen* (Myerstown, PA: Church Center Press, 1940) 101.

high water on the 13th.[25] For all visits that week, he charged one dollar each.[26] The next week, Dr. Muth visited four more times on busy days, again charging one dollar each.[27]

Dr. Muth's daybooks contain no further information about the courtship of Louisa Deppen. The correspondence and conversations that occurred are lost to history. Dr. Muth did note the very warm weather on March 3, 1861, followed by a fire at John Otto's house on the 5th.[28] Curiously, Dr. Muth also saw John Otto as a patient that day, charging only twenty-five cents.[29] Perhaps that was to calm Otto's nerves. *The Sunbury Gazette* later reported that the Ottos were away at a funeral when the fire struck, starting from a stovepipe. Fortunately, no one was home, but it was a total loss, estimated at fifteen hundred dollars.[30]

The next day, March 6, 1861, Dr. Muth sold his mare to "S. Miller," perhaps right-sizing his transportation needs. Dr. Muth continued to see his patients in March, while further south, Abraham Lincoln was sworn in as president, the Confederate capital was declared in Richmond, Virginia, and the Confederates fired on Fort Sumter.

That spring, there was a late snow on April 18. This did not prevent Dr. Muth from seeing five patients that day. The snow also did not ruin the apple blossoms that Dr. Muth noted in his memoranda for May, two weeks later. He recorded their start on the 1st and peak starting on the 5th.[31] Suddenly, Dr. Muth was noticing blossoming trees again. Perhaps his heart was warming.

Dr. Muth married his patient, Louisa Deppen, on June 13, 1861.[32] Reverend J. Fitzinger officiated the ceremony held at Port Trevorton on the west shore of the Susquehanna. This was just across the railroad bridge, passing over White's Island, the Deppen's home at the time. Thus, as the Union was breaking apart, a marital union was forming in a rural valley along the Susquehanna River.

25. Reuben H. Muth, *Physician's Daybooks*, vol. 3, Memoranda for February 1861 (1858–1898, in possession of Lawrence Knorr, Mechanicsburg, Pennsylvania).

26. Ibid., entries for February 11 through February 15, 1861.

27. Ibid., entries for February 17 through February 23, 1861.

28. Ibid., Memoranda for March 1861.

29. Ibid., entries for March 5, 1861.

30. "Fire," *The Sunbury Gazette*, March 16, 1861, 2.

31. Reuben H. Muth, *Physician's Daybooks*, vol. 3, Memoranda for April and May 1861 (1858–1898, in possession of Lawrence Knorr, Mechanicsburg, Pennsylvania).

32. "Married." *Northumberland County Democrat*, June 21, 1861, 3.

Summer 1861 was uneventful for the newlyweds. Mr. and Mrs. Muth attended the Shuey wedding on July 25.[33] High water continued to plague the river on September 29 and October 8.[34] They attended the Alex Snyder / Liz Holshue wedding on October 17 and the Peter Ziegler / Charlotte Snyder wedding two weeks later.[35] The Snyders, Alex and Charlotte, were brother and sister.

The first snow fell on November 15 that year, before Dr. Muth's father-in-law, Abraham Deppen, husked his last corn on December 6. Fortunately, that week was very warm through the tenth. Dr. Muth noted these as the "last warm days of the year."[36]

On December 11, 1861, Dr. Muth noted the death of "Lizzie Shappell."[37] Dr. Muth had been visiting the household of Jacob Shappell from November 29 through December 10, nearly every day.[38] The decedent was likely the fourteen-year-old daughter of Jacob and Elizabeth Shappell.[39]

Two weeks later, on Christmas Eve, the Muths were sleighing.[40] The final entries in Dr. Muth's daybook for 1861 noted a recipe utilizing "a quarter of an ounce of sulphite of lime for every gallon."[41] This was likely a formula for a fungicide for fruit trees. Muth also noted the name of John H. Lick and Lick's Mill in Alviso, Santa Clara County, California.[42] The Lick family was originally from Fredericksburg, Lebanon County, Pennsylvania. John Henry Lick was perhaps the wealthiest person in Lebanon County at the time, thanks to his father, James Lick, who went to California and profited in real estate during the Gold Rush. The James Lick Mill and Lick Observatory remain historic sites in California. Unfortunately, we do not know why Dr. Muth recorded Lick's address. Was it because of a newspaper article or a letter received? Did he have direct correspondence

33. Reuben H. Muth, *Physician's Daybooks*, vol. 3, Memoranda for July 1861 (1858–1898, in possession of Lawrence Knorr, Mechanicsburg, Pennsylvania).

34. Ibid., Memoranda for September and October 1861.

35. Ibid.

36. Memoranda for November and December 1861.

37. Ibid.

38. Reuben H. Muth, *Physician's Daybooks*, vol. 3, entries for November 28 through December 10, 1861 (1858–1898, in possession of Lawrence Knorr, Mechanicsburg, Pennsylvania).

39. US Census Bureau. 1860 United States Federal Census. Census Place: Jackson Township, Northumberland County, Pennsylvania, Dwelling 379, Family 379.

40. Reuben H. Muth, *Physician's Daybooks*, vol. 3, Memoranda for December 1861 (1858–1898, in possession of Lawrence Knorr, Mechanicsburg, Pennsylvania).

41. Ibid. General Memoranda for 1861.

42. Ibid.

with the Lick family? Was he thinking of going West himself prior to his marriage to Louisa? Dr. Muth had seen the "Mother of Elias Desh" as a patient on April 22 and 23, 1858, back in Fredericksburg.[43] This woman was also the mother of John Desh, Barbara Snavely Desh's husband. Thus, a conversation may have been had regarding her grandson, John Henry Lick, the illegitimate son of James Lick and Barbara Snavely, prior to her marriage to Desh. Barbara was not allowed to marry James Lick and subsequently married John Desh from Fredericksburg. James went on to great heights, and his uncle raised John Henry Lick.[44]

David Baer Hackman, the Gold Rush pioneer from Manheim, Pennsylvania, had visited the Lick estate in early October 1854, seven years earlier, when he had started his return trip to Pennsylvania from the Gold Fields. Hackman had some spare time while waiting for the steamer that would take him from San Francisco to Panama for the first ocean leg of his return journey. With some time on his hands and a request from his cousin, A. J. Eby from Manheim, to drop in on their "old bachelor uncle" in "Alveso, Santa Clara, California,"[45] Hackman paid three dollars for an afternoon cruise across the bay from San Francisco to Alviso. When he arrived in Alviso, he asked for directions to the Lick estate and found an impressive operation. While the uncle was out of town, he spent the evening with a cousin and toured the property. Hackman described a lush plantation of six hundred acres run by up to thirty-five employees. Uncle Lick had built a three-and-a-half story mill at the cost of two hundred thousand dollars,[46] a phenomenal sum in those days. Hackman noted there were no women present and three Frenchmen employed in "culinary affairs." Though invited to stay as long as he wished, Hackman left the next morning after spending the night.[47]

Thus, had Muth known about the details of the Lick estate, he may have been intrigued, or perhaps he was just planning to reach out to an old acquaintance.

---

43. Reuben H. Muth, *Physician's Daybooks*, vol. 1, entries for April 22 and 23, 1858 (1858–1898, in possession of Lawrence Knorr, Mechanicsburg, Pennsylvania).

44. Lawrence Knorr, *The Relations of Milton Snavely Hershey* (Mechanicsburg, PA: Sunbury Press, 2009). The Snavely, Eby, and Hackman family trees all intersect with Milton Snavely Hershey, the chocolate magnate who would rise to fame later. It is doubtful Milton ever knew of his distant Lick connection.

45. Lawrence Knorr, *A Pennsylvania Mennonite and the California Gold Rush: The Journal and Letters of David Baer Hackman* (Mechanicsburg, PA: Sunbury Press, 2011), 125–126. David Baer Hackman was this author's great-great-grand-uncle.

46. Ibid., 126.

47. Ibid.

Figure 8. John Henry Lick on a visit to California.

New Year's Day 1862 appeared to be disappointing to Dr. Muth. He noted, "No Sleighing, Windy," that day.[48] Perhaps John Ferster did not heed the wind, because Dr. Muth set his broken collar bone that day.[49] Fortunately, the Muths were able to sled on January 6, 7, and 8 but were likely indoors for the "coldest day" on February 28th.[50] Dr. Muth saw no patients during the last three days of February.

Dr. Muth noted the "first warm day" and "Song of Birds, Robin" on March 9, 1862. Unfortunately, they harkened the death of the elderly Daniel Hilbush, Esquire, who died on March 11 at the age of 82.[51] Hilbush had been in the care of Dr. Muth the week prior.[52] Snow returned on

---

48. Reuben H. Muth, *Physician's Daybooks*, vol. 4, Memoranda for January 1862 (1858–1898, in possession of Lawrence Knorr, Mechanicsburg, Pennsylvania).

49. Ibid., entry for January 1, 1862.

50. Ibid., Memoranda for January and February 1862.

51. Reuben H. Muth, *Physician's Daybooks*, vol. 4, Memoranda for March 1862 (1858–1898, in possession of Lawrence Knorr, Mechanicsburg, Pennsylvania).

52. Ibid., entries for March 1 to 6, 1862.

March 21 and then April 8 through April 10, which Dr. Muth recorded as "10 ½ inches deep."[53] By May, the ground was clear, and Abraham Deppen was able to "finish sewing oats," according to Muth.[54]

June 10, 1862, was moving day for the Muths. Dr. Muth again noted "moved house" on July 11. Perhaps it was actually June 11 that he moved because he saw patients on the other dates.[55] It was likely around this time that Dr. Muth noted the planting of six varieties of pear trees on his property.[56] By the "Public Road S," he planted Sheldon. He also planted White Doyenne, Madeleine, and Bartletts. Next to the flower bed, he planted Vicar of Winkfield, and next to the house, Belle Lucrative.[57] He also noted the months they were expected to produce fruit, ranging from July to December.

On July 6, Dr. Muth logged an extensive wardrobe upgrade with Lewis Charles: 1 pair of shoes, $1.31; 1 suspenders, .15; 4 ½ yards of calico, .63; 1 knife, .12; 1 pair of shoes, $1.45; coat and pants trimmings, $4.12; 1 hat, .50; mending shoes, $1.00; shoestrings, 4 yards, $1.12, for a total of $10.40.[58] This was likely a traveling tailor who cycled through the area in the summer.

On July 13, 1862, with an improved wardrobe, Dr. Muth tended to the birth of his nephew, William S. Deppen, the son of his brother and sister-in-law, Alexander and Catherine Stepp Deppen.[59]

The first snow came on November 7, 1862, and Dr. Muth noted the use of coal oil.[60] On December 6, Muth noted, "High Wind, very cold," prior to butchering on the 9th. For Christmas, the weather had warmed, and the roads were "good."[61]

At some point during the year, Dr. Muth ordered a copy of Thomas P. Kettell's *History of the Great Rebellion*. This book was sold to him by J. R. Hilbush, the "Authorized Agent" for the publisher, "L. Stebbins." The advertisement claimed to be "Complete in One Vol." Dr. Muth promised to pay four dollars upon delivery, which was expected in 1862.[62]

53. Ibid., Memoranda for March and April 1862.
54. Ibid., Memoranda for May 1862.
55. Ibid., Memoranda for June and July, 1862.
56. Ibid., General Memoranda for 1862.
57. Ibid.
58. Ibid., Memoranda for July 1862.
59. Ibid., entry for April 13, 1862.
60. Ibid., Memoranda for November 1862.
61. Ibid., Memoranda for December 1862.
62. Ibid., Inserted promissory note.

The book was published during this timeframe and was in no way a complete record of the Civil War, which was continuing. The Battle of Fredericksburg had been fought in Virginia from December 11 to 15, 1862, another Union defeat.

New Year's Day 1863 did not include sledding due to the weather being "clear and moderate." But there was a "Great Snow" on January 28 and 29.[63] Meanwhile, the local news reported President Lincoln's Emancipation Proclamation, clarifying that it only freed the slaves of "rebel slave-holders."[64]

That chilly winter, Dr. Muth paid for 800 pounds of coal on February 6.[65] This was likely for home heating.

63. Reuben H. Muth, *Physician's Daybooks*, vol. 5, Memoranda for January 1863 (1858–1898, in possession of Lawrence Knorr, Mechanicsburg, Pennsylvania).

64. "Improving," *The Sunbury Gazette and Northumberland County Republican*, January 17, 1863, 2.

65. Reuben H. Muth, *Physician's Daybooks*, vol. 5, Memoranda for February 1863 (1858–1898, in possession of Lawrence Knorr, Mechanicsburg, Pennsylvania).

7

The War Comes Close

In May 1863, Dr. Muth noted the arrival of two preachers, Reverend Waltz on the 2nd and Fritzinger on the 17th.[1] The two were back in June on the 6th and 14th, respectively.[2] Perhaps the church was looking for a new minister at the time.

On June 15th, General Lee's army invaded Pennsylvania. The Sunbury newspaper reported the Confederates arriving in Chambersburg, Pennsylvania.[3] The story noted the threat to Harrisburg and the uncertainty about the invasion plans. The editor of the newspaper promised to keep publishing as long as possible, though many staff members had headed to Harrisburg to aid in the expected defense.[4] Dr. Muth saw no patients from June 17 to the 21st,[5] perhaps preparing for the Deppens and his pregnant wife to move to safer regions. This also may have been when he registered with the provost marshal for potential military service, stating he was a medical doctor, aged 38, from Jackson Township, Northumberland County.[6] Of course, Dr. Muth was 36 at the time, his 37th birthday months away. It is unclear if this incorrect information was intentional on the doctor's part or a clerical error. If intentional and if it

---

1. Ibid., Memoranda for May 1863.

2. Ibid., Memoranda for June 1863.

3. "Pennsylvania Invaded," *The Sunbury Gazette and Northumberland County Republican*, June 20, 1863, 2.

4. "Ourselves," *The Sunbury Gazette and Northumberland County Republican*, June 20, 1863, 2.

5. Reuben H. Muth, *Physician's Daybooks*, vol. 5, entries for June 17 to 21, 1863. (1858–1898, in possession of Lawrence Knorr, Mechanicsburg, Pennsylvania).

6. National Archives and Records Administration (NARA); Washington, D.C.; Consolidated Lists of Civil War Draft Registration Records (Provost Marshal General's Bureau; Consolidated Enrollment Lists, 1863–1865); Record Group: 110, Records of the Provost Marshal General's Bureau (Civil War); Collection Name: Consolidated Enrollment Lists, 1863–1865 (Civil War Union Draft Records); NAI: 4213514; Archive Volume Number: 3 of 7.

led to Dr. Muth avoiding service in the Union Army, there was a severe shortage of physicians at the start of the war, with only 98 in service.[7] According to Adams, over 11,000 surgeons were on the Union payroll at the peak of the war.[8]

The following week, the rebels continued their advance toward Harrisburg. The local newspaper declared the Pennsylvania capital as the objective.[9] Dr. Muth saw two patients over three days from June 25 to 27 and then had no entries the following week, through July 4.[10] Meanwhile, the paper next reported a battle near Gettysburg.[11] The engagement began on July 1, and "I regret to say Maj. Gen. Reynolds was mortally wounded and has since died."[12] The reporter proceeded to tell of the movement of Reynolds' body and Meade's plan to engage the rebels on July 2. Other articles mentioned the movement of rebel forces away from Carlisle, through Mount Holly Springs, towards Gettysburg.[13]

The local newspaper suspended publication until July 18. On that day, two weeks after the victories at Gettysburg and Vicksburg, the news caught up with events.[14] Given the availability of the telegraph, it appears news spread to the populace faster than the print media.

Dr. Muth returned to his patients on July 5, visiting the Emanuel Kempel household. The next day, he stopped there and also tended to the birth of Jacob Wynn.[15]

The following week, Dr. Muth made eleven visits, seeing seven different patients, three of which were obstetrical appointments. The Isaac Kaubel and Sylvester Hilbush households both greeted new family members. Unfortunately for Dr. Muth, it appears his wife, Louisa, had been with child and lost the baby. Dr. Muth recorded an obstetric visit on

7. George Worthington Adams, *Doctor's In Blue: The Medical History of the Union Army in the Civil War* (Baton Rouge, LA: Louisiana State University Press, 1996), 4.

8. Ibid., 9.

9. "The Invasion," *The Sunbury Gazette and Northumberland County Republican*, June 27, 1863, 2.

10. Reuben H. Muth, *Physician's Daybooks*, vol. 5, entries for June 25 to July 4, 1863. (1858–1898, in possession of Lawrence Knorr, Mechanicsburg, Pennsylvania).

11. "Latest News," *The Sunbury Gazette and Northumberland County Republican*, July 4, 1863, 2.

12. Ibid.

13. Ibid.

14. "Escape of General Lee," *The Sunbury Gazette and Northumberland County Republican*, July 18, 1863, 2.

15. Reuben H. Muth, *Physician's Daybooks*, vol. 5, entries for July 5 to July 6, 1863. (1858–1898, in possession of Lawrence Knorr, Mechanicsburg, Pennsylvania). Note that the Jacob Wynn visit is described in detail in the Introduction.

July 16 next to the initials "RHM" and no charge.[16] The old cemetery records at St. Peters Church included an infant Muth son who died and was buried in 1863.[17]

On August 4, 1863, Dr. Muth noted the return of drafted soldiers.[18] He could have been referring to three brothers-in-law, George, age 26; Joseph, age 25; and Alexander, age 23.[19] All three were drafted in June in anticipation of Lee's invasion. It does not appear that either of them actually served for any length of time. This notation occurred during a time when there had been riots in New York and other locales attributed to the draft. The local news described the riot in New York resulting in the death of draft officials and "Twenty Negroes" at the hands of mostly rampaging Irish immigrants.[20] A follow-up article in early August struggled to connect the draft riots to the obvious racial hatred prevalent in New York City at the time. The *Sunbury Gazette* reported that "children of Ham, everywhere throughout the city," were "hunted like wild beasts, and not merely put to death, but in some instances actually hanged and burned."[21] Unrest also smoldered in the Coal Regions of Pennsylvania, fanned by "Copperhead Teaching."[22]

The new year began with hopes for "national prosperity" following the last six months of Union success.[23] One of the first births of 1864 involved the household of Henry Knorr. Dr. Muth logged the birth on Valentine's Day, February 14.[24] Henry Knorr (1835–1901) was the son of David Knorr of Rough and Ready, Schuylkill County, Pennsylvania. He was married to Fietta Dietz (1838–1917). Their son, Michael Knorr (1864–1923), was the newborn.[25]

---

16. Ibid., entries for July 12 to 18, 1863.

17. "Muth: Infant Son," *List of Graves from St. Peters Church, Red Cross, Northumberland County, Pennsylvania, compiled 1992 by Ralph E. French*. The Muth infant was buried in the "Old Section," row 5, position 20.

18. Reuben H. Muth, *Physician's Daybooks*, vol. 5, Memoranda for August 1863. (1858–1898, in possession of Lawrence Knorr, Mechanicsburg, Pennsylvania). Note that the Jacob Wynn visit is described in detail in the Introduction.

19. U.S., Civil War Draft Registrations Records, 1863–1865, Pennsylvania, 14th Class 1, A-K, Volume 1, pages 255 to 257.

20. "The Riots in New York," *The Sunbury Gazette and Northumberland County Republican*, July 18, 1863, 2.

21. "The Great Riots – The Draft," *The Sunbury Gazette*, August 1, 1863, 3.

22. "The Fruits of Copperhead Teaching – The Riots and Murders in the Coal Region," *The Sunbury Gazette*, November 28, 1863, 1.

23. "National Prosperity for the New Year," *The Sunbury Gazette*, January 9, 1864, 1.

24. Reuben H. Muth, *Physician's Daybooks*, vol. 6, entry for February 14, 1864. (1858–1898, in possession of Lawrence Knorr, Mechanicsburg, Pennsylvania).

25. Lawrence Knorr, *The Descendants of Hans Peter Knorr* (Mechanicsburg, PA: Sunbury Press, 2005). Henry Knorr's uncle Heinrich Knorr was this author's ancestor.

Figure 9. Henry Knorr.

Figure 10. Fietta Dietz Knorr.

Figure 11. Michael Knorr (left).

Meanwhile, in Mississippi, General William Tecumseh Sherman and his troops were "moving rapidly inland," currently thirteen miles northeast of Union-occupied Jackson, Mississippi, and "will reduce his lines of communication" and advance "rapidly through the enemy's country."[26]

Times must have been tough for some of Dr. Muth's patients that spring. The payment for Dr. Muth's visits to John Fegley's family on April 3rd and 5th, 1864, was unusual. Rather than cash, Dr. Muth noted "7 Young Chickens" next to the entry.[27]

On May 20, 1864, the *Northumberland County Democrat* newspaper announced that R. H. Muth, M.D., was among the new subscribers to the paper.[28] A few inches above the announcement was an advertisement: "For President: Gen. Geo. McClellan, Subject to the Democratic National Convention."[29] If Dr. Muth was dubious about his political leanings, this subscription certainly showed his alignment. The town also had a Republican-leaning newspaper.

On August 2, the local newspaper reported the burning of Chambersburg, Pennsylvania, that had occurred on July 30, 1864.[30] This time, there was no great alarm through Northumberland County. Dr. Muth and his patients appear unfazed by the Confederate raid to the south, just above the Mason-Dixon Line. Instead, Dr. Muth was a charter member in the formation of the Jackson Horse Detective Company, founded on August 6, 1864, and was elected its president. The company insured subscribers against horse theft.[31]

In the presidential election held three months later, won by Abraham Lincoln over challenger George McClellan, a Democrat, Jackson Township, Northumberland County, Pennsylvania, voted 106 to 50 in favor of McClellan. Overall, Northumberland County tallied 3486 votes for McClellan versus 2686 for Lincoln.[32] It was typical of heavily Pennsylvania Dutch areas to support Democrats, and 1864 was no exception.

---

26. "Brandon," *The Sunbury Gazette*, February 20, 1864, 2.

27. Reuben H. Muth, *Physician's Daybooks*, vol. 6, entries for April 3 to 5, 1864. (1858–1898, in possession of Lawrence Knorr, Mechanicsburg, Pennsylvania).

28. "New Subscribers," *Northumberland County Democrat*, May 22, 1864, 2.

29. "For President:," *Northumberland County Democrat*, May 22, 1864, 2.

30. "The Raid," *The Sunbury Gazette*, August 7, 1864, 2.

31. "From Mahanoy" *Northumberland County Democrat*, February 9, 1899, 4.

32. "Presidential Election Returns for Northumberland County," *The Sunbury Gazette*, November 12, 1864, 2.

The year ended with an understated report in the local Democrat-leaning paper of the capture of Savannah, Georgia: "Sherman seemed to meet with but little opposition from the enemy."[33] Meanwhile, the Republican-leaning newspaper, not subscribed to by Dr. Muth, expounded on Sherman's remarkable accomplishment and "Christmas Gift" to President Lincoln.[34]

The local newspaper reported in its Saturday, February 4, 1865, edition the passage of the 13th Amendment through Congress. The measure had previously passed the Senate and required two-thirds of the House to then move to the states for adoption pending ratification by three-fourths of them. The reporter noted that thirteen Democrat members of the House voted in favor, and the total was two more than needed. Pennsylvania Democrats Bailey and Coffroth voted in the affirmative. "Our member, Miller, of course, voted against it,"[35] he wrote. William H. Miller was a one-term Congressman, representing in the 38th Congress, the 14th District in Pennsylvania, which included Dauphin, Union, Snyder, Northumberland, and Juniata counties. In the 1862 election, he narrowly won the seat, defeating the Speaker of the House, Galusha Grow. Two years later, he narrowly lost to the Republican George F. Miller, no relation, by 100 votes. According to the election results from the prior fall, William H. Miller carried Northumberland County by more than 867 votes.[36] Jackson Township had voted heavily for the Democrat, 95 to 37.[37] Thus, the vote against the amendment was from a lame duck, but he may have shared the sentiments of over seventy percent of his constituents.

By the time William H. Miller was out of the House of Representatives with the seating of the 39th Congress, there was a great flood on the Susquehanna River. Dr. Muth recorded in his journal that the river was the "highest ever known to man."[38] The local paper expanded on the significance of the flood, describing it as "the most destructive freshet that had ever devastated this section of the state since its settlement."[39]

---

33. "Capture of Savannah," *Northumberland County Democrat*, December 30, 1864, 2.
34. "Capture of Savannah," *The Sunbury Gazette, and Northumberland County Republican*, December 31, 1864, 2.
35. "Slavery to be Abolished" *The Sunbury Gazette*, February 4, 1865, 2.
36. "The Congressional vote of the 14th District," *The Sunbury Gazette*, October 22, 1864, 2.
37. "Election Returns for Northumberland County - Official," *The Sunbury Gazette*, October 15, 1864, 2.
38. Reuben H. Muth, *Physician's Daybooks*, vol. 6, Memoranda for March 1865 (1858–1898, in possession of Lawrence Knorr, Mechanicsburg, Pennsylvania).
39. "The Great Freshet" *The Sunbury Gazette*, March 25, 1865, 2.

The water was believed to be about three feet higher than the great flood of 1846.[40] Louisa's parents, Abraham and Mary Deppen, and her brother Joseph were living on the farm on White's Island at the time of the flood, which completely covered the island from March 17 through the 21st. Saw logs that were traveling on the river came through the second-story windows of the house. The family moved to the barn for the following week, having lost nearly all their possessions.[41] This did not deter Dr. Muth from working his usual schedule.

At some point after the flood, the family moved to higher ground near the village of Mahanoy. When Louisa Deppen Muth passed away in 1928, it mentioned she had lived in her home in Mahanoy for 63 years, confirming the couple occupied the house in 1865, after the great flood.[42]

Less than three weeks later, Robert E. Lee surrendered to U.S. Grant at Appomattox Court House on April 9, 1865, following two days of negotiation. The local newspaper reported the news nearly a week later, on April 15.[43] Dr. Muth continued to make his rounds at a normal pace, making 24 visits with 11 patients over the week, including an obstetric visit at John Wentzel's home on April 10.[44] Likely, no one knew as they were reading the Saturday edition of the newspaper on the morning of April 15 that an assassination had occurred the prior evening at Ford's Theater in Washington, D.C. John Wilkes Booth had shot President Abraham Lincoln while he and the First Lady were watching the play *Our American Cousin*. As the morning news was arriving, Abraham Lincoln passed quietly at 7:22 AM on April 15. The *Sunbury Gazette* carried all the details the following Saturday, but, likely, the news had already spread up the Susquehanna.[45] Dr. Muth saw no one on April 18, perhaps a day of mourning, and only Levi Lahr's household for an obstetric visit on the 19th, the declared National Day of Mourning.[46] Aaron Lahr was born that day.[47]

40. Ibid.

41. E. E. Deppen, M. L. Deppen, *Counting Kindred of Christian Deppen* (Myerstown, PA: Church Center Press, 1940), 71.

42. "Red Cross Woman Dies at the Age of Ninety-Three," *Shamokin News Dispatch*, October 10, 1928, 1.

43. "Victory! Victory!" *The Sunbury Gazette*, April 15, 1865, 2.

44. Reuben H. Muth, *Physician's Daybooks*, vol. 6, entries for April 9 to April 15, 1865 (1858–1898, in possession of Lawrence Knorr, Mechanicsburg, Pennsylvania).

45. "The National Calamity" *The Sunbury Gazette*, April 22, 1865, 2.

46. Reuben H. Muth, *Physician's Daybooks*, vol. 6, entries for April 18 to April 19, 1865 (1858–1898, in possession of Lawrence Knorr, Mechanicsburg, Pennsylvania).

47. *Record Book of St. Peters Lutheran Church, Red Cross, PA starting 1841*. Parents: Levi Lahr & wife Mary Ann, Child: Aaron, born 19 Apr 1865, baptism 28 May 1865, Sponsors: His Parents.

January 7, 8, and 9, were especially cold in the Mahanoy area to start 1866.[48] Dr. Muth delivered some medication for Amos Motter for fifteen cents on Sunday, January 7, likely on his way home from church. He then stayed indoors for two days and saw no patients.[49] Four days later, on the 13th, Muth described the weather as completely changed to "warm and pleasant."[50] However, the doctor saw no patients from January 11 to the 18th.[51] This was a rather long stretch for idleness. Perhaps he was under the weather himself.

In March, the Muths must have been expecting chicks because Dr. Muth recorded his hens setting four times during the month. On April 13, Muth noted the planting of potatoes. He purchased nine bushels of oats on the 16th and noted the blossoming plum and peach trees on Sunday, April 22.[52]

Dr. Muth was concerned about the two-week dry spell from May 13 to 27 but used the opportunity to install "post fence" from the 22nd to the 24th. On July 15, Muth was cutting his wheat but noted a lost cow the next day.[53] During these months, Dr. Muth managed to maintain a steady visitation schedule with his patients while also working on his farm.

48. Reuben H. Muth, *Physician's Daybooks*, vol. 7, Memoranda for January 1866 (1858–1898), in possession of Lawrence Knorr, Mechanicsburg, Pennsylvania).
49. Ibid., entries for January 7 to 9, 1866.
50. Ibid., Memoranda for January 1866.
51. Ibid., entries for January 11 to 18, 1866.
52. Ibid., Memoranda for March and April 1866.
53. Ibid., Memoranda for May and July 1866.

8

A Son Is Born

September 3, 1866, was a happy day in the Muth household. With Dr. Muth attending to his wife, Louisa Muth gave birth to Henry Deppen Muth. This was the only appointment of the day for Dr. Muth, though he did see five patients the following day. Dr. Muth then took off September 5th and 6th, likely to spend time with his family.[1] He celebrated his fortieth birthday on the 11th.

Dr. Muth was then back into a busy routine despite the first frost on October 5 and 6.[2] On Saturday, October 6, 1866, he attended a birth at the house of Isaac Lahr.[3] Farmer Isaac was most likely a diehard Democrat because the child was named George McClellan Lahr.[4] About a week later, on October 14, Isaac's grandfather, Johann Georg Lahr, called upon Dr. Muth, who attended him for three weeks, nearly every day. Dr. Muth charged the Lahrs twenty-three dollars for twenty-three visits from October 14 through November 1. On November 1, Dr. Muth saw the elder Lahr twice; thus, he must have been taking extraordinary measures.[5] Unfortunately, Johann Georg Lahr passed that day at age 67.[6]

Nearing the end of 1866, Dr. Muth expressed an interest in animal husbandry, noting what he called the "cow bulling" on November 29th.[7]

---

1. Ibid., entries for September 3 to September 8, 1866.

2. Ibid., Memoranda for October 1866.

3. Ibid., entry for October 6, 1866.

4. "George McClellan Lahr," *Find a Grave*, Memorial ID 39011455, accessed January 5, 2025, https://www.findagrave.com/memorial/39011455/george_mcclellan_lahr.

5. Reuben H. Muth, *Physician's Daybooks*, vol. 7, entries for October 14 to November 1, 1866 (1858–1898, in possession of Lawrence Knorr, Mechanicsburg, Pennsylvania).

6. "John George Lahr," *Find a Grave*, Memorial ID 38943301, accessed January 5, 2025, https://www.findagrave.com/memorial/38943301/john_george_lahr.

7. Reuben H. Muth, *Physician's Daybooks*, vol. 7, Memoranda for November 1866 (1858–1898, in possession of Lawrence Knorr, Mechanicsburg, Pennsylvania).

This was the first instance of many future recordings of his livestock interactions. Also, at the very back of his daybook, he noted the address of A. Rosenberger at 1512 N 4th Street.[8] This name and address remain a mystery. Was this a potential medical student from Philadelphia? In the past, when Dr. Muth omitted the city in an address, he was recording a Philadelphia address. But we cannot be certain of the city, and nearly every town of any size has a Fourth Street. Also, given the use of the first initial rather than the full name, we cannot know if this address was for a man or a woman. Was this a potential business interaction or an old friend from his school days? Or was this a female friend? We cannot know. On March 26, 1867, Dr. Muth noted sending via messenger, money to the German Reformed Church.[9] Perhaps A. Rosenberger was thus affiliated.

Medical historians have written much about the impact of the Civil War on medicine in the United States. Historian Shauna Devine, in her book *Learning from the Wounded: The Civil War and the Rise of American Medical Science*, discusses at length the advent of new procedures and the realization of new knowledge.[10] It is impossible to know to what degree Dr. Muth was in tune with the rapidly changing medical developments of this period, including awareness of microorganisms and the need for sanitation. Perhaps his correspondence with "A. Rosenberger" was related to gathering new knowledge.

That October of 1867, on the 28th, first cousin Edmund J Muth died at only age 25.[11] He was buried in Myerstown. Based on Dr. Muth's visitation records, he did not attend the funeral.[12] Perhaps he was no longer close to his Uncle John or his cousins in Lebanon County. Sadly, young Edmund left a wife and two young children.

The last week of winter in 1868 was eventful. While the Susquehanna again flooded on March 17 and 18, "similar to 1865," Dr. Muth noted his "chicken set" on the 18th. On the 19th, he trimmed his grape

---

8. Ibid., General Memoranda, 1866.

9. Reuben H. Muth, *Physician's Daybooks*, vol. 8, Daily Memoranda for March 24 to 30, 1867 (1858–1898, in possession of Lawrence Knorr, Mechanicsburg, Pennsylvania).

10. Shauna Devine, *Learning from the Wounded: The Civil War and the Rise of American Medical Science* (Chapel Hill, N.C.: University of North Carolina Press, 2014).

11. "Edmund J Muth," *Find a Grave*, Memorial ID 35875894, accessed January 5, 2025, https://www.findagrave.com/memorial/35875894/edmund-j-muth.

12. Reuben H. Muth, *Physician's Daybooks*, vol. 8, entries for October 28 to 31, 1867 (1858–1898, in possession of Lawrence Knorr, Mechanicsburg, Pennsylvania).

vines.[13] The following Friday, Dr. Muth noted the planting of clover seed.[14] However, in the second full week of April, there were snowstorms of two and ten inches,[15] leaving Easter Sunday cold and snowy.

Three months later, Dr. Muth noted "the last voice of the 7 yr Locusts" on July 16, 1868.[16] Then, two weeks later, our budding entomologist noted the appearance of katydids.[17]

The October 9, 1868, edition of the *Northumberland County Democrat* detailed a gruesome injury suffered by eighteen-year-old Abraham Snyder. While attempting to fix an old cider press, he was thrown to the ceiling and then fell hard to the ground after a gear broke.[18] Drs. Muth and Kantz were called to set the bones.[19] Dr. Muth made no mention of visits with Abraham Snyder. There is a visit with "Noah Snyder" on Monday, September 14, for which he charged fifty cents, the fee for a consultation.[20] Dr. Andrew Jackson Kantz (1837–1899)[21] was born in Freeburg, Snyder County, Pennsylvania, and studied medicine with Dr. John C. Beshler. He then practiced in the vicinity of Berrysburg, Dauphin County, Pennsylvania, for thirty-three years, starting circa 1866.[22]

Unfortunately, Dr. Muth's attention changed to the passing of his mother-in-law, Mary Deppen, on November 12, 1868. She was buried on the 14th. The texts read included the "Second Epistle of Paul to Corinthians 4 ch. 18 v."[23] Mary Snyder Deppen's parents were Johann Peter Schneider and Maria Gertrude Maurer Schneider, who emigrated from Bethel Township in Berks County to Northumberland County.[24] Johann Peter's brother was Johann Jacob Schneider of Rehrersburg.[25] Thus, Dr.

13. Reuben H. Muth, *Physician's Daybooks*, vol. 8, Daily Memoranda for March 15 to 21, 1868 (1858–1898, in possession of Lawrence Knorr, Mechanicsburg, Pennsylvania).

14. Ibid., March 22 to 28, 1868.

15. Ibid., April 5 to 11, 1868.

16. Ibid., July 16, 1868.

17. Ibid., July 30, 1868.

18. "Mahanoy Correspondence," *Northumberland County Democrat*, October 9, 1868, 3.

19. Ibid.

20. Reuben H. Muth, *Physician's Daybooks*, vol. 8, entry for September 14, 1868 (1858–1898, in possession of Lawrence Knorr, Mechanicsburg, Pennsylvania).

21. "Andrew Jackson 'A.J.' Kantz," *Find a Grave*, Memorial ID 30549467, accessed January 5, 2025, https://www.findagrave.com/memorial/30549467/andrew-jackson-kantz.

22. "Death of Dr. A. J. Kantz," *Lykens Register*, February 2, 1899, 1.

23. Reuben H. Muth, *Physician's Daybooks*, vol. 8, entry for November 12, 1868 (1858–1898, in possession of Lawrence Knorr, Mechanicsburg, Pennsylvania).

24. "Johann Peter Schneider," *Find a Grave*, Memorial ID 34445042, accessed January 5, 2025, https://www.findagrave.com/memorial/34445042/johann_peter_schneider.

25. "Johann Jacob Schneider," *Find a Grave*, Memorial ID 34127162, accessed January 5, 2025, https://www.findagrave.com/memorial/34127162/johann_jacob_schneider.

Muth may have been welcomed to the Deppen household based on Schneider relatives who had also come from Rehrersburg to Northumberland County. Dr. Muth and Louisa Deppen Muth were likely second or third cousins due to their Schneider/Snyder connections.

Dr. Muth's patient count fell nearly 30% from 1868 to 1869, and his income dipped by over 40% from $863.65 to $513.50.[26] Throughout the year, he was busy each week, but he made no additional notes. Clearly, something was distracting him from the usual happy notations of life on the farm and various flora and fauna and atmospheric experiences.

Ulysses S. Grant was inaugurated on March 4, 1869, as the 18th President of the United States. The Golden Spike was hammered into place near the Great Salt Lake two months later, on May 10, joining the Union Pacific and Central Pacific Railroads to link the continent east and west. Some historians also set this event as the beginning of the Gilded Age.

That summer, there was an attempt to organize the physicians of Northumberland County, Pennsylvania, into a medical association. A meeting was held at 1 PM on Saturday, July 10, 1869, in Sunbury. The first matter of business was to elect Joseph Priestly as president.[27] They planned to create a constitution and bylaws and proceeded to name a committee of physicians from areas other than Mahanoy and Herndon. It appears, from Dr. Muth's journals, that he likely attended this event. He saw no patients from July 8th through the 10th.[28] Neither Dr. Muth nor Dr. Haas, from Mahanoy, were named to the committee. It appears this effort may have fizzled over time; as Herbert Bell noted, "How long this association existed has not been ascertained."[29]

On Friday, September 24, 1869, there was turmoil in the financial markets in New York, such that it became known as "Black Friday." Jay Gould and others attempted to control the gold market but failed due to intervention by the Federal Government. This event was not mentioned in the Northumberland County papers at the time and was not the reason why Dr. Muth's practice had suffered throughout the year.

Dr. Muth's father-in-law seemed unfazed by the financial turmoil. "Hen Patch" reported from Herndon on December 11, 1869, that

26. See Appendix D: "Summary" for Dr. Muth's Career Earnings.
27. "North'd County Medical Association," *Northumberland County Democrat*, July 16, 1869, 3.
28. Reuben H. Muth, *Physician's Daybooks*, vol. 9, entries for July 8 through July 10, 1869 (1858–1898, in possession of Lawrence Knorr, Mechanicsburg, Pennsylvania).
29. Herbert C. Bell, *History of Northumberland County* (Chicago: Brown, Runk, and Co., 1891), 269.

Abraham Deppen, a grain dealer, was "buying it mostly from Snyder Co. and shipping it off on the railroad."[30] Thus, Louisa's father was dealing in more than his own produce.

Dr. Muth was back to noting his plantings again in the spring of 1870. Potatoes were planted on April 8.[31] Ten days later, the doctor noted "High Water,"[32] perhaps on the Susquehanna River.

A short item in the newspaper in July 1870 may be the first mention of the Jackson Horse Detective Company. A horse owned by John Zartman, a harness owned by Jacob Smith, and a buggy and harness owned by Samuel Malick were stolen. The horse, valued at $200, had been insured by the company. The theft happened during the funeral of Zartman's daughter, Mrs. Wilhelmina Brown.[33] The reporter mentioned that the two thieves were tracked east, as far as the Schuylkill County line near Joseph Maurer's farm.[34]

The next paragraph mentioned that local doctors Haas and Muth were very busy this summer.[35] Perhaps the anecdote referred more to Dr. Haas because Muth's ledger was not busier than usual. Dr. Joseph Haas (1830–1905) was born in Sunbury, Pennsylvania, and educated at the Jefferson Medical College in Philadelphia, graduating in 1852. He practiced medicine around Mahanoy for fifty-five years, from about 1850 until he died in 1905. He was described as "a successful physician and a man of pleasing personality."[36] Meanwhile, Dr. Muth noted the arrival of the katydids on July 25.[37]

In the August 12, 1870, edition of the *Northumberland County Democrat*, the Jackson Horse Detective Company posted a reward of up to $175 regarding the theft of a horse on July 15, 1870. One hundred dollars was offered for the arrest and conviction of the perpetrators and seventy-five dollars for the return of the horse described in the advertisement. The advertisement was signed "R.H. Muth, Pres't."[38]

30. "Herndon, Dec, 11, 1869," *The Sunbury Gazette*, December 11, 1869, 3.

31. Reuben H. Muth, *Physician's Daybooks*, vol. 9, Daily Memoranda for April 8, 1870 (1858–1898, in possession of Lawrence Knorr, Mechanicsburg, Pennsylvania).

32. Ibid., for April 18 and 19, 1870.

33. "Mahanoy, Pennsylvania, July 19, 1870" *Northumberland County Democrat*, July 22, 1870, 3.

34. Ibid.

35. Ibid.

36. "Death of Dr. Haas," The Sunbury American, February 3, 1905, 2.

37. Reuben H. Muth, *Physician's Daybooks*, vol. 9, Daily Memoranda for July 25, 1870 (1858–1898, in possession of Lawrence Knorr, Mechanicsburg, Pennsylvania).

38. "New Advertisements," *Northumberland County Democrat*, December 23, 1870, 3.

A December 1870 article mentioned the recovery of a horse belonging to Mr. Zartman that had been stolen in July. The horse was found in Philadelphia and was now the property of the company because it had already paid Zartman "$130 for his loss."[39] The company planned to auction the horse. Dr. Muth was later mentioned as an officer of this organization which was organized as an insurance company against horse theft. Despite the "horsing around" with the Jackson Horse Detective Company, for the year, Dr. Muth recovered about half of the lost patients and revenue through the year.[40]

According to mortality records, Dr. Michael Trion of Northumberland County, Pennsylvania, the cousin of Dr. Jacob Tryon of Rehrersburg, died on January 2, 1871, at age 80. According to Dr. Muth's daybooks for the weeks prior, he logged entries for Michael "Treon" on December 26, 27, 29, and 31, 1870,[41] and January 1 and 2, 1871.[42] The patient was noted as "indigent," and Muth logged a charge of one dollar for each visit. Thus, it is more than likely that Dr. Muth attended to Dr. Michael Trion over his final days. These were the only entries related to Michael "Treon" in Muth's daybooks.

Dr. Muth was elected the church secretary for St. Peters Church at a meeting "in the basement of said church held May 13th, 1871."[43] Daniel Hilbush was elected president. The trustees present included Hilbush, Muth, Peter Bohner, Peter Klock, Abraham Deppen, and Solomon Billman.[44]

Dr. Muth was again quiet about his surroundings for much of 1871. He noted the second annual Avon Park fair to be held from September 19 to the 22nd.[45] Dr. Muth did not mention the location of Avon Park, but a local newspaper printed an article about the fair as it was underway. The fair, held near Lebanon, Pennsylvania, attracted between eight and

---

39. "Mahanoy, Pennsylvania, Dec. 19, 1870," *Northumberland County Democrat*, August 12, 1870, 2.

40. Appendix A: Dr. Muth Career Earnings.

41. Reuben H. Muth, *Physician's Daybooks*, vol. 9, entries for the last week of December 1870 (1858–1898, in possession of Lawrence Knorr, Mechanicsburg, Pennsylvania).

42. Reuben H. Muth, *Physician's Daybooks*, vol. 10, entries for the first week of January 1871 (1858–1898, in possession of Lawrence Knorr, Mechanicsburg, Pennsylvania).

43. *St. Peters Church Board of Trustee Records*, 16, entry for May 13, 1871 (1859–1918, in the possession of St. Peters Church, Red Cross, Pennsylvania).

44. Ibid.

45. Reuben H. Muth, *Physician's Daybooks*, vol. 10, Daily Memoranda for September 17 to 23, 1871 (1858–1898, in possession of Lawrence Knorr, Mechanicsburg, Pennsylvania).

ten thousand patrons. Horse racing was one of the featured events.[46] According to Dr. Muth's daybook, he saw no patients on Friday, September 22, so it is possible he rode the train to and from the event.[47]

By 1872, Dr. Muth was very busy again. His 903 patient visits for the year were the second-most of his career to that point.[48] Thus, it appears Dr. Muth was very focused on his practice and again had little time for his environmental awareness.

One tragic event may have numbed the financial results for the year. Dr. Muth noted his patient, Ben Lahr, committed suicide on Thursday, May 2, 1872.[49] According to his patient log, the doctor had seen Mr. Lahr the day before, charging him seventy-five cents for the visit. According to the newspaper, Benneville Lahr, "of Jackson township, this county, committed suicide by shooting himself on Thursday of last week."[50] Apparently, Mr. Lahr, in his mid-forties, was depressed about his business losses. That day, along with his sister and ten-year-old daughter (Hannah), he grabbed his gun and joined them on a walk to his nephew Isaac's house about one mile away. The ladies objected to him taking his gun, but he told them he planned to shoot a fox, "which would give him pleasure." A short way down the road, Mr. Lahr told his sister he was tired and that she should continue on her own. He told her he would return home with his daughter. After they split, Benneville directed his daughter to a log, where they sat. He then took his own life with his gun, propped on a forked stick, while his daughter sat next to him, "unconscious of his purpose." Lahr was killed instantly, and the daughter ran to nearby friends to tell them of the incident.[51] It is disturbing that Benneville included his daughter in the event. Clearly, this would leave an impression on her for the rest of her life. Perhaps his only remaining pleasure in life was young Hannah, and he wanted to be with her when he died. Mr. Lahr left a wife and three children, the other two older than Hannah.[52]

---

46. "The Avon Park Fair," *Reading Times*, September 22, 1871.

47. Reuben H. Muth, *Physician's Daybooks*, vol. 10, entry for September 22, 1871 (1858–1898, in possession of Lawrence Knorr, Mechanicsburg, Pennsylvania).

48. See Appendix D: "Summary" for Dr. Muth's Career Earnings.

49. Reuben H. Muth, *Physician's Daybooks*, vol. 10, Daily Memoranda for April 28 to May 4, 1872 (1858–1898, in possession of Lawrence Knorr, Mechanicsburg, Pennsylvania).

50. "Shot Himself," *The Sunbury Gazette*, May 10, 1872, 3.

51. Ibid.

52. "Benneville Lahr," *Find a Grave*, Memorial ID 39011245, accessed January 5, 2025, https://www.findagrave.com/memorial/39011245/benneville-lahr.

Perhaps another death may also have tempered Dr. Muth's emotions. Dr. Samuel K. Treichler, his friend and classmate at the University of Pennsylvania, who studied medicine with "the venerable" Dr. Jacob Tryon of Rehrersburg, passed away on October 13, 1872.[53] The obituary mentioned Treichler was a native of Berks County and was "universally respected by his friends and neighbors."[54] Dr. Muth's daybooks are clear on October 15 and October 17, so it is possible he traveled the forty miles to Jonestown, Pennsylvania, for the services.[55] Because he continued to work the other days that week, train rides there and back would have been required.

There is evidence Dr. Muth continued to expand his knowledge of medicine post-graduation. *The Medical and Surgical Reporter* was a weekly journal published by S. W. Butler, M.D. from Philadelphia. Dr. Muth most assuredly subscribed to this journal because these are the same publishers of the daybooks he was using much of the time. The journal was also in the practice of acknowledging its subscribers by listing them on the inside of the front page after their subscription was received. "R. H. Muth" was listed as a subscriber from Pennsylvania in 1873.[56] The cost of the subscription that year was $6 if paid in two installments of $3 each.[57] The issue from late December of that year set the subscription price at $5 if paid in advance and permitted a $1 trial subscription of three months.[58] The publishers also offered *The Half-Yearly Compendium of Medical Science* to supplement the weekly journal for an additional $3 a year.[59] For only 25 cents more, a total of $8.25, a physician could receive both publications and the *Physicians Daily Pocket Record* for the year ($1.50 if purchased individually). Early in his career, Dr. Muth utilized this publisher's daybook from 1867 until 1876, doubling up with two years in each book.[60] This might indicate that he only purchased complete subscriptions every other year. Later in his career, he returned to this publisher's daybook, utilizing it from 1880 to 1884 and 1888

---

53. "Local Affairs," *Reading Times*, Oct 16, 1872, 1.

54. Ibid.

55. Reuben H. Muth, *Physician's Daybooks*, vol. 10, entries for October 15 and 17, 1872 (1858–1898, in possession of Lawrence Knorr, Mechanicsburg, Pennsylvania).

56. S. W. Butler, *The Medical and Surgical Reporter*, Vol. XXVIII, No. 3 (January 18, 1873), ii.

57. Ibid., iv.

58. Ibid., Vol. XXIX, No. 26 (December 27, 1873), xxiii.

59. Ibid.

60. See Appendix A: "Journals" for a list of the daybooks.

to 1890.[61] During those years, he did not double up, recording only one year per book. This might indicate he was back to purchasing the complete subscriptions annually.

On July 25, 1873, the local newspaper complained about "gipsies" in the neighborhood, saying they were "subsisting by fortune-telling, begging, trading horses, and stealing."[62] The reporter suggested a law against them might be beneficial. He also reported that Solomon Tressler was walking about and in the care of Dr. Muth.[63] Solomon (1795–1881) was in his late seventies at the time.[64] He was seen by Dr. Muth nearly every day from June 16 to the 28th.[65] The newspaper of June 13, 1873, recounted an accident involving Solomon Tressler, whereby he was "hurt very badly near Ashland, by the cars crushing his right arm, breaking two or three ribs, &c."[66] According to the reporter, his arm was amputated soon after the accident.[67] Given that Ashland, Schuylkill County, Pennsylvania, is over twenty-five miles east of Dr. Muth's home in Mahanoy, it is most likely he did not perform the amputation. It appears Tressler must have stayed in Ashland and returned home around the 16th of June, and his care was transferred to Dr. Muth.

In September of 1873, a variety of factors led to a prolonged economic slump, which some economists have referred to as the "Long Depression," lasting for many years. Some have referred to this as "The Great Depression" before the events of the following century. At the time, the local news thought the panic had little or no impact on "legitimate business of any description." Rather, it was caused by "speculations in fancy stocks, of which the Northern Pacific Railroad is now regarded at the head of the list."[68] Dr. Muth's practice seemed unaffected by the turmoil. Instead, he had a strong year in 1873 and then the two best years of his career in 1874 and 1875.[69]

61. S. W. Butler, *The Medical and Surgical Reporter*, Vol. XXIX, No. 26 (December 27, 1873), xxiii.

62. "Mahanoy," *Northumberland County Democrat*, July 25, 1873, 3.

63. Ibid.

64. "Solomon Tressler," *Find a Grave*, Memorial ID 38943167, accessed January 5, 2025, https://www.findagrave.com/memorial/38943167/solomon-tressler.

65. Reuben H. Muth, *Physician's Daybooks*, vol. 11, entries for June 16 to June 30, 1873 (1858–1898, in possession of Lawrence Knorr, Mechanicsburg, Pennsylvania).

66. "From the Lower End," *Northumberland County Democrat*, June 13, 1873, 3.

67. Ibid.

68. "The late panic," *Sunbury Gazette*, September 26, 1873, 2.

69. See Appendix D: "Summary" for Dr. Muth's Career Earnings.

The appearance of "R.H. Muth" in the subscribers list of an early issue for 1874 indicates he probably elected to purchase only the journal and not the compendium and daybook.[70] That same year, on the back page of his daybook, Dr. Muth noted a concoction under the heading of "Med. Surgical Reporter Aug. 15, 1874."[71] Beneath that is the note, "For the intense pain of cholera morbus, i.e., the following is useful." He then listed five ingredients for a mixture that was to be administered by the "spoonful every 15 minutes till relieved."[72] The formula and notation were copied almost verbatim from the journal's "Notes and Comments" section.[73] While it is unlikely deadly bacterial cholera was spreading in the Mahantongo Valley of Pennsylvania that year, the local newspaper did print two articles on the subject. The first, in February 1874, noted over 200,000 deaths in Europe.[74] Then, in November, the paper warned of cholera potentially spreading worldwide via pilgrims returning from India.[75] Perhaps the more common experience in Dr. Muth's area was due to the norovirus common in the summer months that results in similar symptoms, but is rarely fatal. Regardless, connecting the weekly journal to notations in a daybook proves the doctor continued to expand his knowledge.

On August 14, 1874, the local newspaper reported an accident involving Moses Wiest and Henry T. Bowman. Apparently, they were attempting to deal with a runaway carriage. Bowman, when attempting to exit the moving carriage, caught his foot on the running board and was dragged over the ground for quite a distance. Wiest stayed with the carriage until the horse was freed when the conveyance hit a telephone pole. Wiest was not severely injured. However, Bowman was taken to the Mahanoy Hotel operated by J.G. Smith, and Dr. Muth was called for.[76] According to the report, the bruises and wounds had caused Bowman's face to swell such that "he could not see."[77] It appears Dr. Muth did not charge for these services as he made no entry in his daybook. Moses

70. S. W. Butler, *The Medical and Surgical Reporter*, Vol. XXX, No. 3 (January 17, 1874), ii.
71. Reuben H. Muth, *Physician's Daybooks*, vol. 11, (back page) (1858–1898, in possession of Lawrence Knorr, Mechanicsburg, Pennsylvania).
72. Ibid.
73. S. W. Butler, *The Medical and Surgical Reporter*, Vol. XXXI, No. 7 (August 15, 1874), 131.
74. "The Cholera Epidemic in Europe," *The Sunbury Gazette*, Feb. 6, 1874, 4.
75. "Cholera in the East," *The Sunbury Gazette*, Nov. 20, 1874, 4.
76. "From the Lower End," *Sunbury Daily*, August 14, 1874, 1.
77. Ibid.

Wiest may have been the Moses Merkel Wiest (1826–1902) who lived at nearby Klingerstown, Schuylkill County, Pennsylvania.[78] Henry T. Bowman (1848–1879) lived in Jordan Township, Northumberland County, Pennsylvania.[79]

On March 18, 1875, Louisa's aunt, Leah Deppen Bower (1815–1875), the wife of Uncle Michael Bower, passed away near Herndon.[80] Dr. Muth had a full schedule of appointments, so perhaps only Louisa attended.[81]

Dr. Muth assisted an unfortunate lad who was the victim of a gruesome accident when a horse kicked him. Apparently, the boy, a son of "Saviary" Brown, had lost most of his upper teeth and had a partially torn tongue. The boy was recovering "as well as expected."[82] According to his patient log, Dr. Muth called on "Vira Brown" on Saturday, August 14, charging three dollars.[83] This was an unusual amount from a non-obstetric visit. Saviry William Brown (1836–1908) was a resident of Herndon for a time.[84] His son, Charles Morris Brown (1872–1959), was only three in 1875.[85] Another son, William Saviry Brown, was six.[86] Either son was the possible victim. Regardless, they both lived to adulthood, so Dr. Muth's care had an impact.

On November 23, 1875, Dr. Muth recorded the butchering of a steer, yielding 425 pounds of beef from a 799-pound animal.[87] This was his last entry for 1875.

78. "Moses Merkel Wiest," *Find a Grave*, Memorial ID 28674352, accessed January 5, 2025, https://www.findagrave.com/memorial/28674352/moses-merkel-wiest.

79. "Henry T. Bowman," *Find a Grave*, Memorial ID 38620383, accessed January 5, 2025, https://www.findagrave.com/memorial/38620383/henry-t-bowman.

80. "Leah Deppen Bower," *Find a Grave*, Memorial ID 46466166, accessed January 5, 2025, https://www.findagrave.com/memorial/46466166/leah-bower.

81. Reuben H. Muth, *Physician's Daybooks*, vol. 12, entries for March 15 to March 20, 1875 (1858–1898, in possession of Lawrence Knorr, Mechanicsburg, Pennsylvania).

82. "Accidents," *Northumberland County Democrat*, September 3, 1875, 3.

83. Reuben H. Muth, *Physician's Daybooks*, vol. 12, entry for August 14, 1875 (1858–1898, in possession of Lawrence Knorr, Mechanicsburg, Pennsylvania).

84. "Saviry William Brown," *Find a Grave*, Memorial ID 46115831, accessed January 5, 2025, https://www.findagrave.com/memorial/46115831/saviry_william_brown.

85. "Charles Morris Brown," *Find a Grave*, Memorial ID 46116090, accessed January 5, 2025, https://www.findagrave.com/memorial/46116090/charles_morris_brown.

86. "William Saviry Brown," *Find a Grave*, Memorial ID 208872330, accessed January 5, 2025, https://www.findagrave.com/memorial/208872330/william_saviry_brown.

87. Reuben H. Muth, *Physician's Daybooks*, vol. 12, Cash Record for 1875 (1858–1898, in possession of Lawrence Knorr, Mechanicsburg, Pennsylvania).

9

The Passing of Ma Muth

Dr. Muth's journal for 1876 only contained patient visits for the first week of January.[1] The year began at a normal pace and then ended abruptly. Perhaps he had received word that back in Rehrersburg, his mother, Anna Maria Muth, was gravely ill. If so, it is almost certain he would have come home immediately and provided whatever care he could. Despite any efforts on the part of her son, Anna Maria Schneider Muth (1806–1876) passed away on May 2, 1876, at sixty-nine years of age. She was buried at the Altalaha Lutheran Church in Rehrersburg, Pennsylvania. Her husband erected a tombstone carved in German.[2]

Assuming Dr. Muth left Northumberland County at this time to tend to his dying mother in Berks County, then he would not have participated in the meeting of the physicians of Northumberland County, held at Sunbury on April 18, 1876, to organize a county medical society. As in 1869, Dr. Joseph Priestly was again elected president.[3] According to Herbert Bell, "this society sustained an intermittent existence of about five years."[4]

The following month, Dr. Muth was back at Mahanoy, performing the duties of treasurer of the church. On June 17th, 1876, he began keeping a simple one-page ledger with a column for "Bills Receivable" and a column for "Bills Payable."[5] The items on the ledger included the collec-

1. Reuben H. Muth, *Physician's Daybooks*, vol. 12, entries for January 1 through January 7, 1876 (1858–1898, in possession of Lawrence Knorr, Mechanicsburg, Pennsylvania).

2. "Anna Maria Schneider Muth," *Find a Grave*, Memorial ID 61620324, accessed January 5, 2025, https://www.findagrave.com/memorial/61620324/anna-maria-muth.

3. "The Physicians of Northumberland County," *The Sunbury Gazette*, April 21, 1876, 3.

4. Herbert C. Bell, *History of Northumberland County* (Chicago: Brown, Runk, and Co., 1891), 269.

5. Reuben H. Muth, Ephemera, item 4, Church Ledger for June 1876 through May 1877 (1876–1924, in possession of Lawrence Knorr, Mechanicsburg, Pennsylvania).

tion and transfer of mission money, payment of salaries to the minister, and other expenses incurred by the presidents and other trustees. The last entry on the ledger was May 21, 1877.[6]

Whatever the excuse for Dr. Muth's hiatus from medical practice in 1876, he was treating patients again on the very first day of 1877, checking in on the household of Samuel Brosius.[7] The pace of Muth's appointments suggests he simply picked up where he left off. Perhaps he and Dr. Haas had a temporary arrangement.

Dr. Muth was back on his sled again in March 1877. He noted "Good Sledding" on March 18, 19, and 20, the last three days of winter.[8] The following month, he planted his potatoes on April 9, 10, and 11.[9] He then estimated the cow bulling had occurred on or about May 30.[10] He cut his wheat that summer on July 2.[11]

That fall, Dr. Muth was still performing the duties of church treasurer as evidenced by instructions on October 6, 1877, from the president of the board of trustees to pay Reverend A. R. Hottenstein his salary of $125 due him on November 1, 1877.[12] Dr. Muth reported a "Fire in Heater" on October 27.[13] The last few weeks of the year, he reported spring-like weather from December 9 to the 29th.[14] It was not a white Christmas in 1877.

As Dr. Muth transitioned from 1877 to 1878, his practice from the prior year had recovered well from his hiatus in 1876. He logged just under eighty percent of the visits and just over eighty percent of the fees tallied in 1875.[15] On New Year's Day, 1878, Dr. Muth saw four patients at the start of a busy week.[16]

---

6. Ibid.

7. Reuben H. Muth, *Physician's Daybooks*, vol. 13, entries for January 1 to January 7, 1877 (1858–1898, in possession of Lawrence Knorr, Mechanicsburg, Pennsylvania).

8. Reuben H. Muth, *Physician's Daybooks*, vol. 13, entries for March 18 to March 20, 1877 (1858–1898, in possession of Lawrence Knorr, Mechanicsburg, Pennsylvania).

9. Ibid., entries for April 9 to April 11, 1877.

10. Ibid., entry for May 30, 1877.

11. Ibid., entry for July 2, 1877.

12. Reuben H. Muth, Ephemera, item 11, Minister's Salary (1876–1924, in possession of Lawrence Knorr, Mechanicsburg, Pennsylvania).

13. Reuben H. Muth, *Physician's Daybooks*, vol. 13, entry for October 27, 1877 (1858–1898, in possession of Lawrence Knorr, Mechanicsburg, Pennsylvania)..

14. Ibid., entries for December 9 to December 29, 1877.

15. See Appendix D: "Summary" for Dr. Muth's Career Earnings.

16. Reuben H. Muth, *Physician's Daybooks*, vol. 14, entries for January 1 to January 7, 1878 (1858–1898, in possession of Lawrence Knorr, Mechanicsburg, Pennsylvania).

During the third week of April 1878, Dr. Muth noted his cherry, peach, and plum trees were in blossom.[17] The apple blossoms followed the next week.[18] Unfortunately for William Wiest, his barn and "a small house adjoining" were consumed by fire "set by an incendiary." The loss was estimated at five hundred dollars.[19] Dr. Muth noted the barn fire in his daybook on May 1, 1878,[20] but he saw no patients that day. Perhaps he was assisting his neighbor with putting out the fire.

During the last full week of July, Dr. Muth noted the return of the katydids. He also marked that the cow bulling had occurred.[21]

The newspaper of August 16, 1878, recounted another potential collaboration of Dr. Muth and Dr. Haas. Andrew Bucher was thrown from a wagon and broke his leg above the ankle. At the time of the accident, which occurred near Urban, Josiah Schwartz was using his threshing machine and was partially blocking the road. Andrew Bucher Senior and his son, Andrew Junior, took the wagon onto Schwartz's field to go around the thresher. Unfortunately, one of the horses was startled and jerked the wagon such that Andrew Junior was thrown off.[22] Both Dr. Muth and Dr. Haas were called for, but it appears Dr. Muth was the one who responded. He logged two appointments with Andrew Bucher on August 15 and 17, noting he had "set fracture."[23] Dr. Muth did not charge for the service.

Later that month, from the 26th to the 30th, Dr. Muth noted the "camp meeting" that was happening.[24] Unfortunately, Dr. Muth did not share the location of the meeting, but apparently, he worked throughout. So, either the camp meeting was very close to Mahanoy so that he could attend at certain times, or he attended to patients at this religious gathering. This was most likely the Herndon Camp Meeting organized by the Evangelical Association that started on the land of his father-in-law,

17. Reuben H. Muth, *Physician's Daybooks*, vol. 14, entries for April 14 to April 20, 1878 (1858–1898, in possession of Lawrence Knorr, Mechanicsburg, Pennsylvania).

18. Ibid., entries for April 21 to April 27, 1878.

19. "Fire at Mahanoy," *Northumberland County Democrat*, May 10, 1878, 3.

20. Reuben H. Muth, *Physician's Daybooks*, vol. 14, entry for May 1, 1878 (1858–1898, in possession of Lawrence Knorr, Mechanicsburg, Pennsylvania).

21. Ibid., entries for July 22 and July 23, 1878.

22. "From Mahanoy, Jackson twp.," *Northumberland County Democrat*, August 16, 1878, 2.

23. Reuben H. Muth, *Physician's Daybooks*, vol. 14, entries for August 15 to August 17, 1878 (1858–1898, in possession of Lawrence Knorr, Mechanicsburg, Pennsylvania).

24. Ibid., entries for August 26 to August 30, 1878.

Abraham Deppen, in 1874. By 1878, the camp moved to land owned by Nathan Brower, who had provided seventy-five tents.[25]

For the last week of October, Dr. Muth noted "Fire in Heater."[26] Given that he has used this phrase before, he probably meant he had started to use the heater in the house rather than had a problem with it. Regardless, "Butcher Day" occurred on November 26, two days before Thanksgiving. This resulted in 158 pounds of beef.[27]

New Year's Day 1879 was relatively quiet, with just one visit to Wilson Drumheller.[28] Young Wilson, only age 18, was the son of Nicholas and Abigail Drumheller, who had lost sons John and William in recent years.[29] Dr. Muth saw Wilson weekly until late March when visits increased to twice a week.[30] Whatever was ailing Wilson Drumheller could not be cured because he passed away on April 8, 1879.[31]

During the first week of May 1879, Dr. Muth recorded the blossoming of pears, peach, plum, and cherry trees.[32] The following week, the apple trees were in bloom, and Dr. Muth recorded unusually high temperatures on his thermometer: 98 degrees on the 14th and 99 degrees on the 15th, followed by rain on the 16th.[33] On the first day of summer, June 21, Dr. Muth noted he mowed his grass.[34] Two days later, he was making hay, and the cow bulling occurred on June 24.[35]

Starting on March 9, 1879, Dr. Muth began treating "Widow Neihart." He saw her on March 9 and 11, and then starting on April 28, he checked in on her two or more times a week through June 14th.[36] Dr. Muth noted her death in his daybook, marking June 24 in his notes, but

25. "Herndon Camp Meeting, 1874–1983," accessed at https://www.lykensvalley.org/herndon-camp-meeting-1874-1983/.

26. Reuben H. Muth, *Physician's Daybooks*, vol. 14, entry for October 20, 1878 (1858–1898, in possession of Lawrence Knorr, Mechanicsburg, Pennsylvania).

27. Ibid., entry for November 28, 1878.

28. Reuben H. Muth, *Physician's Daybooks*, vol. 15, entry for January 1, 1879 (1858–1898, in possession of Lawrence Knorr, Mechanicsburg, Pennsylvania).

29. "Wilson K Drumheller," *Find a Grave*, Memorial ID 46467258, accessed January 12, 2025, https://www.findagrave.com/memorial/46467258/wilson-k-drumheller.

30. Reuben H. Muth, *Physician's Daybooks*, vol. 15, entries for January 8 through April 8, 1879 (1858–1898, in possession of Lawrence Knorr, Mechanicsburg, Pennsylvania).

31. "Died," *Northumberland County Democrat*, May 2, 1879, 3.

32. Reuben H. Muth, *Physician's Daybooks*, vol. 15, entries for May 4 to May 10, 1879 (1858–1898, in possession of Lawrence Knorr, Mechanicsburg, Pennsylvania).

33. Ibid., entries for May 11 to May 17, 1879.

34. Ibid., entry for June 21, 1879.

35. Ibid., entries for June 23 and June 24, 1879.

36. Ibid., entries for March 9 through June 14, 1879.

without recording a visit.[37] Perhaps he checked in on her that day because he had no other visits.

July 15 and 16, 1879, were the hottest days of the year, registering temperatures of 101 degrees and 102 degrees, respectively.[38] Hopefully, the heat abated because Dr. Muth harvested his oats on July 30 and August 1.[39]

Camp Meeting happened at the end of August, from the 24th to the 30th.[40] Again, Dr. Muth continued to see patients, including the birth of his niece, Jane Deppen, the daughter of Alexander Deppen, Louisa's brother.[41] It is difficult to imagine this all occurring in tents on a campground. Given the campground was only a mile or two from Dr. Muth's home, it is more likely he saw patients at his office and participated in the camp meeting when able.

Dr. Muth sewed his wheat on September 23 and then noted "St. Michael" on September 29, 1879.[42] He saw no patients on September 29, the date of Michaelmas or the Feast of St. Michael and All Angels. This was the first time Dr. Muth ever noted this holiday on his calendar.

During the last week of October 1879, Dr. Muth only saw one patient, Jacob Shappell, three times and noted there was a "fire in the heater" on October 31.[43] Five days later, on November 5, three inches of snow fell.[44] This did not prevent Dr. Muth from attending to a birth at the Isaac Lahr home on November 7.[45] Israel Daniel Lahr was born that day[46] for a fee of four dollars.[47]

On Christmas Eve, 1879, Dr. Muth sent a registered letter from Mahanoy to "D. G. Brinton M.D., 115 South Seventh St., Philadelphia." William Weist was the postmaster who signed the receipt.[48] Dr. Daniel

37. Ibid., entry for June 24, 1879.
38. Ibid., entries for July 15 and July 16, 1879.
39. Ibid., entries for July 30 and August 1, 1879.
40. Ibid., entries for August 24 to August 30, 1879.
41. Ibid., entry for August 30, 1879.
42. Ibid., entries for September 23 and September 30, 1879.
43. Ibid., entries for October 26 to November 1, 1879.
44. Ibid., entry for November 5, 1879.
45. Ibid., entry for November 7, 1879.
46. "Israel Daniel Lahr," *Find a Grave*, Memorial ID 52309720, accessed January 5, 2025, https://www.findagrave.com/memorial/52309720/israel_daniel_lahr.
47. Reuben H. Muth, *Physician's Daybooks*, vol. 15, entry for November 7, 1879 (1858–1898, in possession of Lawrence Knorr, Mechanicsburg, Pennsylvania).
48. Reuben H. Muth, Ephemera, item 12, Receipt for a Registered Letter (1876–1924, in possession of Lawrence Knorr, Mechanicsburg, Pennsylvania).

Garrison Brinton was a well-known medical doctor, anthropologist, and publisher from Philadelphia.[49] Dr. Muth's registered letter likely included enclosed funds to purchase the book *The Diseases of Live Stock and Their Most Efficient Remedies*, published by D.G. Brinton in 1879.[50] Perhaps this had been advertised in a medical journal. Of course, this purchase would align with his ongoing livestock husbandry.

As the year ended, Dr. Muth began treating one of the church elders, John Zartman, who was suffering from consumption and "dropsy of the heart."[51] He began treating Zartman on December 27, including three consecutive days on the 29th through the 31st of December.[52] He then treated Zartman every week, sometimes intensely every day, through the first days of March.[53] It appears Dr. Muth may have been attempting to prolong the life of John Zartman or at least reduce his suffering. During his final weeks, Zartman was confined to his chair and bed before succumbing on March 15 at the age of 74.[54]

During the last week of April 1880, Dr. Muth noted the cherry trees were in bloom and there was a frost on the 28th.[55] The potatoes were planted the next week, on May 5.[56] Dr. Muth remarked "Office Cleaning" in his notes from May 17 through the 22nd. This coincided with three obstetric appointments in three days: William Otto on the 18th, George Malick on the 19th, and Sam Hill on the 21st.[57] We do not know if the cleaning was done prior to, during, or after the births of the babies or if this cleaning was just an annual ritual. However, it does appear Dr. Muth may have switched one or more of these appointments to the office rather than traveling.

William C. Otto (1842–1881) was a Civil War veteran. He was married to Mary M. Snyder Otto (1846–1901), who gave birth to Adam

49. "Dr Daniel Garrison Brinton," *Find a Grave*, Memorial ID 4201592, accessed January 5, 2025, https://www.findagrave.com/memorial/4201592/daniel-garrison-brinton.

50. Lloyd V. Tellor, *The Diseases of Live Stock and Their Most Efficient Remedies*, (Philadelphia, PA: D.G. Brinton, 1879).

51. "From Jackson Township," *Northumberland County Democrat*, April 2, 1880, 3.

52. Reuben H. Muth, *Physician's Daybooks*, vol. 15, entries for December 27 through December 31, 1879 (1858–1898, in possession of Lawrence Knorr, Mechanicsburg, Pennsylvania).

53. Reuben H. Muth, *Physician's Daybooks*, vol. 16, entries for January 1 through March 15, 1880 (1858–1898, in possession of Lawrence Knorr, Mechanicsburg, Pennsylvania).

54. "From Jackson Township," *Northumberland County Democrat*, April 2, 1880, 3.

55. Reuben H. Muth, *Physician's Daybooks*, vol. 16, entries for April 25 through May 1, 1880 (1858–1898, in possession of Lawrence Knorr, Mechanicsburg, Pennsylvania).

56. Ibid., entry for May 5, 1880.

57. Ibid., entries for May 16 to May 22, 1880.

Otto[58] one month before the census was taken in Jackson Township, Northumberland County, Pennsylvania, on June 18.[59]

George H. Malick (1839–1908) was a farmer in Jackson Township, married to Caroline Hepler Malick (1842–1923).[60] Their son, George Washington Malick, was born on May 19, 1880.[61]

Regarding the child of Sam Hill, this was the only appointment Dr. Muth ever had with this family.[62] It appears the mother was with Sam, and he paid for the birth since he is listed in the ledger. Sam was likely a transient of some kind, a laborer briefly in the area. Unfortunately, the surname is too common to provide more information.

Meanwhile, in Myerstown, Lebanon County, Pennsylvania, John Muth (1799–1880), the uncle of Dr. Muth, passed away on May 18.[63] John was his father's older brother, who had been treated so well in his grandfather's will. Given how busy Dr. Muth was this week, it is highly unlikely he was aware of the death. If he later sent a letter or visited, there was nothing noted in his daybooks.

During the last week of May, the thermometer hit 103 degrees on May 26th.[64] On Sunday, June 20, Dr. Muth noted visiting his father-in-law, Abraham Deppen. Later that week, on the 26th, he noted "Harvest" but was not specific concerning the produce.[65]

When the census was taken for the village of Herndon on June 11, 1880, Abraham Deppen was boarding with his son, George, who was listed as a "forwarding merchant."[66] It appeared George was picking up the grain dealing previously engaged in by his father, and Abraham had

58. "William C Otto," *Find a Grave*, Memorial ID 46387783, accessed January 5, 2025, https://www.findagrave.com/memorial/46387783/william-c-otto.

59. US Census Bureau. 1880 United States Federal Census. Census Place: Jackson Township, Northumberland County, Pennsylvania, pg. 11, dwelling no. 99.

60. "George H. Malick," *Find a Grave*, Memorial ID 243247595, accessed January 5, 2025, https://www.findagrave.com/memorial/243247595/george_h_malick.

61. "George Washington Malick," *Find a Grave*, Memorial ID 191046540, accessed January 5, 2025, https://www.findagrave.com/memorial/191046540/george_washington_malick.

62. Reuben H. Muth, *Physician's Daybooks*, vol. 16, entry for May 21, 1880 (1858–1898, in possession of Lawrence Knorr, Mechanicsburg, Pennsylvania).

63. "John Muth," *Find a Grave*, Memorial ID 35875897, accessed January 5, 2025, https://www.findagrave.com/memorial/35875897/john-muth.

64. Reuben H. Muth, *Physician's Daybooks*, vol. 16, entry for May 26, 1880 (1858–1898, in possession of Lawrence Knorr, Mechanicsburg, Pennsylvania).

65. Ibid., entries for June 20 to June 26, 1880.

66. US Census Bureau. 1880 United States Federal Census. Census Place: Herndon, Jackson Township, Northumberland County, Pennsylvania, 223, dwelling 133.

yet to move in with the Muths, thus Dr. Muth's need to visit him the previous month.

On August 18, 1880, Dr. Muth logged an obstetric appointment with Joel Heim.[67] Joel Drumheller Heim (1848–1902) and his wife, Mary Louisa Lebo Heim (1855–1910) gave birth to daughter Tamie.[68] At the bottom of Dr. Muth's daybook, he had a notation about "Mrs. Drumheller 7½."[69] Perhaps this was the weight of the baby, and Dr. Muth had confused the surname.

Once again, on September 29, Dr. Muth had no patients. In his daybook, written vertically in the column for that day was the word "Michael."[70] Thus, it appears Dr. Muth, for the second consecutive year, was noting the Michaelmas holiday.

About two weeks later, an advertisement for the sale of land in the *Northumberland County Democrat* of October 15, 1880, indicated that Dr. Muth and Dr. Haas were neighbors. The tract of land for sale was "bounded by lands of G. Smith, Dr. Muth, Dr. Haas."[71]

The following week, on October 18 and 19, Dr. Muth noted "Corn Husking" in his daybook. He did manage to see several patients.[72] This would presume the patients came to him rather than him traveling on days he would be busy at the farm.

The following month, the weather became bitterly cold. Dr. Muth noted a temperature of "15 degrees above zero" on Saturday, November 27, 1880. That day, he saw no patients. The prior day, he had one obstetric appointment with Frank Wolf.[73] On what was probably a very cold Friday, November 26, 1880, the day after Thanksgiving, the young couple of Franklyn T. Wolf (1862–1923) and Sarah Malinda Ferster Wolf (1861–1917) gave birth to their first child, Isaac.[74] It appears the couple was not married yet and came to Muth, who was a church elder.

67. Reuben H. Muth, *Physician's Daybooks*, vol. 16, entry for August 18, 1880 (1858–1898, in possession of Lawrence Knorr, Mechanicsburg, Pennsylvania).

68. "Joel Drumheller Heim," *Find a Grave*, Memorial ID 34482727, accessed January 5, 2025, https://www.findagrave.com/memorial/34482727/joel-drumheller-heim.

69. Reuben H. Muth, *Physician's Daybooks*, vol. 16, entry for August 18, 1880 (1858–1898, in possession of Lawrence Knorr, Mechanicsburg, Pennsylvania).

70. Ibid., entry for September 29, 1880.

71. "Public Sale of Real Estate," *Northumberland County Democrat*, October 15, 1880, 4.

72. Reuben H. Muth, *Physician's Daybooks*, vol. 16, entries for October 18 and October 19, 1880 (1858–1898, in possession of Lawrence Knorr, Mechanicsburg, Pennsylvania).

73. Ibid., entries for November 26 and November 27, 1880.

74. "Franklyn T 'Frank' Wolf" *Find a Grave*, Memorial ID 38962465, accessed January 5, 2025, https://www.findagrave.com/memorial/38962465/franklyn-t-wolf.

We cannot know what was said between the 54-year-old doctor and the 18-year-old father, but it may have included some encouragement to marry the young woman as soon as possible.

During Governor Henry Hoyt's biennial message to the legislature at the beginning of 1881, among many things, he suggested the registration of medical diplomas.[75] He was concerned about the proliferation of diplomas sold to persons who "had not pursued the proscribed course of study, and who were unfitted, by reason of ignorance, to practice medicine."[76]

Interestingly, Dr. Muth's professional fees in 1880 had faded to a level not seen in ten years.[77] Was this due to an increase in charlatans practicing medicine in the area and, perhaps, a lack of trust in physicians?

The first week of May 1881, Dr. Muth noted the blossoms on the cherry and plum trees.[78] The pear trees followed the next week.[79] On May 31, he recorded an "Office Cleaning" and noted "pigs" on June 2, 1881.[80] On Saturday, June 11, Dr. Muth noted "L on visit," perhaps meaning his wife was away.[81] Louisa's trip continued into the next week, ending on the 14th.[82]

On June 15, 1881, the Harrisburg *Patriot-News* announced that Governor Hoyt had signed into law a bill requiring the registration of medical practitioners.[83] Pennsylvania had been slow to register its physicians despite being a leading state for medical education.[84] The new law required the prothonotary for each county to create a register in which to record the credentials of medical practitioners in their counties. The book was to have one page per practitioner and was to note when they left the area or died. Anyone providing medical services "for gain" had to be a graduate of a registered school of medicine and was required to show their diplomas to the prothonotary, or if practicing without a

---

75. "Governor Hoyt's Biennial Message," *The Patriot-News*, January 5, 1881, 3.

76. Ibid.

77. See Appendix D: "Summary" for Dr. Muth's Career Earnings.

78. Reuben H. Muth, *Physician's Daybooks*, vol. 17, entries for May 1 through May 7, 1881 (1858–1898, in possession of Lawrence Knorr, Mechanicsburg, Pennsylvania).

79. Ibid., entries for May 8 through May 14, 1881.

80. Ibid., entries for May 29 to June 4, 1881.

81. Ibid., entry for June 11, 1881.

82. Ibid., entries for June 12 to June 14, 1881.

83. "Two New Laws," *The Patriot-News*, June 15, 1881, 1.

84. Joseph F. Kett, *The Formation of the American Medical Profession: The Role of Institutions, 1780–1860* (New Haven, CT: Yale University Press, 1968), 181–84.

degree, needed to state as such and for how long. The fee to register was one dollar.[85]

Dr. Muth did not see any patients from July 1 through July 8, 1881.[86] On July 2, 1881, President James Garfield was struck in the back by two bullets from a would-be assassin at the Baltimore and Potomac Railway Station in Washington, D.C. The president was returned to the White House, where he was tended to for two months. Dr. Muth's local newspaper described the tragedy in intimate detail.[87] The president was not expected to live but had rallied by the time the story was published six days later.

Dr. Muth may have been preparing for his registration at the protho-notary office in Sunbury, Pennsylvania. He recorded cutting wheat on July 6 and making hay on the 9th. He also started seeing patients again that day, including an obstetrical visit with Lewis Kehres.[88]

At the end of July, Dr. Muth simply noted "Cow" in his journal on July 29.[89] We do not know if this was referring to the purchase of a cow or the birth of one. But it is the first time cows were mentioned in his journal besides the occasional "bulling."

The Sunbury newspaper published an updated listing of the recently registered physicians on August 26, 1881. Dr. Muth was number fifty. He listed his birth town as "Millerburg" rather than Rehrersburg. Mill-ersburg, Berks County, was later renamed Bethel by the postal service. This confirmed the property shuffle that occurred among Dr. Muth's elders early in his life. Dr. Muth also declared his current residence as Jackson Township, Northumberland County, and that he graduated from the University of Pennsylvania on March 31, 1855.[90] In all, 171 physi-cians registered in Northumberland County, Pennsylvania, that summer through 1891, with 116 registering before Jacob S. Krebs, whose career started in 1881.[91]

---

85. Ibid.

86. Reuben H. Muth, *Physician's Daybooks*, vol. 17, entries for July 1 through July 9, 1881 (1858–1898), in possession of Lawrence Knorr, Mechanicsburg, Pennsylvania.

87. "Garfield," *Northumberland County Democrat*, July 8, 1881, 1.

88. Reuben H. Muth, *Physician's Daybooks*, vol. 17, entries for July 1 through July 9, 1881 (1858–1898), in possession of Lawrence Knorr, Mechanicsburg, Pennsylvania.

89. Ibid., entry for July 29, 1881.

90. "The Physician's Register" *The Sunbury Weekly News*, Aug 26, 1881, 2.

91. Hebert C. Bell, *History of Northumberland County, Pennsylvania*, (Brown, Runk & Co, Chicago, 1891), 270–73.

The next month, on September 19, 1881, President James Garfield succumbed from his wounds and was succeeded by Vice President Chester Arthur. The local news reported the death with somberness and great detail.[92]

On November 9, Dr. Muth was back to obscure one-word entries, this time noting "Heiffer" in his journal.[93] Assuming he meant "heifer," this would be a young cow who had yet to give birth. The following week, Dr. Muth noted "Snow, Hail, Sleet" on the 16th. Sadly, he also recorded "Sol dying."[94] Dr. Muth's last patient that week, on Saturday, November 19, was "Sol Tressler," who was listed as indigent.[95] The following week, he saw Tressler again, on the 20th and 22nd. He included a note that "Sollie Died," marking the 23rd of November. That day, he also recorded "Snow, Hail, Sleet."[96] Solomon Tressler (1795–1881) had survived eight years after the amputation of his arm following a terrible accident. He lived to be 86.[97]

Three days before Christmas, Dr. Muth mentioned the rain in his journal.[98] That drippy day, he assisted Isaac Rebuck with the birth of his child.[99] Isaac F. Rebuck (1849–1929) and Amanda Reitz Rebuck (1855–1946) were blessed with their boy Levi.[100] Perhaps this was a nighttime delivery, as Levi's birthdate is listed as the 21st but Dr. Muth recorded the obstetric fee on the 22nd. It was his only appointment that day.[101]

Dr. Muth recorded the weather on Christmas Day as "Mild, Sunshine, and Pleasant." He noted the following day, "Rain, mud. Mild Weather."[102]

92. "The President Dead," *Northumberland County Democrat*, September 23, 1881, 2.

93. Reuben H. Muth, *Physician's Daybooks*, vol. 17, entry for November 9, 1881 (1858–1898, in possession of Lawrence Knorr, Mechanicsburg, Pennsylvania).

94. Ibid., entries for 13 to November 19, 1881.

95. Ibid., entry for November 19, 1881.

96. Ibid., entries for November 20 to November 23, 1881.

97. "Solomon Tressler," *Find a Grave*, Memorial ID 38943167, accessed January 5, 2025, https://www.findagrave.com/memorial/38943167/solomon-tressler.

98. Reuben H. Muth, *Physician's Daybooks*, vol. 17, entry for December 22, 1881 (1858–1898, in possession of Lawrence Knorr, Mechanicsburg, Pennsylvania).

99. Ibid.

100. "Isaac F Rebuck," *Find a Grave*, Memorial ID 34650004, accessed January 5, 2025, https://www.findagrave.com/memorial/34650004/isaac-f-rebuck.

101. Reuben H. Muth, *Physician's Daybooks*, vol. 17, entry for December 22, 1881 (1858–1898, in possession of Lawrence Knorr, Mechanicsburg, Pennsylvania).

102. Ibid., entries for December 25 and December 26, 1881.

Figure 12. Isaac and Amanda Rebuck.

Through December and into January 1882, Dr. Muth checked in on Milton Drumheller twice a week and then three times a week.[103] [104] This included Dr. Muth's only appointment on January 1. On January 10, Dr. Muth noted the death of "H. Drumheller."[105] This would have been Henry Z. Drumheller of Herndon (1847–1882), the son of Nicholas S. Drumheller and husband of Abbie A. Shipe Drumheller.[106] Henry and Abbie had one child, William, who was born in 1880 and was thus a toddler at the time. Milton Drumheller (1831–1902) lived closer to Dr. Muth in Rebuck[107] and was an uncle to Henry. Given that Dr. Muth noted the death of Henry but charged Milton, perhaps Henry convalesced at his uncle's home prior to his passing. Or there was sickness

103. Ibid., entries for December 14 through December 30, 1881.

104. Reuben H. Muth, *Physician's Daybooks*, vol. 18, entries for January 1 through January 14, 1882 (1858–1898, in possession of Lawrence Knorr, Mechanicsburg, Pennsylvania).

105. Ibid.

106. "Henry Z Drumheller," *Find a Grave*, Memorial ID 46467211, accessed January 5, 2025, https://www.findagrave.com/memorial/46467211/henry_z_drumheller.

107. "Milton Drumheller," *Find a Grave*, Memorial ID 34163405, accessed January 5, 2025, https://www.findagrave.com/memorial/34163405/milton-drumheller.

in the family at the same time, and Dr. Muth was simply noting the unfortunate death of a young man in his thirties. There was six inches of snow the next day, January 11, 1882.[108]

Two weeks later, on January 23 and 24, Dr. Muth noted the "coldest days," but then this was followed by rain two days later on the 26th.[109] Dr. Muth had a light schedule early in the week, and when the rain started, he saw no one.

The following week was a snowy one. On Tuesday, January 31, 12 ½ inches of snow were recorded at the Muth residence. Then, on Saturday, the 4th of February, twelve more inches fell. Dr. Muth did not see patients immediately after the first storm or during the second. He had only two appointments in between.[110]

That spring must have been a cold one because even on May 6, Dr. Muth reported "Snow, Sleet, and Rain" in his journal.[111] He saw no patients that day. The following week was rainy, but the pear, peach, plum, and cherry trees were all in bloom.[112] Despite the drippy weather, Dr. Muth saw patients every day.

The following week, during the middle of May, the apple trees were also in bloom. Dr. Muth noted the death of "H Peiffer" on Wednesday, May 17.[113] Dr. Muth had seen Henry Peiffer on the 15th, 16th, and 17th. It must have been a sudden illness because he had not called upon Henry Peiffer in the weeks prior. Henry Peiffer (1806–1882) lived one month past his 76th birthday.[114] He left behind a wife, Sarah Ann Zartman Peiffer (1808–1886), and at least six adult children.

During a light week for Dr. Muth, the third week of May, he planted his corn on the 22nd.[115] Three weeks later, on Monday, June 12, Dr. Muth was in Shamokin to pay "Kutzner and Co."[116] William R. Kutzner (1835–1885) operated a drug and hardware store in Shamokin at the

108. Reuben H. Muth, *Physician's Daybooks*, vol. 18, entries for January 1 through January 14, 1882 (1858–1898, in possession of Lawrence Knorr, Mechanicsburg, Pennsylvania).

109. Ibid., entries for January 24 through January 27, 1882.

110. Ibid., entries for January 31 through February 4, 1882.

111. Ibid., entries for April 30 through May 6, 1882.

112. Ibid., entries for May 7 through May 13, 1882.

113. Ibid., entries for May 14 through May 20, 1882.

114. "Henry Peiffer," *Find a Grave*, Memorial ID 46497942, accessed January 5, 2025, at https://www.findagrave.com/memorial/46497942/henry-peiffer.

115. Reuben H. Muth, *Physician's Daybooks*, vol. 18, entries for May 21 through May 27, 1882 (1858–1898, in possession of Lawrence Knorr, Mechanicsburg, Pennsylvania).

116. Ibid., entry for June 12, 1882.

time.[117] Around that time, his previous partnership had been dissolved and he placed an advertisement in the local newspaper to collect the debts owed and to inform the public he would be operating independently.[118] It appears Dr. Muth's balance may have been $46.02, based on his notation.[119]

On July 27, Dr. Muth noted "pigs bought," now adding a verb to the noun in his notation![120] The following week, on August 6, he noted "Cow B." which could have meant a cow was born, bought, bulled, or butchered. Two days later, he was aware of the "Katy Ditz," referring to the green insects known as katydids. The Dutch spelling is a humorous twist, perhaps.[121] The following week, Dr. Muth recorded a cryptic note, "A D Mt Carmel."[122] "A D" was most likely his father-in-law, Abraham Deppen. Mt. Carmel is a town about twenty-five miles east of Mahanoy, beyond Shamokin. It is most likely Dr. Muth did not accompany his father-in-law due to his patient schedule and instead just noted his absence. Mt. Carmel was the home of Abraham Deppen's son, Joseph Deppen.

During the last week of August, Dr. Muth noted "Cow Bul 2nd time" perhaps meaning the second cow bulling had occurred.[123] Then, during the third week of October, Dr. Muth recorded "Grapes Closing," "Peaches last week," "Lady Bulling" on the 20th, and "First Frost" on the 21st.[124] The Muth farm was clearly quite busy, and the weather was turning.

Dr. Muth noted "Office Cleaning" on November 13, 1882. This followed an obstetric appointment the previous day paid by "Jod. Zartman."[125] The last week of November, Dr. Muth began stable feeding his horses and recorded the first snow on November 26.[126] The butchering day was the 28th of November. Beef weighing 662 pounds alive yielded 346 pounds of meat.[127]

---

117. Hebert C. Bell, *History of Northumberland County, Pennsylvania*, (Brown, Runk & Co, Chicago, 1891), 893.

118. "Dissolution of Partnership," *Sunbury Gazette*, May 5, 1882, 2.

119. Reuben H. Muth, *Physician's Daybooks*, vol. 18, entries for May 21 through May 27, 1882 (1858–1898, in possession of Lawrence Knorr, Mechanicsburg, Pennsylvania).

120. Ibid., entries for July 23 to July 29, 1882.

121. Ibid., entries for August 6 to August 12, 1882.

122. Ibid., entries for August 13 to August 19, 1882.

123. Ibid., entries for August 27 to September 2, 1882.

124. Ibid., entries for October 15 to October 21, 1882.

125. Ibid., entries for November 12 and November 13, 1882.

126. Ibid., entries for November 26 to December 2, 1882.

127. Ibid., last page of journal.

January of 1883 started cold. On the 23rd and 24th, Dr Muth recorded temperatures of only two degrees above zero.[128] Somehow, he managed to keep a few appointments.

On Saturday, February 10, 1883, Dr. Muth provided obstetric services for Sam Treon, charging three dollars.[129] Samuel Treon (1844–1923) was the husband of Catherine Reitz Treon (1844–1919)[130] and the son of Joseph Treon and Sarah Shutt Treon, who were both deceased by 1857.[131] George Samuel Treon (1883–1963) was born on this day.[132] He would later marry Anna Elizabeth Deppen, a niece of Dr. Muth and Louisa.

One month later, on March 10, the Muths enjoyed sleighing thanks to "Deep Snow."[133] Two weeks later, on Thursday, March 22, which was Maundy Thursday, Dr. Muth cut his grape vines. The next day, Good Friday, he wrote, "Snowing on Good Friday."[134] Perhaps there was snow on the ground as the parishioners attended Easter services that Sunday.

On May 1 and 2, 1883, Dr. Muth planted his potatoes and sewed his oats. He saw no patients on the 1st and only one on the 2nd.[135] Meanwhile, in Brooklyn, a great bridge was opened to the public on May 24, 1883. The local newspaper conveyed some amazing statistics about this engineering feat and boasted, "These figures outstrip any other bridge figures the world has ever seen."[136]

J.H.B. reporting from Rebuck, July 21, 1883, mentioned the Muth and Haas homes in the same sentence. "First of all, we passed the houses of our doctors, Haas and Muth, who are always busy and have plenty to do. Everything about their cool and shady homes is looking No. 1 in style."[137]

Noah Klock's little boy fell from a wagon and broke an arm, according to the local news on August 31, 1883. Dr. Muth was summoned and

---

128. Reuben H. Muth, *Physician's Daybooks*, vol. 19, entries for January 21 through January 27, 1883 (1858–1898, in possession of Lawrence Knorr, Mechanicsburg, Pennsylvania).

129. Ibid., entry for February 10, 1883.

130. "Samuel Treon," *Find a Grave*, Memorial ID 34693553, accessed January 5, 2025, https://www.findagrave.com/memorial/34693553/samuel_treon.

131. *Northumberland County Wills, 1834–1871*, Nos. 4 and 5., Northumberland County Registrar of Wills, Sunbury, Pennsylvania.

132. "George S Treon," *Find a Grave*, Memorial ID 34684226, accessed January 5, 2025, https://www.findagrave.com/memorial/34684226/george-samuel-treon.

133. Reuben H. Muth, *Physician's Daybooks*, vol. 19, entries for March 4 to March 10, 1883 (1858–1898, in possession of Lawrence Knorr, Mechanicsburg, Pennsylvania).

134. Ibid., entries for March 18 to March 24, 1883.

135. Ibid., entries for May 1 to May 2, 1883.

136. "Figures of the Great Bridge," *The Sunbury Weekly News*, June 8, 1883.

137. "From Mahanoy," *Northumberland County Democrat*, July 27, 1883.

tended to the boy. He was "doing as well as expected," said the doctor.[138]
Noah Klock (1840–1920) lived in Herndon. His son, Harvey, was born
in 1879 and was about four years old at the time.[139] Dr. Muth charged
Noah three dollars on Saturday, August 11, 1883. He then followed up
with several visits through early September.[140]

The following month, on September 8th, Dr. Muth tended to a birth
in his brother-in-law George Deppen's family.[141] That day, Dr. Muth's
niece, Nettie I. Deppen, was born.[142]

Two weeks later, Dr. Muth noted the "Lady Bulling" on the 22nd.[143]

On October 5, 1883, the local newspaper recounted a story of the
burning of a little boy: "The youngest boy of H. A. Hilbush of Little
Mahanoy Township was hurt considerable last week by pouring hot
water over his body." Dr. Muth was summoned to attend to the child.[144]
Henry Adam Hilbush (1836–1909) was a farmer who had a son named
Herbert Henry Hilbush, who was born June 22, 1882.[145] Thus, the lad
would have been only about sixteen months old. Dr. Muth made no
entry in his daybook for this event, so he likely did not charge.

Dr. Muth appeared to be out of town, not seeing patients, from
Wednesday, October 10 through Sunday, October 14, 1883. He noted
he was "At Lebanon Fair" on Thursday the 11th.[146] Two weeks later, Dr.
Muth noted "Grapes and Peaches" and "Office Cleaning" on the 23rd.
He saw only two patients all week.[147] Butchering Day was November
19, 1883. That day, a steer weighing 780 pounds yielded 427 pounds
of meat and 54 pounds of hide.[148] He also recorded a recipe for lice
extermination, an elixir to be spread on the "infested animal,"[149] again

138. "From Mahanoy," *Northumberland County Democrat*, August 31, 1883.
139. "Noah Klock," *Find a Grave*, Memorial ID 46378509, accessed January 5, 2025, https://www.findagrave.com/memorial/46378509/harvey_klock.
140. Reuben H. Muth, *Physician's Daybooks*, vol. 19, entries for August 18 to September 7, 1883 (1858–1898, in possession of Lawrence Knorr, Mechanicsburg, Pennsylvania).
141. Ibid., entry for September 8, 1883.
142. "Nettie I Deppen Rubendall," *Find a Grave*, Memorial ID 46415767, accessed January 5, 2025, https://www.findagrave.com/memorial/46415767/nettie_i_rubendall.
143. Reuben H. Muth, *Physician's Daybooks*, vol. 19, entry for September 22, 1883 (1858–1898, in possession of Lawrence Knorr, Mechanicsburg, Pennsylvania).
144. "Other Items," *Northumberland County Democrat*, October 5, 1883.
145. "Henry Adam Hilbush," *Find a Grave*, Memorial ID 39186213, accessed January 5, 2025, https://www.findagrave.com/memorial/39186213/henry_adam_hilbush.
146. Reuben H. Muth, *Physician's Daybooks*, vol. 19, entries for October 10 through October 14, 1883 (1858–1898, in possession of Lawrence Knorr, Mechanicsburg, Pennsylvania).
147. Ibid., entries for October 21 through October 27, 1883.
148. Ibid., last page of journal for 1883.
149. Ibid.

illustrating his interest in veterinary medicine, performed in caring for his own livestock.

On December 14, Dr. Muth noted another "Lady Bulling."[150] Three days later, he noted the first snow.[151] He recorded nothing about the death of his father, Frederick Muth, in Rehrersburg that occurred that same day. The local newspaper in Berks County contained a very brief obituary: "Frederick Muth, who died in Rehrersburg at the advanced age of 88 years, was formerly in the mercantile business and had been a Justice of the Peace for many years. He was a good surveyor and, by strict attention to business, accumulated quite a fortune. He owned a nice farm at the western end of Rehrersburg and a smaller one in Bethel township."[152]

At Myerstown, Lebanon County, Dr. Muth reimbursed his nephew, John Henry Muth, $5.97 on Christmas Eve for a list of unusual items.[153] It appears Dr. Muth had traveled to Myerstown, Lebanon County, for four days from the 21st of December through Christmas Eve and purchased a blanket, a pair of shirts, a fur, a half-gallon of syrup, a pinafore burner, a Lucifer chimney, and four pounds of raisins. He had no patients logged in his daybook.[154] Perhaps, having missed the funeral of his father, he was picking up a handful of keepsakes related to his late parents and the old homestead.

In January, despite Dr. Muth being the eldest child, his brother and brother-in-law, George K. Muth and Henry Kurr, were made administrators of the estate.[155] Dr. Muth made no additional entries in his daybook throughout the winter, but he did affix his signature when settling his father's estate. Six children divided $6954.05. Less fees, each received $1154.[156]

On April 11, 1884, the local paper reported that Henry D. Muth, along with Frank Reitz and David Hottenstein, were "heading to the Freeburg Academy in a few days."[157] David Hottenstein was the son of Reverend Aaron Hottenstein from St. Peter's Church.[158] Frank Reitz was

---

150. Ibid., entry for December 14, 1883.

151. Ibid., entry for December 17, 1883.

152. "The late Frederick Muth," *Reading Times*, December 28, 1883, 1.

153. Reuben H. Muth, Ephemera, item 13, Myerstown December 24, 1883 (1876–1924, in possession of Lawrence Knorr, Mechanicsburg, Pennsylvania).

154. Reuben H. Muth, *Physician's Daybooks*, vol. 19, entries for December 21 to December 24, 1883 (1858–1898, in possession of Lawrence Knorr, Mechanicsburg, Pennsylvania).

155. "Court," *Reading Times*, January 31, 1884, 4.

156. *Berks County Wills, 1883*, 42, Berks County Registrar of Wills, Reading, Pennsylvania.

157. "From Mahanoy," *Northumberland County Democrat*, April 11, 1884, 4.

158. "David Hottenstein," *Find a Grave*, Memorial ID 38976168, accessed January 5, 2025, https://www.findagrave.com/memorial/38976168/david-hottenstein.

likely the son of Godfrey Reitz,[159] a local farmer. The Freeburg Academy
was a school in Freeburg, Snyder County, Pennsylvania. Perhaps the payment of this tuition was related to the recent inheritance.

By late April, Dr. Muth was commenting again, noting the plum,
peach, and cherry blossoms.[160] On July 16, Dr. Muth recorded that "Joe
Deppen was here," most likely his brother-in-law.[161]

J.R.H., reporting on July 24, 1884, described the improved conveyance the local doctors were using. Wrote J.R.H.: "Both our doctors,
Muth and Haas, are visiting their patients, the former in a brand-new
buggy, and the latter with his coming fresh out of the shop, appearing
almost as new, too."[162] It appears both doctors were doing well and were
now staying out of the weather when traversing the countryside.

The next "Lady Bulling" was recorded on October 13, 1884. Later
in the week, on Saturday, October 18, Dr. Muth noted "Public Sale of
Homestead."[163] This was most likely the farm on the west end of Rehrersburg, near Millersburg, Berks County, where Dr. Muth spent his first
few years. The last peaches for the year were picked for the final week of
October.[164] The first snow fell a week before Thanksgiving, on Wednesday, November 19, 1884.[165] "Butcher Day" was Tuesday, November 25.
A steer weighing 740 pounds yielded 405 pounds of meat.[166]

As 1884 gave way to 1885, Dr. Muth had visited only 116 households the prior twelve months, his lowest activity since 1869 and his
second-lowest since moving to Northumberland County.[167] Either he
was allowing his practice to ebb, or he was facing stiffer competition.

Dr. Muth made no additional entries in his journal through most
of 1885, noting only bull activity on August 19.[168] However, he clearly
recorded the upcoming board meeting at St. Peter's Church on the first

---

159. "Godfrey Reitz," *Find a Grave*, Memorial ID 34697571, accessed January 5, 2025, https://www.
findagrave.com/memorial/34697571/godfrey_reitz.

160. Reuben H. Muth, *Physician's Daybooks*, vol. 20, entries for April 27 through May 3, 1884 (1858–
1898, in possession of Lawrence Knorr, Mechanicsburg, Pennsylvania).

161. Ibid., entry for July 16, 1884.

162. "From Mahanoy," *Northumberland County Democrat*, August 1, 1884, 4.

163. Reuben H. Muth, *Physician's Daybooks*, vol. 20, entries for October 12 through October 18, 1884
(1858–1898, in possession of Lawrence Knorr, Mechanicsburg, Pennsylvania).

164. Ibid., entries for October 26 to November 1, 1884.

165. Ibid., entry for November 19, 1884.

166. Ibid., last page of journal for 1884.

167. See Appendix D: "Summary" for Dr. Muth's Career Earnings.

168. Reuben H. Muth, *Physician's Daybooks*, vol. 21, entry for August 19, 1885 (1858–1898, in possession of Lawrence Knorr, Mechanicsburg, Pennsylvania).

Saturday of September the 5th.[169] He then recorded another "bulling" on September 8th and "Harry Traded" on September 9th.[170] Perhaps Harry was the bull!

169. Ibid., entries of August 30 to September 5, 1885.
170. Ibid., entries for September 8 and September 9, 1885.

10

Where Is H.D.?

During the second to last week of October 1885, Dr. Muth noted the last of the peaches and grapes and the "Absence" of "H.D." for four days, from October 21 through the 24th.[1] Of course, "H.D." was his son's initials. Was there a problem at the Freeburg Academy that semester? Young Henry Deppen Muth was only nineteen at the time. Perhaps he was expected to be at home. He again records H.D.'s "Absence" two weeks later, from November 16 to the 18th. The first snow then fell on the 19th.[2] This odd notation continues the next week, from November 26 through the 28th. Snow had fallen from the 23rd to the 25th, over "Butcher Day" on the 24th. Dr. Muth also recorded the "Burning of B F Latsha Barn."[3] Benjamin Franklin Latshaw (1845–1923) was a resident of Jackson Township at the time.[4] The fire amounted to a loss of $2500.[5]

H.D. was absent again the following week, on Sunday and Monday, the 29th and 30th.[6] It seems unlikely Dr. Muth had regular, timely attendance reports from school. It is more likely Dr. Muth was keeping tabs on his son, who was away from home for stretches of time, perhaps asserting his independence.

On December 29th, 1885, Dr. Muth again sent a registered letter to D.G. Brinton in Philadelphia.[7] This was likely for another book but

---

1. Ibid., entries for October 18 through October 24, 1885.

2. Ibid., entries for November 16 to November 19, 1885.

3. Ibid., entries for November 22 to November 28, 1885.

4. "Benjamin Franklin Latshaw," *Find a Grave*, Memorial ID 46471539, accessed January 5, 2025, https://www.findagrave.com/memorial/46471539/benjamin-franklin-latshaw.

5. "Local Shorts," *The Sunbury Weekly News*, December 4, 1885, pf 3.

6. Reuben H. Muth, *Physician's Daybooks*, vol. 21, entries for November 29 and November 30, 1885 (1858–1898, in possession of Lawrence Knorr, Mechanicsburg, Pennsylvania).

7. Reuben H. Muth, Ephemera, item 14, Registry Receipt (1876–1924, in possession of Lawrence Knorr, Mechanicsburg, Pennsylvania).

likely not a medical book. Brinton had just written and published his work about the Natives of southeastern Pennsylvania titled *The Lenâpé and Their Legends*.[8] Perhaps this was set next to his book on the Civil War.

The "Mystery of H.D." continued into the new year. Dr. Muth noted "H.D." on January 22nd and 23rd but did not include any other information. Perhaps he was tired of writing the word "Absence."[9] H.D. was then noted the following week for the 24th and 25th, making the entire (assumed) absence a length of four days.[10]

The cherry and plum trees were in bloom during the third week of April.[11] The next week, the apple trees were also blooming, and Dr. Muth planted his potatoes on April 30th. "H.D." was again marked for three days, from Monday the 26th to Wednesday the 28th.[12]

Before digging in for his potatoes, Dr. Muth stopped by J.H. Laudenslager, Agent, in Herndon to place an order for the second volume in cloth of *Wood's Reference Hand-Book of the Medical Sciences*.[13] By 1886, the set had just reached eight volumes, published from 1881 to 1885.[14]

One week later, Dr. Muth noted, for the first time, "House Cleaning," which lasted for two weeks. This was much more than just the regular periodic office cleaning.[15] H.D. was out again at the end of the week on Saturday, the 22nd,[16] and again on Monday, Tuesday, and Saturday the following week.[17]

Mrs. Muth's uncle, Isaac Deppen (1817–1886), died on May 27, 1886, in Mifflintown, Juniata County, Pennsylvania.[18] A trip to Mifflintown for the funeral would have involved a train ride of over fifty miles. Dr. Muth continued to see patients through Monday, May 31, but had an open schedule on Tuesday, June 1, 1886.[19] Perhaps the family traveled that day.

8. Daniel G. Brinton, *The Lenâpé and Their Legends* (Philadelphia, PA: D.G. Brinton, 1885).

9. Reuben H. Muth, *Physician's Daybooks*, vol. 22, entries for January 22 and January 23, 1886 (1858–1898, in possession of Lawrence Knorr, Mechanicsburg, Pennsylvania).

10. Ibid., entries for January 24 and January 25, 1886.

11. Ibid., entries for April 18 to April 24, 1886.

12. Ibid., entries for April 25 to May 1, 1886.

13. Reuben H. Muth, Ephemera, item 15, To William Wood & Company (1876–1924, in possession of Lawrence Knorr, Mechanicsburg, Pennsylvania).

14. "A Reference Handbook of the Medical Sciences," *Civil War Medical Books*, accessed December 31, 2024, http://www.civilwarmedicalbooks.com/Reference_Handbook_Medical_Sciences.html.

15. Reuben H. Muth, *Physician's Daybooks*, vol. 22, entries for May 9 to May 22, 1886 (1858–1898, in possession of Lawrence Knorr, Mechanicsburg, Pennsylvania).

16. Ibid.

17. Ibid., entries for May 23 to May 29, 1886.

18. "Short Locals," *Juniata Sentinel and Republican*, June 2, 1886, 3.

19. Reuben H. Muth, *Physician's Daybooks*, vol. 22, entries for May 30 to June 5, 1886 (1858–1898, in possession of Lawrence Knorr, Mechanicsburg, Pennsylvania).

There were many Deppen relations from the area, so it could have been a large group riding the rails to Mifflintown. However, there was no mention of this in the Northumberland County papers. Of course, if "H.D." had been expected to attend his great uncle's funeral, he was absent again from the 28th through the supposed travel day of June 1.[20]

Dr. Muth was back to his husbandry activities, noting "Calf Lady" on June 20.[21] He appears to have been more interested in the bovine activities and the whereabouts of his son, completely ignoring the call for physicians to join an association for the county. A meeting was held on July 12, 1886, in Milton, Northumberland County, Pennsylvania, to attempt to revive the medical association started previously. This time, Dr. A. S. Cummings of Shamokin was elected president,[22] rather than Joseph Priestley, who had died in 1883.[23] It is nearly impossible that Dr. Muth attended the meeting given that he saw patients on the day of the meeting.[24] H.D. was away for another long weekend, from Saturday, July 31, through Monday, August 2nd.[25] While gone, H.D. missed the "Lady Bul." on Monday.[26]

It appears there may have been a difficult delivery at the George Deppen house on August 2. Dr. Muth had delivered a daughter, Nettie, three years earlier to George and Mary Ann Deppen, but Mrs. Deppen was now in her 39th year. Nephew Lawrence Deppen was born that day,[27] but Dr. Muth returned for three more visits later in the week to follow up.[28] Both Mary Ann and the baby lived for many more years, so the results were positive.

At the end of August, Dr. Muth noted the eclipse on Sunday, August 29, 1886.[29] Either the newspaper or Dr. Muth got the day wrong when

20. Ibid.

21. Ibid., entry for June 20, 1886.

22. "Neighboring Notes," *Northumberland County Democrat*, July 23, 1886, 1.

23. "Dr Joseph Priestley," *Find a Grave*, Memorial ID 225692022, accessed January 12, 2025, https://www.findagrave.com/memorial/225692022/joseph-priestley.

24. Reuben H. Muth, *Physician's Daybooks*, vol. 22, entries for July 12 to July 13, 1886 (1858–1898, in possession of Lawrence Knorr, Mechanicsburg, Pennsylvania).

25. Ibid. entries for July 31 through August 7, 1886.

26. Ibid.

27. "Lawrence D Deppen," *Find a Grave*, Memorial ID 46318966, accessed January 5, 2025, https://www.findagrave.com/memorial/46318966/lawrence_d_deppen.

28. Reuben H. Muth, *Physician's Daybooks*, vol. 22, entries for August 2 to August 7, 1886 (1858–1898, in possession of Lawrence Knorr, Mechanicsburg, Pennsylvania).

29. Ibid., entry for August 26, 1886.

the local news reported, "There will be a total eclipse of the sun next Saturday."[30] The *Philadelphia Times* placed the eclipse on Sunday morning but reported it was too cloudy to observe.[31]

Three days later, on the first of September, Dr. Muth again arranged to purchase a volume of *Wood's Reference Hand-Book of the Medical Sciences*. This time, he ordered volume three, again in cloth, for six dollars.[32]

Dr. Muth's 60th birthday passed on September 11, and then H.D. was missing again from Friday, October 1, 1886, through Sunday, October 3.[33] Perhaps most unsettling to the father was his absence from church. Where was this twenty-year-old lad going? Perhaps Dr. Muth was hesitant to confront his son because of his own misbehavior in his college days. It appears he may have had a falling-out with his father and the family afterward. One can imagine the mother, Mrs. Muth, not worrying so much about her son. "He has to find his way," she might have said to the worried father. As an only child and son, H.D. was likely a spoiled "mama's boy," given his father's busy career.

During the third week of October, Dr. Muth reported he "Discarded the Fly Nettes" and was "Putting up Stove in Office."[34] The nets were likely not for fishing but rather to keep the bugs away from him and his patients while working. The stove in the office certainly signified he planned to spend more time there rather than in his buggy, traveling the roads during colder weather. The stove was in place just in time, as the first snow fell on Saturday, November 6.[35]

A steer and a hog were butchered on November 23. Dr. Muth recovered 336 pounds of meat from a 724-pound steer. The hog weighed 365 pounds.[36] Thursday, November 25, was Thanksgiving. It snowed all day, and Dr. Muth saw no patients.[37]

The Friday, December 10, 1886, edition of the *Northumberland County Democrat* reported that Dr. Muth, Isaac Reitz, John Tressler, J. R. Hilbush, and Samuel Zartman were "in Sunbury attending court as

30. "Sunbury Siftings," *Northumberland County Democrat*, August 20, 1886, 1.

31. "The Sun's Eclipse," *The Philadelphia Times*, August 30, 1886, 2.

32. Reuben H. Muth, Ephemera, item 16, To William Wood & Company (1876–1924, in possession of Lawrence Knorr, Mechanicsburg, Pennsylvania).

33. Reuben H. Muth, *Physician's Daybooks*, vol. 22, entries for October 1 through October 3, 1886 (1858–1898, in possession of Lawrence Knorr, Mechanicsburg, Pennsylvania).

34. Ibid., entries for October 17 to October 23, 1886.

35. Ibid., entry for November 6, 1886.

36. Ibid., last page of the journal for 1886.

37. Ibid., entry for November 25, 1886.

witnesses in some criminal suits."[38] Perhaps they were providing details on some horse theft cases in the area in conjunction with the Jackson Horse Detective Company.

On December 25, Dr. Muth seemed disappointed when he noted, "No Sleighing on Christmas." Perhaps most of the snow from late November had melted.[39] The following day, Second Christmas, was a Sunday. Dr. Muth saw Jeremiah Treon (1861–1942),[40] the grandson of Dr. Frederick Treon (1803–1870), who had served the community years ago. Jeremiah was also the grandnephew of the late Dr. Michael Tryon (1790–1871), whom Dr. Muth had replaced.[41] Born this day was Bertha A. Treon.[42] Of course, H.D. was nowhere to be found on New Year's Eve.[43]

Affixed to the inside flap of Dr. Muth's 1886 daybook were two items. One, printed in red, advertised for the "Woman's Infirmary, Maternity Home, James O'Reilly, Margaret Hoppe." It was located at 303 West 42nd Street, New York.[44] The advertisement urged the doctor to "Paste this in your Memoranda Book for future reference." Dr. Muth did, and we cannot know why he continued to be interested in the convalescence of wayward women.

The other item was a newspaper clipping in Pennsylvania Dutch titled "Ich Wot Ich Ware Ein Bauer by Nyun."[45] This translates to "I Wish I Were a Farmer by Anonymous." According to folklorists Boyer, Buffington, and Yoder, this song was first published in 1875 in a compilation of folk songs edited by Abraham Reeser Horne, a professor at the Keystone State Normal School at Kutztown, Pennsylvania (now Kutztown University.)[46] The song is quite humorous. Dr. Muth clipped the item, which included the title and portions of the first and fourth verses. The translation is as follows, thanks to the folklorists, "I wish I were a

38. "Mahanoy," *Northumberland County Democrat*, December 10, 1886, 4.

39. Ibid., entry for December 25, 1886.

40. Ibid., entry for December 26, 1886.

41. "Jeremiah 'Jerry' Treon," *Find a Grave*, Memorial ID 51078484, accessed January 5, 2025, https://www.findagrave.com/memorial/51078484/jeremiah_treon.

42. "Bertha A Treon Champion," *Find a Grave*, Memorial ID 185773999, accessed January 5, 2025, https://www.findagrave.com/memorial/185773999/bertha_a_champion.

43. Reuben H. Muth, *Physician's Daybooks*, vol. 22, entry for December 31, 1886 (1858–1898, in possession of Lawrence Knorr, Mechanicsburg, Pennsylvania).

44. Ibid., inside back flap.

45. Ibid.

46. Walter E. Boyer, Albert F. Buffington, and Don Yoder, *Songs Along the Mahantongo* (Hatboro, PA: Folklore Associates, Inc., 1964), 103–105.

farmer and had a homestead farm, with horses, green and yellow cows, and a wife to keep me warm. A nice brown brindled Moolie-bull, in my barnyard I keep, Alpaca Geese, a Borzert Dog, and Cochin-Shanghai Sheep!"[47]

This article indicated Dr. Muth remained fluent in Pennsylvania Dutch and that he had a sense of humor. The absurdities of the song were probably enough to tickle his ribs each time he referred to it. These are the only song lyrics he ever attached to any of his daybooks. Of course, the comment about the wife might be telling. Dr. Muth, now sixty, had only one child with Louisa, and that was over twenty years ago. Probably unknown to Dr. Muth, the song was actually written by Dr. Ezra Grumbine, the boy he knew back in Fredericksburg when he called on his father's home as a young doctor.[48] The song had become very popular with the Pennsylvania Dutch, and Ezra was beginning to show prowess in more than his medical career.

Dr. Muth's practice in 1886 was greatly improved from the previous year, grossing over eight hundred dollars in fees, his best performance over the last ten years. He also reached a peak of 161 households visited, the highest amount in his late career. Now past his sixtieth birthday and without a son to pass the business to, it appears Dr. Muth began to fade quietly beginning in early 1887.[49]

Dr. Muth was in his garden on April 11, 1887, and saw no patients.[50] The following month, the house cleaning occurred in the first two weeks of May.[51] On Friday, May 13, he was summoned to attend to Mrs. Schlegel. Dr. Muth recorded an extraordinary fee of ten dollars that day, eight to ten times the normal visitation fee.[52] This indicated he had to travel a good distance and may have seen more than one patient. He recorded "Rudy Schlegel" as the one paying the fee, despite a note that "Mrs. Schlegel" was to be seen. However, recent news reports discussed problems with Rudy's brother's family. The family of Daniel Schlegel of Snydertown had been dealing with typhus. Mrs. Schlegel had been severely ill earlier in

47. Ibid., 104–5.
48. Ibid., 103.
49. See Appendix D: "Summary" for Dr. Muth's Career Earnings.
50. Reuben H. Muth, *Physician's Daybooks*, vol. 23, entry for April 12, 1887 (1858–1898, in possession of Lawrence Knorr, Mechanicsburg, Pennsylvania).
51. Ibid., entries for May 1 to May 14, 1887.
52. Ibid., entry for May 13, 1887.

the year but survived. Two of the four children then became ill and were slowly recovering, while the other two were now "battling with the fever for several weeks."[53] Snydertown was roughly eighteen miles due north of Mahanoy, requiring four hours or more by buggy or perhaps a bit less by train and taxi. Perhaps Rudy had seen the news report that morning and rushed to ask Dr. Muth if he could help. Besides Daniel and his wife, the newspaper mentioned Rosie, 6; Nathan, 8; James, 7; and Ella, 14. Nathan Charles Schlegel (1877–1918) appears to have survived but perhaps succumbed during the 1918 influenza epidemic at only age 41.[54] No information could be found for the other children.

On May 15, Dr. Muth noted "Lady calving," and he was planting his corn the next day.[55] "J.R.H." reported on May 17, 1887, that "both our doctors, Haas and Muth, went in the direction of Dornsife this morning, no doubt to see patients."[56] This almost comical quip seems to hint that the reporter found it humorous that the two doctors were going in the same direction. Were they mistakenly both heading to the same patient? Often, there were reports of multiple doctors being called to a scene. The only patient on Dr. Muth's register that day was "Mrs. Goodman," for whom he charged one dollar.[57] Perhaps the two raced to collect that one dollar. If so, Dr. Muth won this time. Could "J.R.H." have been fellow Mahanoy resident, surveyor, and Justice of the Peace, Jacob Romberger Hilbush?[58]

At the end of the month, Dr. Muth's father, Frederick Muth's estate was finally settled. The executors sold the farm on the west end of Rehrersburg, including the ancient Inn at Tolheo, which was the home of Gottfried Rehrer, the founder of Rehrersburg.[59] The proceeds were to be split among the six heirs, as before.[60] Later that week, H.D. was again

53. "The family of Daniel Schlegel," *Northumberland County Democrat*, May 13, 1887, 4.

54. "Nathan Charles Schlegel," *Find a Grave*, Memorial ID 102923475, accessed January 5, 2025, https://www.findagrave.com/memorial/102923475/nathan-charles-schlegel.

55. Reuben H. Muth, *Physician's Daybooks*, vol. 23, entries for May 15 and May 16, 1887 (1858–1898, in possession of Lawrence Knorr, Mechanicsburg, Pennsylvania).

56. "Mahanoy," *Northumberland County Democrat*, May 20, 1887, 4.

57. Reuben H. Muth, *Physician's Daybooks*, vol. 23, entry for May 17, 1887 (1858–1898, in possession of Lawrence Knorr, Mechanicsburg, Pennsylvania).

58. "Jacob Romberger Hilbush," *Find a Grave*, Memorial ID 38974922, accessed January 5, 2025, https://www.findagrave.com/memorial/38974922/jacob-romberger-hilbush.

59. Dolores Hill, Sandra Kauffman, Barbara Loose, Carol Mehler, Barry Miller, and Jodie Ziegler, *History of Rehrersburg* (Rehrersburg, PA: Andulhea Heritage Center, 2019), 28.

60. *Berks County Property Records, 1887*, Book 174, Page 428, Berks County Recorder of Deeds, Reading, Pennsylvania.

missing for a long weekend, from Saturday, June 4, through Monday, June 6.[61] He repeated the behavior from Saturday, June 18, through Tuesday, June 21.[62]

Dr. Muth was back to monitoring the husbandry, noting "Dolly Bul." on June 27.[63] Perhaps the cow's name was Dolly! "Lady Bulling" followed on July 23rd.[64] And perhaps the other cow was named Lady!

Dr. Muth noted and then crossed out "camp meeting" the first week of August 1887. The following week, he had a light schedule of only three visits with two patients. Two of the appointments were with "Rudy Schlegel." The doctor also noted "Camp Meeting Communion" on August 10.[65] It appears Dr. Muth did not attend the camp meeting except for communion. Perhaps he was checking in on the Schlegel children.

On the husbandry front, Dr. Muth seemed happy to note "Little Pigs" on Friday, August 13, 1887.[66] He saw no patients that day, so he may have been busy in the stye. Nearly three weeks later, on the 30th, he noted "Mag Bulling."[67] And now we may have a third cow named "Mag." Outside the barn, in the field, the wheat was sown by September 9.[68] Dr. Muth noted "St. Michael" on the 29th of September, again recording Michaelmas.[69] He did see one patient that day, Mary Bower.

It appears Dr. Muth was also raising chickens. During the first full week of November, he recorded "Chickens sold for $4.32."[70] He also noted "15 Rooster."[71] That's a lot of roosters to have in one place, given their natural aggressiveness. It is probably best he sent them off! Butchering Day was November 29. Dr. Muth noted 332 pounds of beef obtained from a 640-pound steer. He also noted the hog, dressed at 400 pounds.[72]

For the first time in six months, H.D. was noted again from Thursday, December 15, through Saturday, December 17, 1887.[73] Two weeks

61. Reuben H. Muth, *Physician's Daybooks*, vol. 23, entries for June 4 through June 6, 1887 (1858–1898, in possession of Lawrence Knorr, Mechanicsburg, Pennsylvania).
62. Ibid., entries for June 18 through June 21, 1887.
63. Ibid., entry for June 27, 1887.
64. Ibid., entry for July 23, 1887.
65. Ibid., entries for July 31 to August 13, 1887.
66. Ibid., entry for August 13, 1887.
67. Ibid., entry for August 30, 1887.
68. Ibid., entry for September 9, 1887.
69. Ibid., entry for September 29, 1887.
70. Ibid., entries for November 6 to November 12, 1887.
71. Ibid.
72. Ibid., Cash Account
73. Ibid., entries for December 15 to December 17, 1887.

later, after Christmas, he was gone again from December 27 through the 30th.[74] What was Henry Deppen Muth up to?

Sometime at the end of the year, after he recorded his butchering tabulations, Dr. Muth made a curious notation at the back of his day-book. He made two tallies of funds that achieved the same result: "189 Trade Dollars, 18 Louisa, 37 A Deppen," summing to $244, less a 2.44 discount, yielding $241.56, and then simply "244 Trade Dollars" less the 2.44 discount, yielding the same answer, which was "Paid Aug 23, 1883."[75] Why did Dr. Muth recount this four-year-old transaction? This was at a time months before his father died, so it likely had nothing to do with that situation. Given the tallying of funds from his wife Louisa and his father-in-law, "A Deppen," it appears the three were purchasing something for the farm, perhaps livestock. The initial illustration also showed over three-quarters of the funds presumably coming from Dr. Muth and not his wife and in-law. Was there a dispute of some kind in the household? The other interesting tidbit was regarding the notation of "Trade Dollars." The Coinage Act of 1873 had ended the production of the silver dollar for general circulation, then the Liberty Seated Variety. This caused some turmoil in the silver market and was a contributing factor to the subsequent economic slump. As part of the act, the government began minting what were called "Trade Dollars" to be used for export transactions. These coins were minted from 1873 to 1885, overlapping the reintroduction of the silver dollar for general circulation in 1878, the Morgan variety. So, by August 23, 1883, the family could have been using a variety of silver dollar coins. Instead, Dr. Muth noted "Trade Dollars," indicating the family had continued to hoard the largest silver coins available when they were no longer being made for general circulation or Dr. Muth was engaged in a small transaction of international trade. The former seems more likely than the latter.

As for why the recounting of the transaction was done four years later, it is curious that there was a line item for Louisa's contribution of only eighteen dollars. Was it customary for husband and wife to keep separate funds even after more than twenty years of marriage? Most likely not.

The last page of the 1887 daybook included a listing of wheat and flour transactions for the year. Dr. Muth logged providing seven bushels

---

74. Ibid., entries for December 26 to December 31, 1887.
75. Ibid., Cash Account for 1887.

of wheat early in the year and then noted a draw of bags of flour on a regular, mostly monthly, basis.[76] These were probably transactions with the local grist mill. The flour log continued into January 1888. Dr. Muth drew bags for January, February, and April.[77]

The first five days of February 1888, H.D. was marked out,[78] again for two days in March, Thursday and Friday, the 22nd and 23rd,[79] then for three days in April, the 7th through the 9th, which was Saturday through Monday.[80]

On May 2, 1888, a brief story appeared that young Henry D. Muth was now engaged in a coal business with A. Z. Drumheller and L. Bucher. They had taken coal out of the Mahanoy Creek, where others had given up before on account of all the water.[81] Mr. Drumheller was likely Albert Zartman Drumheller (1850–1910), who was quite a bit older than Henry Muth.[82] L. Bucher may have been Andrew L. Bucher (1860–1941).[83] Andrew was a junior, so he may have been using his middle name. He was also the lad thrown from the wagon ten years prior as a teenager. It does not appear this scheme amounted to much and may have been hatched by Zartman, but it may explain some of H.D.'s recent absences. H.D. was away again from Thursday, May 10, through Saturday, May 12.[84]

Dr. Muth's role as President of the Jackson Horse Detective Company was prominent in the local paper on May 18, 1888.[85] Muth, along with Secretary E. R. Hilbush and Treasurer Daniel Hetrick, had $470 on hand to help recover stolen horses and prosecute the thieves.[86]

Young Henry Deppen Muth, now twenty-two years old, was lauded in the local newspaper for the work he had done to the home of Mrs.

76. Ibid., Cash Account for 1887, last page.
77. Reuben H. Muth, *Physician's Daybooks*, vol. 24, Cash Account for 1888, last page. (1858–1898, in possession of Lawrence Knorr, Mechanicsburg, Pennsylvania).
78. Ibid., entries for February 1 through February 5, 1888.
79. Ibid., entries for March 22 and March 23, 1888.
80. Ibid., entries for April 7 through April 9, 1888.
81. "Mahanoy," *Northumberland County Democrat*, May 2, 1888, 4.
82. "Albert Zartman Drumheller," *Find a Grave*, Memorial ID 38943627, accessed January 5, 2025, https://www.findagrave.com/memorial/38943627/albert-zartman-drumheller.
83. "Andrew L. Bucher," *Find a Grave*, Memorial ID 38916147, accessed January 5, 2025, https://www.findagrave.com/memorial/38916147/andrew-bucher.
84. Reuben H. Muth, *Physician's Daybooks*, vol. 24, entries for May 10 through May 12, 1888 (1858–1898, in possession of Lawrence Knorr, Mechanicsburg, Pennsylvania).
85. "Mahanoy," *Northumberland County Democrat*, May 18, 1888, 4.
86. Ibid.

Harriett Dunkelberger in June 1888.[87] Her house was repainted, shutters added to the windows, and the barn enlarged and painted whitewashed.[88] Apparently, the young man was not intending to follow his father into the medical field or on the farm, and was instead working with his hands.

Dr. Muth's first husbandry activity was logged on June 21, noting "Dolly Bul. 1st time."[89]

On Sunday, July 8, Louisa's niece, Agnes M. Deppen, the daughter of her brother, Alexander Deppen, married Grant Bolig, who was the stationmaster at Dornsife, a stop or two north on the railroad.[90] The couple were married at their home in Dornsife. Dr. Muth saw a patient that day, so perhaps Louisa attended, or he worked around the wedding schedule. Dornsife is about two and a half miles north of Mahanoy, an easy carriage ride after church.

The following month, on August 20th, "Dollie" was at it again with her bull.[91] "Mag Bul." was then noted on September 5.[92] H.D. must have been done painting houses for the summer because his father marked him away from Saturday, September 15, through Monday, September 17.[93] Dr. Muth noted the "Firemans Parade Sept 20, 1888" on this same page, which was a page before the event.[94] This was probably a notation recording back in July when the notice of the parade occurred in the local newspaper. The parade was to be held at Shamokin.[95] It appears Dr. Muth did not attend, given his patient schedule that day.[96]

Brother-in-law George Deppen added another member of the household on Saturday, September 8, 1888, as Dr. Muth assisted.[97] Nephew A. Earl Deppen was born on this day.[98]

87. "Mahanoy," *Northumberland County Democrat*, June 22, 1888, 4.

88. Ibid.

89. Reuben H. Muth, *Physician's Daybooks*, vol. 24, entries for June 21, 1888 (1858–1898, in possession of Lawrence Knorr, Mechanicsburg, Pennsylvania).

90. "Marriages," *Sunbury Weekly News*, July 20, 1888, 3.

91. Reuben H. Muth, *Physician's Daybooks*, vol. 24, entry August 20, 1888 (1858–1898, in possession of Lawrence Knorr, Mechanicsburg, Pennsylvania).

92. Ibid., entry for September 5, 1888.

93. Ibid., entries for September 15 through September 17, 1888.

94. Ibid.

95. "A Firemens Parade at Shamokin," *Northumberland County Democrat*, July 13, 1888, 1.

96. Reuben H. Muth, *Physician's Daybooks*, vol. 24, entry September 20, 1888 (1858–1898, in possession of Lawrence Knorr, Mechanicsburg, Pennsylvania).

97. Ibid., entry for September 8, 1888.

98. "A Earl Deppen," *Find a Grave*, Memorial ID 46115501, accessed January 5, 2025, https://www.findagrave.com/memorial/46115501/a-earl-deppen.

H.D. was gone for two days in October, the 15th and 16th.[99] Dr. Muth recorded "Thunder" on Friday the 19th and saw no patients.[100] Perhaps the thunderstorms deterred business. H.D. was gone for five days the following month, from Monday, November 12, through Friday, November 16, 1888.[101] On the day H.D. left, November 12, Dr. Muth purchased a steer from Isaac B. Tressler & Co. of Mahanoy weighing 558 pounds. The bill noted, "from Isaac Reitz to Dr. R.H. Muth."[102]

H.D. was back for Butcher Day on the 20th. Dr. Muth obtained 558 pounds after dressing, according to his daybook.[103] Given the receipt from Tressler's, it appears Dr. Muth had Isaac Reitz process the animal for him, arranged by Tressler.

Before the year was out, Dr. Muth subscribed to *The Philadelphia Record* newspaper through January 1, 1890, at the cost of $3.10. He received a penny postcard as a receipt.[104]

99. Reuben H. Muth, *Physician's Daybooks*, vol. 24, entries for October 15 and October 16, 1888 (1858–1898, in possession of Lawrence Knorr, Mechanicsburg, Pennsylvania).

100. Ibid., entry for October 19, 1888.

101. Ibid., entries for November 12 through November 16, 1888.

102. Reuben H. Muth, Ephemera, item 19, Isaac B. Tressler & Co (1876–1924, in possession of Lawrence Knorr, Mechanicsburg, Pennsylvania).

103. Reuben H. Muth, *Physician's Daybooks*, vol. 24, entry November 20, 1888 (1858–1898, in possession of Lawrence Knorr, Mechanicsburg, Pennsylvania).

104. Reuben H. Muth, Ephemera, item 21, *The Philadelphia Record* (1876–1924, in possession of Lawrence Knorr, Mechanicsburg, Pennsylvania).

11

Dr. Thayer's Private Lying-In Institute and Sanitarium

Tucked in the back of the daybook was an advertisement printed on pink paper, probably an insert in one of his medical journals, promoting "Dr. Thayer's Lying-In Institute and Sanitarium," located in Fort Wayne, Indiana. According to the text in the advertisement, this was a home for "troubled women" who were pregnant.[1] This was the second such institution tracked by Dr. Muth, including the New York home affixed to a prior daybook. It appears Dr. Muth was concerned about out-of-wedlock pregnancy. At the time, he could not have known about the trouble Dr. Frederick Thayer would be involved in five years later.

The first indication something was wrong with Dr. Frederick Thayer was when a warrant for his arrest was issued on April 20, 1893, accusing the doctor of abandoning a child on the doorstep of a nearby Bloomingdale resident.[2] While Dr. Thayer appeared to escape justice at that point, on September 19, a horrendous report appeared in the paper linking him to the death of one of his patients, Emma S. Baer, who had been treated poorly and may have been strangled.[3] That afternoon, Dr. Thayer was questioned by the coroner at the institute he started in 1881[4] and denied seeing any markings on the body and suggested she died from a fever.[5]

---

1. "Dr. Thayer's," advertisement, circa 1888, found in Reuben H. Muth, *Physician's Daybooks*, vol. 24 (1858–1898, in possession of Lawrence Knorr.)
2. "To Be Arrested," *The Fort Wayne News and Sentinel*, April 20, 1893, 1.
3. "Was It Murder?" *The Fort Wayne News and Sentinel*, September 19, 1893, 1.
4. "Dr. Frederick Thayer," *The Fort Wayne Journal Gazette*, January 19, 1893, 3.
5. "A Mystery," *The Fort Wayne Journal Gazette*, September 20, 1893, 4.

The undertaker's testimony of no markings on the body influenced the coroner to declare Emma Baer had died from puerperal fever.[6]

Based on additional information detectives had collected, Dr. Thayer was arrested on September 30, 1893, and charged with manslaughter for the death of Miss Emma Baer at his Lying-In Institute. Dr. Thayer denied the charges and was released on a one-thousand-dollar bond.[7] Detectives had determined Dr. Thayer and his housekeeper, Maggie, had been covering up an adoption ring and also tacked on a manslaughter charge for Emma Baer.[8] Maggie was described as "cool, foxy, guarded, and sly."[9] The reporter also related that detectives had learned of Emma Baer's statements of mistreatment prior to her death, including being strapped down to a bed.[10]

On October 9, 1893, Dr. Thayer was again arrested, this time for reusing a "Columbian stamp." The postmaster had noticed Dr. Thayer had reused a canceled stamp and had him arrested and bound over for $500.[11] Why would a successful physician reuse a canceled two-cent stamp? It appeared the authorities were really scrutinizing the doctor in every way possible. The doctor protested his innocence and blamed his near-sightedness on the mistake.[12]

Dr. Thayer was not convicted either time but was arrested again in 1895 when another baby was found with a mistreated mother.[13] Detectives were called to check on the shrieks of a woman at Dr. Thayer's institute, only to find a near-smothered baby and a severely ill teenage woman. The police hastily inspected the property and found a secret stairwell in the house behind which was a room with trunks full of baby items and a wardrobe full of women's clothing. In the barn was a "huge furnace with a large pot covered with a thin scum of tar."[14] The doctor was arrested and questioned. He denied the allegations and stated he had closed his hospital, and the couple that were remaining were guests who had asked to stay. Dr. Thayer was sent to jail, and the investigation into

6. "Puerperal Fever," *Fort Wayne Weekly Journal*, September 21, 1893, 5.
7. "Dr. Thayer," *The Fort Wayne Journal Gazette*, October 1, 1893, 8.
8. Ibid.
9. Ibid.
10. "Oh! Doctor!" *Fort Wayne Weekly Journal*, October 5, 1893, 8.
11. "In a New Role," *The Fort Wayne News and Sentinel*, October 11, 1893, 1.
12. "Once More," *The Fort Wayne Journal Gazette*, October 12, 1893, 4.
13. "Gave No Bonds," *Fort Wayne Daily News*, August 2, 1895, 1.
14. Ibid.

reports of a "crematory" on the property was unfounded. The cauldron was believed to be used to concoct Dr. Thayer's medicines.[15] Dr. Thayer was sent to jail for twenty days and fined twenty-five dollars for cruelty to a child.[16]

On August 8, Dr. Thayer was released after posting a bond and serving seven days in jail.[17] He believed he would be acquitted in a higher court. Apparently, the neighbors did not like the institute in their neighborhood and were always suspicious of it.[18] After his appeal, Dr. Thayer had his day in court in December, denying all charges.[19] Unfortunately, he lost again and was fined $50 and sentenced to thirty days in prison. Because he was now penniless, it was expected he would spend three months in jail. The medical profession believed the doctor was innocent.[20] Dr. Thayer was either a perfectly innocent, well-meaning practitioner of women's medical services, or the neighbors were right to suspect malfeasance, perhaps including murder and abortions, covered up in his cauldron.

H.D.'s absences continued in 1889. He was away on several occasions early in the year, On January 1st and 2nd, 20th through the 22nd, and the 25th through the 30th.[21] In February, H.D. was out from Wednesday the 6th through Friday the 8th.[22]

The Muths must have acquired a piano at the beginning of April 1889, based on an entry in the daybook. H.D. was also noted to be in Myerstown from Friday April 5th through Monday, April 8th, perhaps visiting Muth relatives there.[23]

Dr. Muth was called to the home of Washington Otto on Friday, April 19, 1889. Otto was severely injured at the train depot at Otto Station when he was pinched between a wagon wheel and the platform. Otto was "confined to bed and is doing as well as can be expected."[24] Dr. Muth saw Washington Otto nearly every day for the next week.[25]

15. "Went to Jail," *Fort Wayne Weekly Sentinel,* August 2, 1895, 1.

16. "Sent to Jail," *Fort Wayne Weekly Sentinel,* August 3, 1895, 1.

17. "Out on Bonds," *Fort Wayne Daily News,* August 9, 1895, 1.

18. Ibid.

19. "He Denies It," *Fort Wayne Daily News,* December 17, 1895, 1.

20. "Goes To Jail," *Fort Wayne Daily News,* December 18, 1895, 1.

21. Reuben H. Muth, *Physician's Daybooks,* vol. 25, entries for January 1 through January 31, 1889 (1858–1898, in possession of Lawrence Knorr, Mechanicsburg, Pennsylvania).

22. Ibid., entries for February 6 through February 8, 1889.

23. Ibid., entries for April 1 through April 8, 1889.

24. "From Mahanoy" *Northumberland County Democrat,* Apr 19, 1889, 4.

25. Reuben H. Muth, *Physician's Daybooks,* vol. 25, entries for entries for April 19 through April 28, 1889 (1858–1898, in possession of Lawrence Knorr, Mechanicsburg, Pennsylvania)

(Dr. Thayer's Private Lying-In Institute and Sanitarium.)

Figure 13. Pictures from Dr. Thayer's advertisement.

Later in April, the cherry, plum, and peach trees were in bloom before the four days of rain from the 25th through the 28th.[26] At the end of May, H.D. was away again from Thursday, the 30th, through Saturday, June 1. Dr. Muth noted "High Water" on the first and second.[27] Little did Dr. Muth know, as he awoke that Saturday morning, there had also been high water in Johnstown, Pennsylvania, over 160 miles west-southwest of Mahanoy. The initial news reports were sensational, expecting upwards

---

26. Ibid., entries for April 21 through April 28, 1889.
27. Ibid., entries for May 28 through June 2, 1889.

of 15,000 deaths from the deluge caused by heavy rains and the breach
of the South Fork Dam on the Conemaugh River.[28] Dr. Muth continued
seeing patients as usual during the ensuing weeks. By the 21st of June,
authorities were still unsure how many people were lost in the flood. By
one estimate, of the 29,600 inhabitants of the area, 12,730 remained
unaccounted for.[29] By mid-July, the coroner had determined the South
Fork Fishing and Hunting Club responsible due to its neglect of the
dam.[30] Eventually, it would be learned that the loss of life, while great,
was much less than 15,000. However, as recounted by Willis Fletcher
Johnson, there was "desolation so complete, so relentless, so dreadful
that it is absolutely beyond the power of language fairly to tell the tale."[31]

H.D. was away again from July 19 through the 21st.[32] The next
month, it was mother's turn, as Louisa Muth was away at Mount Carmel
from August 15th to the 17th.[33] Dr. Muth noted the camp meeting on
Friday, August 24th, during which he saw no patients.[34] The next week,
he noted "Mag Bul. 1st time," on Friday, August 30. H.D. was away
again during this time, from the 29th through the 31st.[35]

In another medical collaboration, most likely on September 16th,
Dr. Muth and Dr. Krebs joined to perform surgery on Mrs. Daniel Reed.
The doctors removed a three-pound tumor from her leg. The surgery was
successful and "she bore up heroically while the operation lasted and is
at present doing quite well."[36] Perhaps this was implying the surgery was
done without anesthesia. The reporter had filed his report on September
23, and the operation had occurred the prior week. Dr. Muth logged
appearing at the Daniel Reed home on September 16 with a follow-up
two days later. He did not charge for the visits.[37] Given that the report

28. "Overwhelmed," *The Sunbury American*, June 7, 1889, 1.

29. "At the Stricken City," *The Sunbury American*, June 21, 1889, 1.

30. "South Fork Club Guilty," *Northumberland County Democrat*, July 12, 1889, 3.

31. Willis Fletcher Johnson, *History of the Johnstown Flood, Illustrated* (Philadelphia, PA: Edgewood Publishing Company, 1889), 80.

32. Reuben H. Muth, *Physician's Daybooks*, vol. 25, entry for July 19 to 21, 1889 (1858–1898, in possession of Lawrence Knorr, Mechanicsburg, Pennsylvania).

33. Ibid., entries for August 15 to 17, 1889.

34. Ibid., entry for August 23, 1889.

35. Ibid., entries for August 29 to 31, 1889.

36. "Our Herndon Letter," *The Sunbury Weekly News*, September 27, 1889, 2.

37. Reuben H. Muth, *Physician's Daybooks*, vol. 25, entry for September 16 to 18, 1889 (1858–1898, in possession of Lawrence Knorr, Mechanicsburg, Pennsylvania).

came from Herndon, the patient was likely Caroline Rubendale Reed (1827–1900), who was married to Daniel Reed (1820–1894).[38]

Dr. Jacob S. Krebs (1861–1938) was thirty-five years younger than Dr. Muth and likely called upon him to assist with his patient. Dr. Krebs was born in Snyder County and attended the Freeburg and New Berlin Academies. He was a graduate of the Medico-Chirurgical College in Philadelphia. After his marriage to Rachel Wetzel of Snyder County on March 1, 1881, he started a medical practice in Herndon, about four miles west of Mahanoy, along the Susquehanna River. The newspaper declared Dr. Krebs was "the first physician to locate in that rural section."[39] The reporter also mentioned how Dr. Krebs used a horse and sulky to get to patients "over rough and muddy rural highways" before he started using an automobile.[40]

Dr. Muth carefully wrote a notation about dropsy in his journal the week after the visit with Dr. Krebs: "The following is a broad rule. Dropsy of the feet alone means heart; dropsy of the belly alone means liver; and dropsy of all the body means kidneys."[41] Perhaps the young physician shared the information.

H.D. was next away for six days in November, from Monday, the 18th, through Saturday, the 23rd.[42] November 26 was Butcher Day, yielding 356 pounds of beef and 818 pounds of pork from two hogs.[43] Said the local news, "Many sausages are being made in and around our town, and some good-sized hogs are butchered." Reporter J.R.H. confirmed the combined weight of Dr. Muth's hogs.[44] A month later, Dr. Muth noted "Christmas warm and pleasant, roads muddy."[45]

At the back of his 1889 journal, Dr. Muth penciled the definition of "limited" as it relates to a business entity and its limited liability.[46] Perhaps he was contemplating upscaling from his sole proprietorships.

---

38. "Caroline Rubendale Reed," *Find a Grave*, Memorial ID 46398816, accessed January 5, 2025, https://www.findagrave.com/memorial/46398816/caroline_reed.

39. "Dr. J. S. Krebs Dies at Home," *Shamokin News-Dispatch*, June 10, 1938, 2.

40. Ibid.

41. Reuben H. Muth, *Physician's Daybooks*, vol. 25, entry for September 22 to 28, 1889 (1858–1898, in possession of Lawrence Knorr, Mechanicsburg, Pennsylvania).

42. Ibid., entries for November 18 to November 23, 1889.

43. Ibid., last page of journal, 1889.

44. "Mahanoy," *Northumberland County Democrat*, December 6, 1889, 4.

45. Reuben H. Muth, *Physician's Daybooks*, vol. 25, entries for December 22 to December 28, 1889 (1858–1898, in possession of Lawrence Knorr, Mechanicsburg, Pennsylvania).

46. Ibid., last page of journal, 1889.

He also glued a news clipping from September highlighting the miraculous survival of sextuplets, weighing a combined eight pounds. The event occurred in Idaho and was reported from Salt Lake City, Utah.[47]

From January 20th through the 28th, 1890, Michael Bower, Louisa's uncle who was married to her Aunt Leah, was in the care of Dr. Muth.[48] Unfortunately, Uncle Michael passed away on January 29 at Herndon.[49] Their daughter had married Washington Otto, making him an in-law as well. Given his open schedule on January 31, Dr. Muth likely attended the funeral.[50]

Dr. Muth notes H.D. was away with "Lenker" from February 11 through the 13th, 1890.[51] Perhaps his son was finally sharing the company he was keeping.

On March 5, Dr. Muth arranged to replenish his supply of hypodermics from John Wyeth and Brother, Manufacturing Chemists from Philadelphia.[52] These would have been for the various vaccinations that Dr. Muth performed.

One month later, on April 16, Dr. Muth was in his garden planting radishes. His only appointment of the day was his brother-in-law, George Deppen.[53] The following week, he planted potatoes on the 22nd and recorded a bulling on the 23rd.[54] H.D. was then gone from May 2 to May 5, 1890.[55]

By mid-May, it appeared Dr. Muth was now raising geese. He noted "Geese set" on May 12, May 19, and May 24.[56] H.D. exited for four days, from Saturday, May 24 through Tuesday, May 27. "Little Pigs" then arrived on May 31, 1890.[57] The husbandry activity was more exciting at this time. Following Dolly's "bulling" on June 6, "Magie" was

47. Ibid.

48. Reuben H. Muth, *Physician's Daybooks*, vol. 26, entry for January 20 to January 31, 1890 (1858–1898, in possession of Lawrence Knorr, Mechanicsburg, Pennsylvania).

49. "Michael Bower," *Find a Grave*, Memorial ID 46466131, accessed January 5, 2025, https://www.findagrave.com/memorial/46466131/michael_bower.

50. Reuben H. Muth, *Physician's Daybooks*, vol. 26, entry for January 20 to January 31, 1890 (1858–1898, in possession of Lawrence Knorr, Mechanicsburg, Pennsylvania).

51. Ibid., entries for February 13 to February 15, 1890.

52. Reuben H. Muth, Ephemera, item 20, John Wyeth and Brother (1876–1924, in possession of Lawrence Knorr, Mechanicsburg, Pennsylvania).

53. Reuben H. Muth, *Physician's Daybooks*, vol. 26, entry for April 16, 1890 (1858–1898, in possession of Lawrence Knorr, Mechanicsburg, Pennsylvania).

54. Ibid., entries for April 22, and April 23, 1890.

55. Ibid., entries for May 2 through May 9, 1890.

56. Ibid., entries for May 12 through May 24, 1890.

57. Ibid., entries for May 24 through May 31, 1890.

calving on June 9. At least we know her name was Magie. H.D. was away from June 10 through the 12th.[58]

Louisa's uncle, William Deppen, died on June 13, 1890.[59] Uncle William was not a patient of Dr. Muth's, as he lived about seven miles southwest at Hickory Corners, closer to Dalmatia. Perhaps Louisa attended the funeral.

The next month, on the 17th, Dolly was "bulled" for the second time.[60] The following week, Dr. Muth's brother-in-law, Samuel Snyder, the husband of his sister, Anna Maria, passed away at Rehrersburg.[61] Dr. Muth saw Albert Heller on the 25th and then no one else until Monday the 28th. Thus, it is very plausible he returned to western Berks County for this funeral held at Altalaha Church in Rehrersburg.

Mag was "bulled" again on Wednesday, August 20, one day before the camp meeting on the 21st. Dr. Muth continued to see patients throughout the camp meeting, so it must have been local.[62]

The following month, H.D. was away for six days from Thursday, September 18, through Tuesday, September 23.[63] He was away again for three days from October 13 through the 15th.[64] He then was away November 6 through November 8[65] and November 22 through the 24th.[66] Butcher Day was November 25, yielding 755 pounds of pork from two hogs and 449 pounds of beef from one steer after dressing.[67]

The Northumberland County Medical Society was finally formed on December 2, 1890, at the courthouse in Sunbury.[68] Dr. Muth had an open day on December 2, so it is very possible he traveled to Sunbury to attend the meeting.[69] He was not elected as one of the officers.

58. Ibid., entries for June 6 through June 12, 1890.

59. "William Deppen," *Find a Grave*, Memorial ID 39931396, accessed January 5, 2025, https://www.findagrave.com/memorial/39931396/william-deppen.

60. Reuben H. Muth, *Physician's Daybooks*, vol. 26, entry for July 17, 1890 (1858–1898, in possession of Lawrence Knorr, Mechanicsburg, Pennsylvania).

61. "Samuel Snyder," *Find a Grave*, Memorial ID 32416113, accessed January 5, 2025, https://www.findagrave.com/memorial/32416113/samuel-snyder.

62. Reuben H. Muth, *Physician's Daybooks*, vol. 26, entries for July 17 to July 23, 1890 (1858–1898, in possession of Lawrence Knorr, Mechanicsburg, Pennsylvania).

63. Ibid., entries for September 18 through September 23, 1890.

64. Ibid., entries for October 13 through October 15, 1890.

65. Ibid., entries for November 6 through November 8, 1890.

66. Ibid., entries for November 22 through November 24, 1890.

67. Ibid., last page of journal for 1890.

68. Herbert C. Bell, *History of Northumberland County* (Chicago: Brown, Runk, and Co., 1891), 269.

69. Reuben H. Muth, *Physician's Daybooks*, vol. 26, entry for December 2, 1890 (1858–1898, in possession of Lawrence Knorr, Mechanicsburg, Pennsylvania).

During "institute week," H. D. Muth, Frank A. Lahr, and Col. J. H. Robenolt of Jackson Township stopped in at the newspaper office in Sunbury and "paid their respects."[70] Apparently, "H.D." was passing through on his way home or on his way out in the week before Christmas.

H.D.'s first absence in 1891 was from January 19 through the 21st.[71] He was next away the first week of April for five days, from Friday the 3rd through the 7th. Dr. Muth planted clover seed on the 8th and was gardening on the 9th but managed to see several patients.[72]

70. "Personal," *Northumberland County Democrat*, December 25, 1890, 1.

71. Reuben H. Muth, *Physician's Daybooks*, vol. 27, entries for January 19 to January 21, 1891 (1858–1898, in possession of Lawrence Knorr, Mechanicsburg, Pennsylvania).

72. Ibid., entries for April 3 through April 9, 1891.

12

Jackson Horse Detective Company

Dr. Muth's role as President of the Jackson Horse Detective Company was again mentioned in the local paper on May 7, 1891.[1] Muth, along with Secretary E. R. Hilbush and Treasurer Daniel Hetrick, was "financially OK" with $475.81 on hand.[2] H.D. was in Myerstown in May on the 8th and 9th, likely visiting Muth relations.[3] He was then away elsewhere, from May 17 through the 25th.[4]

Dolly was "bulled" on June 9.[5] Then, nearly three weeks later, word came of the passing of Dr. Muth's cousin, Richard Muth, at Myerstown on June 28. Perhaps Henry had gone to visit him back in May. Richard Muth (1822–1891) was Dr. Muth's oldest cousin, the son of his Uncle John Muth.[6] Dr. Muth saw no patients on the following two days, so he may have attended the funeral.[7]

The husbandry was back in action on Saturday, July 25, when Mag was "bulled."[8] The following Friday, August 1, 1891, Dr. Muth noted a "Celebration." Given that there were no obvious large celebrations reported in the news, this must have been a family celebration of some sort to remain unattributed.

---

1. "From Mahanoy," *Northumberland County Democrat*, May 7, 1891, 4.

2. Ibid.

3. Reuben H. Muth, *Physician's Daybooks*, vol. 27, entries for May 8 to May 9, 1891 (1858–1898, in possession of Lawrence Knorr, Mechanicsburg, Pennsylvania).

4. Ibid., entries for May 17 through May 25, 1891.

5. Ibid., entry for June 9, 1891.

6. "Richard Muth," *Find a Grave*, Memorial ID 35875899, accessed January 5, 2025, https://www.findagrave.com/memorial/35875899/richard-muth.

7. Reuben H. Muth, *Physician's Daybooks*, vol. 27, entries for June 29 to June 30, 1891 (1858–1898, in possession of Lawrence Knorr, Mechanicsburg, Pennsylvania).

8. Ibid., entry for July 25, 1891.

Dr. Muth seemed concerned about losing or mislaying on August 13 a due bill from "J B Tressler" for "49 ½ lbs Lard," for which he was to be paid $4.45 per pound.[9] H.D. was away on the 12th and 13th and could not help find it.[10] Dr. Muth turned sixty-five on September 11.

On Sunday night, October 4, 1891, there was a great fire in Dornsife, less than three miles north of Mahanoy, one stop on the railroad up from Otto Station. William M. Zartman of Dornsife lost his barn in the conflagration.[11] William M. Zartman (1852–1926) was the son of Abraham Zartman and lived on his father's farm into middle age. Thus, this could have been the barn built by old Abraham.[12] At the same time, Grant Bolig, Louisa's nephew and the ticket agent and operator of the Philadelphia and Reading Railroad (at nearby Otto Station), broke one of his legs while assisting with the fire. The news reported that Dr. Muth set the bone.[13] According to his journal, Dr. Muth cared for his nephew starting on the 4th through the 10th, seeing him four times in seven days.[14]

H.D. was next gone the first week of November, from the 2nd through the 8th.[15] Butcher Day was then on November 24. One steer was dressed, yielding 411 pounds of meat from 740 pounds of live weight.[16]

The following month, Dr. Muth recorded his chimney dimensions.[17] Perhaps he was planning to have them rebuilt or swept before Christmas. Afterall, he had not been nearly as busy all year as a physician. He recorded the fewest households visited since he came to Northumberland County, and his income had dropped to its lowest level since the Civil War.[18]

H.D. was first away in February 1892 from the 9th to the 13th.[19] March 26th was a busy day on the farm as Dolly birthed a calf and the geese were setting. Dr. Muth saw two patients regardless.[20] Two weeks

---

9. Ibid., entry for August 13, 1891.

10. Ibid., entry for August 12 to August 13, 1891.

11. "From Mahanoy," *Northumberland County Democrat*, October 15, 1891, 4.

12. "William Michael Zartman," *Find a Grave*, Memorial ID 52589518, accessed January 5, 2025, https://www.findagrave.com/memorial/52589518/william-michael-zartman.

13. "From Mahanoy," *Northumberland County Democrat*, October 15, 1891, 4.

14. Reuben H. Muth, *Physician's Daybooks*, vol. 27, entries for October 4 to October 10, 1891 (1858–1898, in possession of Lawrence Knorr, Mechanicsburg, Pennsylvania).

15. Ibid., entries for November 2 to November 8, 1891.

16. Ibid., last page of the journal for 1891.

17. Ibid., entries for December 6 to December 12, 1891.

18. See Appendix D: "Summary" for Dr. Muth's Career Earnings.

19. Reuben H. Muth, *Physician's Daybooks*, vol. 28, entries for February 9 to February 13, 1892 (1858–1898, in possession of Lawrence Knorr, Mechanicsburg, Pennsylvania).

20. Ibid., entry for March 26, 1892.

later, Dr. Muth was in the garden on April 9th and saw no patients that day.[21]

On April 11, Dr. Muth was at the Grant Bolig home where his wife's niece, Agnes, gave birth to Ethel Harriett Bolig.[22] Clearly, the father, Grant Bolig, had recovered from the broken leg he had suffered.

Two weeks later, Dr. Muth planted his potatoes in the garden and the field on the 26th and 27th of April. He had no patients while gardening on the 26th but a full schedule the next day.[23] The following week, the first week of May, the peaches, cherries, and plums were all in bloom.[24] On the 9th of May, Dollie was "bulled."[25]

H.D. was out of the house at the beginning of June, on the 4th and 5th. Mag was "bulled" on June 11.[26] H.D. was then gone from July 23rd through the 24th[27] and again from September 30th through October 4th.[28]

It appears Dr. Muth did no butchering this year. Instead, he purchased a Holstine steer weighing 720 pounds from Isaac B. Tressler on October 8, 1892. J. M. Weist weighed the animal and there was no notation about dressing it.[29] Finally, just before Christmas, H.D. left from December 19 through the 22nd.[30]

H.D. was away for five days in January 1893, from the 23rd to the 27th, and then the 30th and 31st.[31] The following week, he was gone again on Tuesday the 7th and Wednesday the 8th of February.[32] His absences seemed to be more frequent and regular. He was gone again from February 28 through March 2.[33]

21. Ibid., entry for April 10, 1892.

22. E. E. Deppen, M. L. Deppen, *Counting Kindred of Christian Deppen* (Myerstown, PA: Church Center Press, 1940), 72.

23. Reuben H. Muth, *Physician's Daybooks*, vol. 28, entries for April 26 to April 27, 1892 (1858–1898, in possession of Lawrence Knorr, Mechanicsburg, Pennsylvania).

24. Ibid., entries for May 1 to May 6, 1892.

25. Ibid., entry for May 9, 1892.

26. Ibid., entries for June 4 to June 11, 1892.

27. Ibid., entries for July 23 to July 24, 1892.

28. Ibid., entries for September 30 to October 4, 1892.

29. Reuben H. Muth, Ephemera, Item 24, Isaac B. Tressler & Co. (1876–1924, in possession of Lawrence Knorr, Mechanicsburg, Pennsylvania).

30. Reuben H. Muth, *Physician's Daybooks*, vol. 28, entries for December 19 to December 22, 1892 (1858–1898, in possession of Lawrence Knorr, Mechanicsburg, Pennsylvania).

31. Reuben H. Muth, *Physician's Daybooks*, vol. 29, entries for January 23 to January 31, 1893 (1858–1898, in possession of Lawrence Knorr, Mechanicsburg, Pennsylvania).

32. Ibid., entries for February 7 through February 8, 1893.

33. Ibid., entries for February 28 through March 2, 1893.

Around this time, Dr. Muth tallied the billing history of services rendered to George Deppen and his family from 1889 until late February 1893.[34] It appears brother-in-law George never paid Dr. Muth, as there was a beginning balance of $14.25, followed by itemized charges of much more. Why was he suddenly tallying this? Had there been a dispute or misunderstanding?

Dr. Muth noted a "Board of Trustees Meeting" for Saturday, March 4, 1893.[35] This was surely for the St. Peters Church in Mahanoy. Perhaps the conversation that evening considered the financial turmoil that was emanating from New York and around the country, as some major banks and corporations were on the brink of failure.

H.D. was away on March 7 and 8. Dr. Muth marked this with red ink for an unknown reason. Perhaps he was becoming more concerned. Two weeks later, H.D. was gone again, this time for three days, from Monday the 20th to Wednesday the 22nd of March.[36]

At the end of April, Dr. Muth planted his radishes and potatoes. He saw only two patients that week. Meanwhile, H.D. took off on Saturday, the 29th and was gone through the 1st of May.[37] The following week, Dr. Muth noted the blossoming pear, peach, and cherry trees.[38] The apples followed in bloom the next week.[39] Meanwhile, in Chicago, the World's Fair was underway, also known as the Columbian Exposition, honoring the four hundredth anniversary of the discovery of the Americas.[40] The great fair would run through October.

Back on the farm, Dr. Muth planted corn the third week of May.[41] H.D. was out the door again in early June, from the 5th to the 10th and then the 12th to the 16th.[42]

The camp meeting was much longer in 1893, or Dr. Muth was able to attend. He marked his calendar from Tuesday, August 8, through

---

34. Reuben H. Muth, Ephemera, item 23, 1889, March 29 account Bal. 14.25 (1876–1924, in possession of Lawrence Knorr, Mechanicsburg, Pennsylvania). Note: This was determined to be George Deppen and his family based on the various dates of visits and associated charges. All lined up with the daybooks.

35. Ibid., entry for March 4, 1893.

36. Ibid., entries for March 20 through March 22, 1893.

37. Ibid., entries for April 23 through May 1, 1893.

38. Ibid., entries for May 7 through May 13, 1893.

39. Ibid., entries for May 14 through May 20, 1893.

40. "The Fair Full-Blown," *Public Press* (Northumberland, Pennsylvania), Mary 12, 1893, 1.

41. Reuben H. Muth, *Physician's Daybooks*, vol. 29, entries for May 21 to May 27, 1893 (1858–1898, in possession of Lawrence Knorr, Mechanicsburg, Pennsylvania).

42. Ibid., entries for June 5 through June 16, 1893.

Thursday, August 17. During the ten days, he continued to see patients, including a birth, and logged "Mag-" on the 16th.[43] This was likely some husbandry activity.

13

A Surprise Marriage

It appears that Dr. Muth was unaware that his son, Henry Deppen Muth, married Lulu Herrold on Tuesday, November 14, 1893.[1] The couple had registered for a marriage license the day before with Samuel Zartman, who was the Justice of the Peace for Jackson Township, residing at Otto Station, close to the Muth farm. The record in the book had the unusual notation "Do Not Publish."[2] The new daughter-in-law was the daughter of Frederick and Matilda Herrold.[3] Lulu had just turned nineteen years old. Matilda Herrold passed away in 1881 when Lulu was only seven. At the time, Frederick Herrold was a farmer living in Chapman, Snyder County, across the Susquehanna.[4] By 1900, Frederick Herrold was still found in Chapman Township,[5] so it was highly unlikely the Herrolds lived anywhere else in between.

What is most remarkable about this relationship is the distance between Henry and Lulu. Assuming she was living in Chapman Township with her father, one or the other would need to travel thirty miles, likely by rail, up to Sunbury and then down the other side of the Susquehanna River. The Trevorton Bridge that crossed the Deppen land on White's Island was gone by 1870, greatly lengthening the trip to the

---

1. *Northumberland County Marriage Dockets, v. 6–7, 1893–1896*, number 4872, Northumberland County Courthouse, Sunbury, Pennsylvania.

2. Ibid.

3. "Lulu Herrold Muth," *Find a Grave*, Memorial ID 38972687, accessed January 5, 2025, https://www.findagrave.com/memorial/38972687/lulu-muth.

4. US Census Bureau. 1880 United States Federal Census. Census Place: Chapman Township, Snyder County, Pennsylvania, pg. 74, dwelling 242.

5. US Census Bureau. 1900 United States Federal Census. Census Place: Chapman Township, Snyder County, Pennsylvania, pg. 118, dwelling 87.

other shore. Given the travel distance, there would certainly be a need for at least two or three days to travel, meet, and spend time together. Perhaps Lulu was working in Sunbury as a domestic, as many young women did, especially if their father was widowed. Her older sister continued to live with her father, making Lulu a candidate to earn money for the household.

Figure 14. Uncle George Snyder.

Dr. Muth first marked "H.D." absent in 1885, eight years prior. This would mean Lulu was only about eleven at the time. It is impossible that Henry was out and about with such a young girl. The earlier escapades probably had more to do with friends and his business ideas at the time. However, the more intense, recent absences were very likely candidates for their rendezvous.

Apparently oblivious to the activity at the Justice of the Peace, for five consecutive days, from November 13 through the 17th, Dr. Muth called upon Uncle George Snyder.[6] Uncle George (1813–1893) was married to Louisa's Aunt Sarah (1811–1897).[7] He was also likely the nephew of Dr. Muth's grandfather on his mother's side. If correct, this would make Reuben and Louisa Muth second cousins. Unfortunately, Uncle/Cousin George Snyder passed away on November 24, two months past his eightieth birthday. It was a very busy time for Dr. Muth, perhaps preventing him from attending the funeral. Certainly, Louisa did.

Butchering Day was November 28, 1893. Dr. Muth dressed a steer, yielding 414 pounds of beef from a live weight of 740 pounds. Two hogs yielded 689 pounds in total.[8]

Across the Susquehanna River in Mifflintown, Louisa's Aunt Sarah, the widow of Isaac Deppen, was gravely ill. She died on December 8,

6. Reuben H. Muth, *Physician's Daybooks*, vol. 29, entries for November 13 through November 17, 1893 (1858–1898, in possession of Lawrence Knorr, Mechanicsburg, Pennsylvania).

7. "George Snyder," *Find a Grave*, Memorial ID 46318400, accessed January 5, 2025, https://www.findagrave.com/memorial/46318400/george-snyder.

8. Reuben H. Muth, *Physician's Daybooks*, vol. 29, Cash Accounts, 1893 (1858–1898, in possession of Lawrence Knorr, Mechanicsburg, Pennsylvania).

1893.[9] Dr. Muth's daybook was filled with patients; thus, it is impossible that he attended this funeral so far away. This is also likely one that Louisa missed, too, especially given the news that her Uncle John Deppen had passed away on December 11, 1893. John Deppen (1815–1893) was not in the care of Dr. Muth but rather a doctor in Herndon, perhaps Dr. Krebs.[10] Dr. Muth's schedule for December 14 was very light, with only one patient, meaning he most assuredly attended this funeral held at St. Peters in Mahanoy.[11]

After a six-month hiatus of marking his son away, Dr. Muth logged a five-day absence in December, from the 10th through the 14th.[12] It appears Henry Deppen Muth may have completely missed the death and funeral of his great uncle.

Christmas 1893 was unusual weather-wise for the Mahantongo Valley. Dr. Muth wrote: "Dec. 25, 1893: Christmas, a beautiful green day, snow visible, Thermometer 65 degrees at Noon. Roads little muddy."[13] There would be no sleigh rides this Christmas.

In late January 1894, H.D. left the homestead again from the 27th through the 29th.[14] The following week, on February 8th, the husbandry activity yielded a calf.[15]

Two months later, on April 3, 1894, Dr. Muth was in his garden and working a light schedule in his office.[16] Much to his chagrin, on the 10th and 11th, there was a deep snow, perhaps raising concerns about the plants.[17] The following week, Dr. Muth noted the arrival of "Little Pigs"[18] and then recorded two "bullings," with Mag on the 24th and Dolly on the 28th.[19]

9. "Sarah Shaffer Deppen," *Find a Grave*, Memorial ID 59854698, accessed January 5, 2025, https://www.findagrave.com/memorial/59854698/sarah-deppen.

10. "John Deppen," *Find a Grave*, Memorial ID 38942145, accessed January 5, 2025, https://www.findagrave.com/memorial/38942145/john-deppen.

11. Reuben H. Muth, *Physician's Daybooks*, vol. 29, entries for December 14, 1893 (1858–1898, in possession of Lawrence Knorr, Mechanicsburg, Pennsylvania).

12. Ibid., entries for December 10 through December 14, 1893.

13. Ibid., entry for December 25, 1893.

14. Reuben H. Muth, *Physician's Daybooks*, vol. 30, entries for January 27 through January 29, 1894 (1858–1898, in possession of Lawrence Knorr, Mechanicsburg, Pennsylvania).

15. Ibid., entry for February 8, 1894.

16. Ibid., entry for April 3, 1894.

17. Ibid., entries for April 10 and April 11, 1894.

18. Ibid., entry for April 17, 1894.

19. Ibid., entries for April 24 and April 28, 1894.

On May 16, 1894, Reverend A. R. Hottenstein from St. Peters Church in Mahanoy signed the marriage certificate attesting to the wedding that had occurred on November 14, 1894.[20] Of course, this would be impossible to do so. Reverend Hottenstein was most assuredly referring to the marriage that occurred in front of the Justice of the Peace the prior November. Or Reverend Hottenstein performed the wedding back in November but did not sign the certificate for six months. Given that Dr. Muth was a member of the board of trustees for the church and had worked very closely with Reverend Hottenstein, it is impossible that the Reverend would conceal such a thing from Dr. Muth. The most plausible explanation is the couple was married by the Justice of the Peace but also wanted to have a wedding sanctioned by the church. The latter happened on Wednesday, May 16, 1894. Let's hope Henry and Lulu informed the family before Reverend Hottenstein felt compelled to do so.

On May 21, 1894, Dr. Muth reported flooding in his journal, and then H.D. headed out at the end of the week, on the 26th, not returning until the 27th.[21] Dr. Muth saw only one patient that week before H.D. headed out again on June 2nd for three days until the 4th. But he was gone again for the 6th and 7th.[22]

For most of the summer of 1894, Dr. Muth, nearing 68 years of age, worked a light schedule and noted no farm work. He also made no mention of H.D. and his travels. This probably meant he was finally aware of his son's marriage. One can only imagine what Louisa thought about the situation. Perhaps she knew more than Dr. Muth.

Dr. Muth's next concern was the camp meeting that started on August 21 and ran through the 25th.[23] Louisa's niece, Emma Deppen, the daughter of her brother Alexander Deppen, was married to Nolan Wiest on Saturday evening, August 25, 1894.[24] Dr. Muth delivered a baby that day for Aaron Shafer's family,[25] so he could have been present if the baby had been delivered earlier in the day. Regardless, Louisa likely

20. *Northumberland County Marriage Dockets, v. 6–7, 1893–1896,* number 4872, Northumberland County Courthouse, Sunbury, Pennsylvania.

21. Reuben H. Muth, *Physician's Daybooks,* vol. 30, entries for May 21 through May 27, 1894 (1858–1898, in possession of Lawrence Knorr, Mechanicsburg, Pennsylvania).

22. Ibid., entries for June 2 through June 7, 1894.

23. Ibid., entries for August 21 through August 25, 1894.

24. "Mahanoy Matters," *The Daily Item* (Sunbury, Pennsylvania), August 30, 1894, 2.

25. Reuben H. Muth, *Physician's Daybooks,* vol. 30, entry for August 25, 1894 (1858–1898, in possession of Lawrence Knorr, Mechanicsburg, Pennsylvania).

attended. Perhaps the wedding waited until the end of the camp meeting or was a way to cap the event.

Finally, on September 19 and 20, Dr. Muth recorded "potatoes" and "seeding."[26] Then, Louisa's father, Abraham Deppen, lost a valuable horse on September 23 "after an illness of two days."[27] Most likely, this horse was stabled at the farm where Dr. Muth and his family also lived. Dr. Muth may have checked on the animal, but there is no log entry.[28]

Across the road, at Dr. Haas's residence, "young friends of the neighborhood" gave his son, Will Haas, a surprise birthday party on Friday, September 29, at which he received many presents. "After enjoying themselves to a late hour, all returned to their respective homes well-pleased."[29] William H. Haas (1862–1933) was born on September 10, so a party nearly three weeks later would have been quite a surprise. Or, perhaps the news was late coming, and it actually occurred on the 14th. Given that this was Will's thirty-second birthday, Henry Deppen Muth, a few years younger, may have attended. Dr. Muth marked "H.D." gone from September 29 through October 1.[30]

H.D. was missing again for three days, from October 29 to the 30th.[31] Butchering Day was November 27 this year. A 740-pound steer yielded 404 pounds of beef. Two hogs yielded 652 pounds of pork.[32]

On December 4, 1894, Dr. Muth noted an obstetric visit in his daybook under the description of "Muth Henry (W)."[33] Apparently, he was able to know his new daughter-in-law a little better as he delivered his first grandchild, a granddaughter named Mary Louisa Muth.[34]

It appears Henry, wife, and newborn may have left the homestead on December 17 and 18, as Dr. Muth notes H.D.'s absence. He also noted they were away over Christmas, from the 25th through the 27th.[35] Dr.

26. Ibid., entries for September 19 through September 20, 1894.

27. "Mahanoy Matters," *The Daily Item* (Sunbury, Pennsylvania), October 3, 1894, 4.

28. Reuben H. Muth, *Physician's Daybooks*, vol. 30, entries for September 21 through September 23, 1894 (1858–1898, in possession of Lawrence Knorr, Mechanicsburg, Pennsylvania).

29. "Mahanoy Matters," *The Daily Item* (Sunbury, Pennsylvania), October 3, 1894, 4.

30. Ibid., entries for September 29 through October 1, 1894.

31. Ibid., entries for October 29 through October 30, 1894.

32. Reuben H. Muth, *Physician's Daybooks*, vol. 30, Cash Accounts for 1894 (1858–1898, in possession of Lawrence Knorr, Mechanicsburg, Pennsylvania).

33. Reuben H. Muth, *Physician's Daybooks*, vol. 30, entry for December 4, 1894 (1858–1898, in possession of Lawrence Knorr, Mechanicsburg, Pennsylvania).

34. "Mary Louisa Muth," *Find a Grave*, Memorial ID 46387012, accessed January 5, 2025, at https://www.findagrave.com/memorial/46387012/mary_louisa_updegrove.

35. Reuben H. Muth, *Physician's Daybooks*, vol. 30, entries for December 17 through December 27, 1894 (1858–1898, in possession of Lawrence Knorr, Mechanicsburg, Pennsylvania).

Muth recorded a "Christmas Snowstorm" in his journal lasting from the 25th through the 29th.[36] The Muth grandparents were certainly concerned about their newborn grandchild at this time. Perhaps only Henry was venturing out, leaving Lulu and Louise at the farm.

H.D. was away for three days in January 1895, from the 12th to the 14th[37] and two weeks later, from the 26th to the 28th.[38] Dr. Muth noted the birth of a calf on February 7th.[39] Then, in early March, Henry was away twice for two days during the same week, on March 1st and 2nd and then the 5th and the 6th.[40] He is away again on April 20 and 21.[41]

Regarding the farm, the cherries and plums were in bloom the first days of May. Dolly met with her bull on May 3rd. H.D. was away for another weekend, from May 11 to May 12.[42]

Henry Deppen Muth was away in Ohio from May 20 to May 25.[43] This was probably to visit Deppen relatives rather than his wife's side of the family.

The following month, Dr. Muth recorded that Meg had her calf on June 19.[44] The rest of the summer, H.D. was next away from Saturday, August 10, through Wednesday, August 14,[45] and Dr. Muth was at the camp meeting held from August 20 through the 28th.[46]

As autumn neared, H.D. was away for two days in September on the 9th and 10th[47], and Dr. Muth recorded the first frost on September 15.[48]

Butcher Day was November 26, 1895. Dr. Muth recorded 386 pounds of beef dressed from 615. He also noted two hogs totaling 744 pounds of pork.[49]

Dr. Muth also included several curious notations at the back of his journal. One item was the address of Dr. John B. Deaver at 1634 Walnut

---

36. Ibid., entries for December 25 through December 29, 1894.

37. Reuben H. Muth, *Physician's Daybooks*, vol. 31, entries for January 12 through January 14, 1895 (1858–1898, in possession of Lawrence Knorr, Mechanicsburg, Pennsylvania).

38. Ibid., entries for January 26 through January 28, 1895.

39. Ibid., entry for February 7, 1895.

40. Ibid., entries for March 1 through March 6, 1895.

41. Ibid., entries for April 20 through April 21, 1895.

42. Ibid., entries for May 1 through May 12, 1895.

43. Ibid., entries for May 20 through May 25, 1895.

44. Ibid., entry for June 19, 1895.

45. Ibid., entries for August 10 through August 14, 1895.

46. Ibid., entries for August 20 through August 28, 1895.

47. Ibid., entries for September 9 through September 10, 1895.

48. Ibid., entry for September 15, 1895.

49. Ibid., Cash Accounts for 1895.

Street in Philadelphia.[50] Dr. John Blair Deaver Sr. was a leading surgeon at the time in Philadelphia and a fellow University of Pennsylvania Alumnus.[51] He also mentioned "S. H. Kennedy Ext. Pines canadensis (White)."[52] Perhaps Dr. Muth was planning to purchase some pine trees for around the farm. Another notation was "41673.57 for 1895."[53] This appears to be a monetary figure but is probably too great a number for the value of his holdings. It is more than likely the value of Abraham Deppen's accounts. If so, why was he recording the value of his father-in-law's holdings? Was Louisa aware he was doing so? Did he tabulate this in conjunction with old Abraham Deppen, or did he count the money clandestinely when Abraham was away?

Before Christmas, Henry was away from December 18th to the 20th.[54] The following week, he was away over Christmas, from the 24th through the 29th.[55] Perhaps Dr. Muth and Louise were home alone while the young couple was with her father and sister across the river.

50. Ibid., Cash Accounts for 1895.

51. "Dr. John Blair Deaver Sr." *Find a Grave*, Memorial ID 89336532, accessed January 5, 2025, https://www.findagrave.com/memorial/89336532/john-blair-deaver.

52. Ibid., Cash Accounts for 1895.

53. Ibid.

54. Reuben H. Muth, *Physician's Daybooks*, vol. 31, entries for December 18 through December 20, 1895 (1858–1898, in possession of Lawrence Knorr, Mechanicsburg, Pennsylvania).

55. Ibid., entries for December 24 through December 29, 1895.

14

Semi-Retirement

Dr. Muth, now sixty-nine, appears to have settled into semi-retirement. He was not as active on the farm, perhaps indicating young Henry was taking on a more prominent role. He also was not as busy as a doctor, perhaps letting his practice ebb.

When Dr. Muth marked H.D. away in February 1896, it was likely to note he would be away from the 10th through the 12th rather than he was sneaking out.[1] The next month, a snow of ten inches fell at the farm on March 10, 1896.[2] Two weeks later, H.D. was gone again for three days from the 23rd through the 25th[3] and again from April 8th through the 10th.[4] The cherries, pears, and plums were then in bloom starting on the 19th of April.[5]

During the first week of May, Dr. Muth noted the dogwood trees in bloom for the first time.[6] He had not mentioned these trees previously, so they may have been planted recently. Dr. Muth noted the potato planting that week, too.[7] The dogwoods remained in bloom the following week when he saw to the corn planting on May 11.[8] H.D. was then away later in the month, from May 24th through the 26th,[9] and then June 9th and 10th.[10] The animal husbandry picked up on June 15 with the arrival

---

1. Reuben H. Muth, *Physician's Daybooks*, vol. 32, entries for February 10 through February 12, 1896 (1858–1898, in possession of Lawrence Knorr, Mechanicsburg, Pennsylvania).
2. Ibid., entry for March 10, 1896.
3. Ibid., entries for March 24 through March 26, 1896.
4. Ibid., entries for April 8 through April 10, 1896.
5. Ibid., entries for April 19 through April 25, 1896.
6. Ibid., entries for May 3 through May 9, 1896.
7. Ibid.
8. Ibid., entries for May 7 through May 16, 1896.
9. Ibid., entries for May 24 through May 26, 1896.
10. Ibid., entries for June 9 through June 10, 1896.

of "Little Pigs." A "Red Cow Calf" was born in the barn on Saturday, June 20.[11]

Louisa's sister-in-law, Eve Hoffman Deppen (1841–1896), died on June 18. She was buried at St. Peters at Mahanoy, likely on the 21st.[12] Dr. Muth's schedule was clear, permitting him to attend.

The week after the funeral, a "line fence" was put up at the farm.[13] In early August, H.D. was out for two days, on the 5th and 6th,[14] and then three days from September 4th to the 6th.[15]

Dr. Muth quietly celebrated his seventieth birthday on September 11. On September 19 and 20, H.D. was away for a "shirting."[16] This was likely a fitting with a tailor.

October 3, 1896, was an exciting day on the Muth farm. That day, Dr. Muth delivered his grandson, who was his namesake, Reuben Harris Muth.[17] H.D. now had two children to raise and a wife to care for. Perhaps the naming of the grandson was a way for the father-son relationship to come full circle. Clearly, it had been strained in the past with Dr. Muth's almost neurotic tracking of his son's "absences." Rather than his son doing things behind his back, the thirty-year-old was front and center and taking on a more prominent role. Louisa and great-grandpa Abraham Deppen were likely both over the moon.

H.D. was next away on November 18 and 19, perhaps to take the newborn across the river to his in-laws in Snyder County,[18] but was back for Butcher Day on the 24th. Dr. Muth noted 436½ pounds of beef dressed from an 824-pound steer.[19] That Christmas, the whole, now enlarged, family was together on the farm.

A calf was born on January 8, 1897, the same day H.D. headed out for two days on the 8th and 9th.[20] The following Friday, the 16th,

---

11. Ibid., entries for June 14 through June 20, 1896.

12. "Eve E Hoffman Deppen," *Find a Grave*, Memorial ID 38942353, accessed January 5, 2025, https://www.findagrave.com/memorial/38942353/eve-e-deppen.

13. Reuben H. Muth, *Physician's Daybooks*, vol. 32, entries for June 21 to June 27, 1896 (1858–1898, in possession of Lawrence Knorr, Mechanicsburg, Pennsylvania).

14. Ibid., entries for August 5 through August 6, 1896.

15. Ibid., entries for September 4 through September 6, 1896.

16. Ibid., entries for September 19 through September 20, 1896.

17. Ibid., entry for October 3, 1896.

18. Ibid., entries for November 18 through November 19, 1896.

19. Ibid., Cash Accounts for 1896.

20. Reuben H. Muth, *Physician's Daybooks*, vol. 33, entries for January 8 to January 9, 1897 (1858–1898, in possession of Lawrence Knorr, Mechanicsburg, Pennsylvania).

calves were sold.[21] At the start of February, Dolly had her "bulling" on the 5th.[22]

On February 18, 1897, Louisa's sister-in-law, Sarah Deppen Snyder, the widow of her late brother George, passed away. She was buried in Herndon.[23] H.D. was away when the funeral was likely held on the 21st, but Dr. Muth's schedule was very light.[24]

H.D. was away for five days in March, from the 10th through the 14th,[25] but he was back in time for Dolly's barn activity on the 18th.[26] On March 31, Dr. Muth saw no patients and was in the garden.[27]

H.D. was away for the weekend of April 17 and 18, and then it was "cold" on the 20th.[28] Hopefully, Dr. Muth was not in the garden too soon!

The following week, the peaches, plums, and cherries were in bloom. Dr. Muth was confident enough to plant his potatoes and corn on Monday the 26th. Then, on Tuesday the 27th, he scribbled "Cold Snow Windy." From the distressed and hurried appearance of his scrawl, he was very concerned he had made a mistake.[29]

H.D. was away on Tuesday and Wednesday for two consecutive weeks, from May 10 to May 19. Dr. Muth must have been installing a new stove at the time because he noted, "stove plate, 30 inches for window, 39 inches from wall."[30]

The little pigs arrived on Friday, June 9.[31] Was granddaughter Mary Louisa, now in her third year, old enough to play with a piglet?

Dr. Muth recorded the "Sale at Smiths" for August 3, 1897.[32] This was most likely referring to the men's and women's apparel "Clearance Sale" happening at H.B. Smith's department store in Sunbury.[33] Perhaps this was a trip for the whole family or just Louisa and her daughter-in-law.

21. Ibid., entry for January 16, 1897.

22. Ibid., entry for February 5, 1897.

23. "Sarah Deppen Snyder," *Find a Grave*, Memorial ID 46318380, accessed January 5, 2025, https://www.findagrave.com/memorial/46318380/sarah-snyder.

24. Reuben H. Muth, *Physician's Daybooks*, vol. 33, entries for February 18 to February 22, 1897 (1858–1898, in possession of Lawrence Knorr, Mechanicsburg, Pennsylvania).

25. Ibid., entries for March 10 through March 14, 1897.

26. Ibid., entry for March 18, 1897.

27. Ibid., entry for March 31, 1897.

28. Ibid., entries for April 18 through April 20, 1897.

29. Ibid., entries for April 25 through May 1, 1897.

30. Ibid., entries for May 10 through May 19, 1897.

31. Ibid., entry for June 9, 1897.

32. Ibid., entry for August 3, 1897.

33. "H.B. Smith," *The Daily Item* (Sunbury, Pennsylvania), August 3, 1897, 4.

On Dr. Muth's seventy-first birthday, September 11, 1897, the local headlines were about a massacre of striking miners at Lattimer, Pennsylvania. Sixteen protesting miners were slain and thirty-eight injured when sheriff's deputies opened fire on them after they approached the phalanx of lawmen. All the dead were "foreigners."[34]

H.D. was next away for Mondays and Tuesdays on September 27th and 28th and again on October 25th and 26th.[35] He then exited again just before Thanksgiving, from November 22nd to the 24th.[36] Henry missed Butcher Day on the 23rd. Dr. Muth recorded 334 pounds of beef dressed from a 690-pound steer. He also processed two hogs for a total of 755 pounds of pork.[37]

H.D. and family were away this Christmas, from the 25th through the 27th. Dr. Muth noted Christmas Eve was "cold and windy." Christmas Day was "Clear, cold, no wind, very little snow."[38] It appears he was missing his grandchildren, looking out the windows at the weather a bit too much.

A calf was born on December 28th, and New Year's Eve brought "Rain and Snow."[39] Also, on the final page of the Cash Accounts, Dr. Muth noted "$36233.46" with no explanation and included odd dimensions for a ladder, "20 ft Long, 4 in Breadth, 1 3/8 thick." Finally, he included an address for John and Salzer Seed Co. of LaCross, Wisconsin. He mentioned they were "Seed Growers and Florists."[40]

Henry Deppen Muth was away for two or three days each of the weeks of January.[41] Perhaps he was working out of town for a stretch.

The headline in the local newspaper for March 1 announced the belief the battleship USS *Maine* was deliberately blown up in Havana Harbor.[42] There were now rumblings of a coming war against Spain.

---

34. "Strikers and Deputies Battle Near Hazleton," *Mount Carmel Item* (Sunbury, Pennsylvania), September 11, 1897, 1.

35. Reuben H. Muth, *Physician's Daybooks*, vol. 33, entries for September 27 to October 25, 1897 (1858–1898, in possession of Lawrence Knorr, Mechanicsburg, Pennsylvania).

36. Ibid., entries for November 22 through November 24, 1897.

37. Ibid., Cash Accounts for 1897.

38. Ibid., entries for December 24 through December 27, 1897.

39. Ibid., entries for December 28 through December 31, 1897.

40. Ibid., Cash Accounts for 1897.

41. Reuben H. Muth, *Physician's Daybooks*, vol. 34, entries for January 1 to January 31, 1898 (1858–1898, in possession of Lawrence Knorr, Mechanicsburg, Pennsylvania).

42. "Maine Was Blown Up," *The Daily News* (Mt. Carmel, Pennsylvania), March 1, 1898, 1.

A week later, Dolly was out for her "bulling" on March 9.[43] Dr. Muth then noted "cellar window opened" the last week of winter.[44] The reason was not clear.

On April 11, Dr. Muth was gardening and saw two patients that day, including Henry Tressler and J. H. Wentzel.[45] It must have been a pleasant spring because the cherry blossoms came early, during the third week of April.[46] But the weather turned the next week after planting the potatoes in the field. Dr. Muth reported "Snowing, Rain, Sleet."[47]

On May 2, the local papers announced the attack by Admiral Dewey on the Spanish fleet the previous week at Cuba, resulting in a route of the Spanish.[48] Two weeks later, the headlines announced the capture of "Porto Rico" by Captain Sampson of the cruiser USS *New York*.[49]

In late June, the news reported, "R. K. Muth, of Mahanoy, transacted business in town Friday."[50] This was certainly R.H. Muth, and it was likely his last trip to Sunbury on June 24, 1898.

First cousin Jefferson Muth, who was born three weeks after Reuben, died on July 2, 1898. Reuben likely attended this funeral in Myerstown, as his daybook was bereft of patients from July 1 through July 6,[51] though he notes a temperature of 105 degrees on July 3rd.[52] "H.D." likely did not attend, as the local news reported he was ill at the time: "Constable H.D. Muth, Abraham Zartman, Martin Rebuck and wife, who have been very ill, are improving."[53] This was also the first mention of Henry Deppen Muth as the local constable for Jackson Township. Dr. Muth recorded the arrival of "Little Pigs" on Saturday, July 9.[54]

On August 12, 1898, the local newspaper announced that peace talks with Spain were underway in Madrid.[55]

---

43. Reuben H. Muth, *Physician's Daybooks*, vol. 34, entry for March 9, 1898 (1858–1898, in possession of Lawrence Knorr, Mechanicsburg, Pennsylvania).

44. Ibid., entries for March 13 through March 19, 1898.

45. Ibid., entry for April 11, 1898.

46. Ibid., entries for April 17 through April 23, 1898.

47. Ibid., entries for April 24 through April 30, 1898.

48. "The Maine Is Being Remembered," *The Daily Item* (Sunbury, Pennsylvania), May 2, 1898, 2.

49. "Sampson Has Taken Porto Rico," *The Daily News* (Mt. Carmel, Pennsylvania), May 13, 1898, 2.

50. "Personal Paragraphs," *The Daily Item* (Sunbury, Pennsylvania), June 24, 1898, 1.

51. Reuben H. Muth, *Physician's Daybooks*, vol. 34, entries for July 2 through 6, 1898 (1858–1898, in possession of Lawrence Knorr, Mechanicsburg, Pennsylvania).

52. Ibid.

53. "From Mahanoy," *Northumberland County Democrat*, July 14, 1898, 4.

54. Reuben H. Muth, *Physician's Daybooks*, vol. 34, entry for July 9, 1898 (1858–1898, in possession of Lawrence Knorr, Mechanicsburg, Pennsylvania).

55. "Spain Assents," *The Daily News* (Mt. Carmel, Pennsylvania), August 12, 1898, 1.

On August 16, 1898, Louisa's sister-in-law, Mary Ann Mertz Deppen (1847–1898), the wife of George Deppen, passed away. She was buried at Herndon.[56] It appears the family attended the funeral, given Dr. Muth's open schedule.[57]

The following week, Dr. Muth's brother-in-law, Henry Kurr (1828–1898), the husband of his sister Eliza Muth Kurr, passed away in Rehrersburg.[58] Dr. Muth did not travel the long distance to Berks County for this funeral, as evidenced by his patient schedule.[59]

Figure 15. Galen Reitz.

As Reuben's 72nd birthday approached on September 11, 1898, he had seventeen visits the previous week and even two on the 11th, including Sam B. Smith and Widow Reitz.[60]

J.R.H. reported in the local news on September 27 that "Postmaster Isaac B. Tressler and his brother John, Constable H.D. Muth and J.R. Hilbush made a business trip to Sunbury yesterday."[61] Thus, "J.R.H." was likely reporting about himself in the third person.

On October 31, 1898, Dr. Muth was called to the farm of Galen Reitz[62] to assist with the birth of baby Claude Clarence Reitz, born November 1.[63] Dr. Muth logged a three-dollar fee for the services. It was the last birth that he attended in his long career. Unfortunately, baby Claude only lived less than three years.

Dr. Muth's visitation record slowed after the middle of November. Thanksgiving Day was Thursday, November 24, a stretch of nine days

56. "Mary Ann Mertz Deppen," *Find a Grave*, Memorial ID 46318466, accessed January 5, 2025, https://www.findagrave.com/memorial/46318466/mary-ann-deppen.

57. Reuben H. Muth, *Physician's Daybooks*, vol. 34, entries for August 16 to August 20, 1898 (1858–1898, in possession of Lawrence Knorr, Mechanicsburg, Pennsylvania).

58. "Henry Kurr," *Find a Grave*, Memorial ID 32409950, accessed January 5, 2025, https://www.findagrave.com/memorial/32409950/henry-kurr.

59. Reuben H. Muth, *Physician's Daybooks*, vol. 34, entries for August 24 to August 30, 1898 (1858–1898, in possession of Lawrence Knorr, Mechanicsburg, Pennsylvania).

60. Ibid., entries for September 4 through 11, 1898.

61. "From Mahanoy," *Northumberland County Democrat*, September 29, 1898, 4.

62. Reuben H. Muth, *Physician's Daybooks*, vol. 34, entries for October 31 through November 1, 1898 (1858–1898, in possession of Lawrence Knorr, Mechanicsburg, Pennsylvania).

63. "Claude Clarance Reitz," *Find a Grave*, Memorial ID 39060508, accessed January 5, 2025, https://www.findagrave.com/memorial/39060508/claude_clarence_reitz.

without any visits.[64] The November 24, 1898, newspaper reported that Dr. Muth was sick and confined to his house, providing the excuse for the lapse in his schedule.[65] Unfortunately, this was the beginning of his final illness. On the 25th, Dr. Muth saw Abraham Schlegel Senior and charged him twenty-five cents.[66] This was likely for medication. Abraham, now 78, was six years older than Dr. Muth and would live another four years.[67] This was Dr. Muth's final patient of his forty-three-year career. At the back of his journal, Dr. Muth noted

Figure 16. Abraham Schlegel.

there was snow on Thanksgiving Day, the 24th, and then on the 26th.[68]

For Butcher Day, November 29, Dr. Muth noted the yield of 352 pounds of beef dressed from a 645-pound steer. He also noted 715 pounds of pork produced from two pigs. It was "A Pleasurable Day, Pleasant, Snow on the Ground."[69] These were the last entries he ever wrote in his daybooks.

On December 15, the local newspaper reported on the treaty with Spain: "The treaty alienates from Spain and puts in the possession or under the protection of the United States more than 2,000 islands, with nearly 200,000 square miles of territory and 10,000,000 inhabitants."[70] Dr. Muth, born during the John Quincy Adams administration, when the United States was mostly east of the Mississippi River, and the West had yet to be tamed, was likely reading in his rocker the accounting of how his country now not only connected east and west with the Golden Spike but had far-reaching colonies in the Caribbean Sea and Pacific

---

64. Reuben H. Muth, *Physician's Daybooks*, vol. 34, entries for November 16 through 24, 1898 (1858–1898, in possession of Lawrence Knorr, Mechanicsburg, Pennsylvania).

65. "From Mahanoy," *Northumberland County Democrat*, November 24, 1898, 4.

66. Reuben H. Muth, *Physician's Daybooks*, vol. 34, entry for November 25, 1898 (1858–1898, in possession of Lawrence Knorr, Mechanicsburg, Pennsylvania).

67. "Abraham Wentzell Schlegel" *Find a Grave*, Memorial ID 16065936, accessed January 5, 2025, https://www.findagrave.com/memorial/16065936/abraham-wentzell-schlegel.

68. Reuben H. Muth, *Physician's Daybooks*, vol. 34, Cash Accounts for 1898 (1858–1898, in possession of Lawrence Knorr, Mechanicsburg, Pennsylvania).

69. Ibid.

70. "The Treaty and the People," *Northumberland County Democrat*, December 15, 1898, 2.

Ocean. His country had grown from a vulnerable survivor of two wars with Great Britain to a global superpower on the cusp of the Twentieth Century. Perhaps he gazed at his two young grandchildren and tried to imagine the world they would behold in their lifetimes. But then, he was probably distracted by weakness and a wicked cough. Pneumonia may have been setting in.

The local paper noted that many were sick in the area, including Dr. Muth, as 1899 began.[71] Two weeks later, the paper again reported Dr. Muth among the many sick who were suffering from "the grippe and other ailments."[72] Another local paper noted the travel of "Dr. Sminky of Gratz," who passed through Mandata on his way to Mahanoy to tend to Dr. Muth.[73] This may have been a young doctor, Alfred H. Smink, later of Shamokin, who had a remarkable career.[74]

---

71. "From Mahanoy," *Northumberland County Democrat*, January 12, 1899, 4.
72. "From Mahanoy," *Northumberland County Democrat*, January 26, 1899, 4. Note that the grippe was an archaic term for influenza.
73. "Mandata," *Sunbury Daily*, February 1, 1899, 6.
74. "Dr. A. H. Smink Dies Suddenly at Residence," *Shamokin News-Dispatch*, January 17, 1941.

15

Doctors Must Die, Too

Finally, on January 27, 1899, Dr. Muth's death was reported "due to a protracted and lingering illness. Doctors must die, too."[1] Another paper, printing a brief obituary, marked the day of death as "last Saturday evening," which would have been the 28th of January.[2] The tombstone at St. Peter's Church is engraved with January 28, 1899, aged 72 years, 4 months, and 17 days. Reverend Hottenstein officiated his internment in the cemetery at St. Peter's Church in Red Cross, Northumberland County, Pennsylvania.[3]

The flu must have been especially bad that winter because at 7 o'clock on February 1, 1899, Dr. Andrew Jackson Kantz passed away at the age of 62 "of pneumonia resulting from an attack of grip."[4] He married his third wife, Miss Ella Kramer of Millersburg, while on his deathbed.[5]

About one week after Dr. Muth's funeral, on Monday, February 6, 1899, the newspaper reported, "H.D. Muth, of the lower end of the county, was in town Monday."[6] This was probably to make a court filing regarding his father's estate. The next day, on February 7, 1899, Louisa renounced any claim to the estate and Letters of Administration were granted in the name of their son, Henry Deppen Muth. The estate was valued at $3000.[7]

1. "Herndon Happenings," *The Sunbury Gazette*, January 27, 1899, 14.
2. "From Mahanoy," *Sunbury Daily*, February 1, 1899, 6.
3. "Dr. Reuben H Muth" *Find a Grave*, Memorial ID 38942306, accessed January 5, 2025, https://www.findagrave.com/memorial/38942306/reuben-h-muth.
4. "Death of Dr. A. J. Kantz," *Lykens Register*, February 2, 1899, 1.
5. Ibid.
6. "Personal Paragraphs," *The Daily Item* (Sunbury, Pennsylvania), February 6, 1899, 1.
7. *Northumberland County, Pennsylvania, Will Book 9*, Page 248, Northumberland County Registrar of Wills, Sunbury, Pennsylvania.

Dr. Muth may have had the last word regarding his college scandal at Marshall College. In fine print in his obituary, it clearly stated, "He was a graduate of Marshall College."[8] Maybe he had been forgiven after all.

Afterword

Dr. Muth's estate appraisers J.G. Smith, H.D. Muth, and J.R. Hilbush[9] headed to Sunbury together in early February 1899, likely to file the appraisal."[10] Not long after, Henry Deppen Muth's notice to collect all debts owed to the late doctor's estate appeared in the newspaper.[11]

Sometime in late March or early April, H.D. Muth and his grandfather, Abraham Deppen, were both ill and confined to the house. The article misidentified Abraham as H.D.'s uncle. Regardless, H.D. was "improving and can walk out when the weather is favorable."[12]

With Dr. Muth's passing early in 1899, the Jackson Horse Detective Company adjusted its officers. Muth had been the president since its founding in 1864, "with an interruption of two or three years."[13] At its annual meeting, J. R. Reitz was president, E. R. Hilbush, secretary, and I. B. Tressler, treasurer. They reported that no horse thefts had occurred with the company since 1870. The company still had $570 on hand.[14] Only two horses had been stolen from the company, and both were recovered.[15]

Meanwhile, old Abraham Deppen was unable to shake his illness. Concerned about his health, grandson Joseph Deppen Jr., of Mt. Carmel, a student at Bucknell, visited Grandfather Abraham, Aunt Louisa Muth, and cousin Henry Deppen Muth and his family over July 4th.[16]

Henry Deppen Muth, now an ex-constable, appeared to be settling down as the new "man of the farm" and had begun a different line of work. In early August, he was at "Herndon Manufacturing in Herndon, preparing their new planning mill for work." Henry was referred to as "an expert in cutting and arranging the steam and water pipes and is well-prepared with tools for doing such work."[17] In later months, Henry was working in the area as an industrial pipefitter.

---

8. "From Mahanoy," *Sunbury Daily*, February 1, 1899, 6.

9. "From Mahanoy," *Northumberland County Democrat*, March 2, 1899, 4.

10. "From Mahanoy," *Northumberland County Democrat*, February 16, 1899, 4.

11. "Administrator's Notice," *Northumberland County Democrat*, February 23, 1899, 2.

12. "From Mahanoy," *Northumberland County Democrat*, April 13, 1899, 4.

13. "From Mahanoy," *Northumberland County Democrat*, February 9, 1899, 4.

14. "From Mahanoy," *Northumberland County Democrat*, May 11, 1899, 4.

15. "From Mahanoy," *Northumberland County Democrat*, February 9, 1899, 4.

16. "From Mahanoy," *Northumberland County Democrat*, July 6, 1899, 4.

17. "From Mahanoy," *Northumberland County Democrat*, August 3, 1899, 4.

Soon after Henry started working at Herndon Manufacturing, Abraham Deppen died on August 13, 1899, at the Muth home. He was lauded as "one of the wealthiest men of the lower end." Abraham's funeral was held at St. Peters Church at 9:30 AM on August 17, 1899.[18] A few weeks later, his estate was valued at $57,540.69,[19] exceeding the number in the back of Dr. Muth's earlier journal by over ten thousand dollars.

When son Henry Deppen Muth passed on July 13, 1943, the obituary, printed next to a map of the allied landing in Sicily, mentioned incorrectly he was the son of "James Muth," a "pioneer physician in the lower end of Northumberland County." He had spent his entire life on the family farm, leaving a wife, the former Lulu Herrold, son Reuben Muth of Gratz, and daughter Mrs. Albert Updegrove or Hendon, and seven grandchildren.[20]

Lulu then passed on February 4, 1962, at age 87.[21] She left an estate of more than twenty thousand dollars plus real estate to friends and family. In the end, she was living with her uncle George and aunt Anne Treon of Sunbury. Charles E. Muth and John Updegrove, grandchildren, were named the executors.[22]

On June 23, 1962, there was an estate auction at Red Cross (formerly Mahanoy), Pennsylvania, for the late Lulu Muth.[23] Apparently, the house was a time capsule from the time of Dr. Muth. Listed among the contents for sale were medical equipment, a medical journal for 1860, and "antiques of Dr. Muth, who died in 1899, consisting of quilts, dry sinks, cherry tables, spool bed, oil lamps, flour chest, chests, desks, corner cupboard, pictures: large selection of antiques, dishes, tinware, etc."[24]

Over fifty years later, the author acquired the entire set of doctor's journals for $230 plus shipping from eBay. The listing said: "Antique Visiting Country Doctor Pocket Ledger List Mahanoy PA 1858–1898 Old Book."[25] The auction closed at 3:08 PM on September 26, 2013.

---

18. "Death of Abraham Deppen," *Northumberland County Democrat*, August 14, 1899, 1.
19. "From Mahanoy," *Northumberland County Democrat*, August 31, 1899, 4.
20. "Rural Man Found Dead in His Bed," *Shamokin News-Dispatch*, July 14, 1942, 3.
21. "Elderly Resident of Red Cross Dies," *Shamokin News-Dispatch*, February 5, 1962, 3.
22. "Muth Estate to Relatives, Friend," *The Daily Item*, February 20, 1962, 8.
23. "Public Sale of Estate of Lulu Muth," *The Daily Item*, June 22, 1962, 19.
24. Ibid.
25. "Antique Visiting Country Doctor Pocket Ledger List Mahanoy PA 1858–1898 Old Book," eBay Listing for Item# 300781949802, accessed January 13, 2025 at https://www.ebay.com/itm/300781949802?ViewItem=&item=300781949802.

16

Language and Trust

Reuben Harris Muth, M.D., who lived from 1826 until 1899, was born into a Pennsylvania Dutch community in rural Pennsylvania that was known to resist assimilation to the English language. Muth, who was educated at Marshall College and the University of Pennsylvania's medical school, was a prominent physician and church member in rural Mahanoy, Northumberland County, Pennsylvania, during the latter half of the 19th century. The thirty-four traveling physician's daybooks and additional papers and ephemera, likely by his hand, are written in English. This demonstrates the adoption of the English language, not as evident in prior generations of his family. Despite growing up in a German-speaking household and eventually moving to a remote corner of the Pennsylvania Dutch community in the Mahantongo Valley, Muth adopted the English language and used it in his practice. He is an example of English language assimilation in the mid-19th century.

During the colonial period, Benjamin Franklin, the polymath of the founding fathers of the United States, voiced his concerns about the inundation of German immigrants into Pennsylvania. His letter to Peter Collinson on May 9, 1753, provides insight into his fears about the prevalence of German speakers in the Pennsylvania colony, who were becoming more numerous during this period of peak immigration. In particular, he mentions the resistance of the Germans to utilizing English even in official documents and court proceedings.[26] This letter was written before Franklin collaborated with the German immigrant Conrad

---

26. Benjamin Franklin to Peter Collinson, May 9, 1753 in *[The Papers]; The Papers of Benjamin Franklin. 4. July 1, 1750, through June 30, 1753* (New Haven: Yale University Press, 1961), 477–86.

Weiser as the two negotiated the Treaty of Carlisle with the Iroquois Confederacy that November. The letter also predates Franklin's experiences in the American Revolution with such German immigrants as Peter and Frederick Muhlenberg. Regardless, Franklin's opinions expressed at that time illustrate the impact of the German immigrants on Pennsylvania, especially their language.

After the American Revolution, there was continued evidence of resistance to assimilation among the Germans. Harry M. Tinkcom, in his work, *The Republicans and Federalists in Pennsylvania, 1790–1801*, refers to the first popular society to be formed in Pennsylvania, the German Republican Society.[27] This organization, formed in 1793, while patriotic, decided to maintain its records and communications in German. The hope was to unite the German-speaking population of Pennsylvania into a political force.

According to Mark L. Louden, Ph.D., in his book *Pennsylvania Dutch: The Story of an American Language*, language assimilation by the Lutheran and Reformed German speakers was gradual, while the Anabaptists continued to resist. Louden provides examples of how families, like the Muths, would have spoken Pennsylvania Dutch among themselves but used English when dealing with outsiders. Eventually, English took over the educational and commercial discourse. Louden provides an overview of this transition during the early republic led by prominent Pennsylvania German clergy and political leaders.[28]

Given that Dr. Muth was not famous, how to confirm his identity and affiliation with the Pennsylvania Dutch culture? Herbert C. Bell was the author or co-author of several local or topical histories in the 19th century. In his *History of Northumberland County*, there is a brief biographical entry about Dr. Reuben H. Muth that provides a good starting point with some basic information about his life, education, and practice. According to Bell, Dr. Muth was born in Berks County, Pennsylvania, and attended Marshall College in Mercersburg before studying medicine with Dr. Lewis Rogers of Schuylkill County. Muth subsequently graduated from the University of Pennsylvania with his medical degree in

27. Harry Marlin Tinkcom, *The Republicans and Federalists in Pennsylvania, 1790–1801* (Harrisburg, PA: Pennsylvania Historical and Museum Commission, 1950), 83.

28. Mark L. Loudon, *Pennsylvania Dutch: The Story of an American Language* (Baltimore: Johns Hopkins University Press, 2016), 127–30.

1855. He then practiced in Fredericksburg, Lebanon County, and then Northumberland County following the passing of his wife in 1860.[29]

Further documentation of Reuben H. Muth's German heritage was uncovered by Reverend Frederick S. Weiser, a graduate in history from Gettysburg College who later entered the seminary and became an ordained minister in the Lutheran Church. For many years, Weiser continued his interest in history by being the archivist for the Gettysburg Lutheran Seminary and by providing translations of early German church records.[30] One of the records Reverend Weiser translated was for the congregation in Stouchsburg, Pennsylvania, about seven miles south of Rehrersburg, in Berks County. Among the many items is the baptismal record of Reuben H. Muth, proving the doctor was born into a Pennsylvania German congregation, his baptism occurring on December 17, 1826, and was sponsored by grandparents Friedrich and Catt. Elis. Muth. Reuben is listed as the son of Friedrich and Maria Muth, born on September 11, 1826.[31]

Newspaper columnist Schuyler Brossman mentioned a call for information concerning the Muths. In an article from 1981, he states there are tombstones at the Lutheran Church in Rehrersburg, including Friedrich, born September 11, 1773; wife Elizabeth, died September 11, 1846, aged 73 years; and Elizabeth, nee Schucker, born April 30, 1755, the wife of Friedrich Muth, died October 26, 1848, aged 93 years, five months, and 26 days.[32] A later article by Brossman provided further detail concerning Friedrich Muth, stating he lived across the street from the Altalaha Lutheran Church in Rehrersburg. He sold a tract of land to the congregation, which was then used as the cemetery.[33] Local historian George M. Meiser included a description of Frederick Muth's activities in Rehrersburg in his *The Passing Scene Volume 10*. According to Meiser, Frederick Muth was an important dealer in lumber that was brought "over the mountain to Rehrersburg" via wagons.[34] The location of

29. Herbert C. Bell, *History of Northumberland County* (Chicago: Brown, Runk, and Co., 1891), 1234.

30. Stephanie Bowen, *Guide to the Frederick Weiser '57 papers* (Gettysburg: Gettysburg College, 2013), 2.

31. Frederick S. Weiser, *Records of Pastoral Acts at Christ Lutheran Church, Stouchsburg, Pennsylvania* (Birdsboro, PA: The Pennsylvania German Society, 1990), 20.

32. Schuyler Brossman, "Surname File Genealogists' Boon." *Sunday-The Daily News*, March 22, 1981, 6E. https://www.newspapers.com/clip/55031899/sunday-the-daily-news/.

33. Schuyler Brossman, "Researcher tracing Muths from Lebanon, Berks counties." *The Daily News*, February 22, 1993, 7. https://www.newspapers.com/clip/55030995/the-daily-news/.

34. George M. Meiser and Gloria Jean Meiser, *The Passing Scene Volume 10* (Reading, PA: The Historical Society of Berks County, 1997), 155.

Friedrich Muth, the father of Reuben H. Muth, is further confirmed by
the 1862 map of Marion and Tulpehocken Townships in Berks County.
This map contains the property of Frederick Muth, Esquire, next to the
church in Rehrersburg.[35]

The first mention of Reuben H. Muth in official records since his
birth is the 1850 U.S. Census. The "Mood" family is found in Tulpehocken Township, Berks County. Father Frederick, a farmer, is listed as
50 years of age. His wife, Mary C., is listed as aged 43. Reuben is 23 years
old and has attended school in the last year. Five younger siblings are
mentioned as well as a farmhand.[36] It should be noted Frederick Muth's
property was valued much higher than his immediate neighbors. The
spelling of the family name by the census taker, Mr. Seibert, is also of
interest. It is spelled the way the name is pronounced by German speakers (the "u" is long, and the "h" is silent).

The Altalaha Lutheran Church, situated in Rehrersburg, Tulpehocken Township, Berks County, was founded on or before 1757. For
most of its early history, services were conducted in German.[37] A visit to
the cemetery confirmed the tombstone for the father of Reuben Muth,
Frederick Muth, is inscribed in German and provides context for the
language preferences of the Muth family by generation.[38] Many other
tombstones from before 1900 are inscribed in German, illustrating that
the Muth family's adherence to German was not an isolated occurrence.

As mentioned, the 1850 census indicated Reuben Muth had been
attending school. Though all evidence from his early life points to German being prevalent during his upbringing, Muth later used English in
all his records and correspondence. It is likely his formal English language training occurred at school. Abraham Reeser Horne was the principal of the Keystone State Normal School at Kutztown, who published
the *Pennsylvania German Manual* in 1875 to teach English to children
familiar with Pennsylvania Dutch. Susan R. Severs, a schoolteacher from
Lancaster County, Pennsylvania, reprised Horne's efforts while teaching

35. *Township Map of Berks County, Pennsylvania, from Actual Surveys*, (Philadelphia: H.F. Bridgens, 1862). https://www.loc.gov/item/2003625159/.

36. U.S. Census Bureau, 1850 United States Census, Tulpehocken Township, Berks County, Pennsylvania, roll 752, page 49A, lines 4–12.

37. Frederick S. Weiser, *Tulpehocken Church Records, 1730–1800: Christ (Little Tulpehocken) Church and Altalaha Church, Rehrersburg* (Breinigsville, PA: Pennsylvania German Society, 1982), 1–3.

38. Frederick Muth tombstone, 1883. Inscription carving. Altalaha Lutheran Cemetery, Rehrersburg, Pennsylvania. Viewed August 8, 2020.

Amish school children English during the 1950s and 1960s. The authors provide insight into the survival of the Pennsylvania Dutch language among the Anabaptists despite its decline among the Lutheran and Reformed Dutch.[39] The experiences described by Severs and Horne are likely similar to that of Reuben Muth. Given the article focuses primarily on the period after Muth was out of school, it also indicates he likely continued to encounter the Pennsylvania Dutch language with rural inhabitants of the region.

Dr. Ezra Grumbine, in his *Stories of Old Stumpstown*, recounted the habits of the Pennsylvania Dutch inhabitants of Lebanon County before the Civil War. Stumpstown was ten miles west of Rehrersburg. Grumbine, a physician, mentioned the resistance to formal medical care in the community and their reliance on folk medicine.[40] Growing up in an affluent family, it appears Reuben's interest in practicing medicine might have been related to wanting to improve the quality of medical care in the community. Drs. Heindel and Foster contributed an article regarding America's first German medical school, the Allentown Academy, in Allentown, Pennsylvania. This school provided instruction and a journal in both German and English, but its focus was homeopathy, which aligned closely with the superstitions of Pennsylvania Dutch Powwow.[41] These practices, also known as *braucheri*, were common among the rural people of Pennsylvania Dutch country. Based on books such as *Der Lange Verborgene Freund* (English: *The Long Hidden Friend*) by folk healer Johann Georg Hohman, practitioners known as "powwow doctors" performed rituals to heal ailments or cure misfortunes. According to local reports, they were kept quite busy and did not charge a specific fee, accepting gifts from twenty-five cents to two dollars.[42] On one occasion, a particular folk healer, "Dr. Wilhelm" of Raubsville, near Allentown, Pennsylvania, had 138 patients lined up in one day! One farmer credited Dr. Wilhelm with curing his sore throat. Apparently, the crowds formed on specific days of the month, as the doctor's powers were strongest on

---

39. Susan R. Severs & Abraham R. Horne. "Anglicizing the Pennsylvania Dutch: 1966 and 1875." *Pennsylvania Folklife* 16, no. 3 (Spring 1967): 46.

40. Ezra Grumbine. *Stories of Old Stumpstown: A History of Interesting Events, Traditions, and Anecdotes of Early Fredericksburg Known for Many Years as Stumpstown* (Lebanon, PA: Lebanon County Historical Society, 1910), 227–28.

41. Ned D. Heindel & Natalie I. Foster. "The Allentown Academy: America's First German Medical School." *Pennsylvania Folklife* 30, no. 1 (Autumn 1980): 2–8.

42. "Pennsylvania Superstitions," *Northumberland County Democrat*, August 1, 1890, 1.

the first Friday of any new moon.[43] According to David W. Keibel, the author of *Powwowing Among the Pennsylvania Dutch*, formally trained physicians, called "regulars" by the powwowers, were often at odds with their mystical brethren.[44]

As mentioned previously, Muth chose the University of Pennsylvania for medical training, illustrating his alignment with mainstream medical practices in addition to his assimilation to English. After he completed his medical training, Dr. Muth settled in Fredericksburg, Lebanon County, also known as Old Stumpstown. Grumbine confirmed Muth's education at the University of Pennsylvania and his brief marriage to Margaret Hauer of Fredericksburg, who died of consumption. According to Grumbine, Muth arrived in 1855 and was only in the area for a few years before moving to Northumberland County.[45]

Muth's move to Northumberland County is documented in local newspapers. According to Muth's obituary, he married the daughter of Abraham Deppen and practiced medicine in the region for over 40 years.[46] Mrs. Louisa Muth's obituary from 26 years later confirmed her maiden name as Deppen. She was the widow of Dr. Reuben H. Muth and had lived at her residence for 65 years. She also had a son named Henry.[47]

As mentioned earlier, there were dozens of pieces of ephemera relating to the lives of Dr. Reuben H. Muth or his son, Henry L. Muth.[48] Included are original church records, purchase receipts, drug formulae, bank drafts, and correspondence with the University of Pennsylvania Alumni Association. Every item is either handwritten or printed in English, further proving that Dr. Muth utilized English in his business and volunteer interactions.

Regarding the physician's logs, all the handwritten entries were written in English. When studying the Cummings map of 1874, which provides

43. Ibid.

44. David W. Keibel, *Powwowing Among the Pennsylvania Dutch: A Traditional Medical Practice in the Modern World* (University Park, PA: Penn State University Press, 2007), 73–74.

45. Ezra Grumbine. *Stories of Old Stumpstown: A History of Interesting Events, Traditions, and Anecdotes of Early Fredericksburg Known for Many Years as Stumpstown* (Lebanon, PA: Lebanon County Historical Society, 1910), 230.

46. "From Mahanoy." *Northumberland County Democrat*, February 2, 1899, 4. https://www.newspapers.com/clip/48405870/northumberland-county-democrat/.

47. "Red Cross Woman Dies At The Age of 93." *Shamokin News-Dispatch*, October 10, 1928, 1. https://www.newspapers.com/clip/55033034/obituary-for-louise-muth-aged-93/.

48. Reuben H. Muth, and Henry L. Muth papers and records, 1876–1924. Private collection of Lawrence Knorr, Mechanicsburg, Pennsylvania. See Table 2 in the Appendix for a list of the artifacts.

a snapshot of the geography of Northumberland County, Pennsylvania, and its prominent residents, the residence of R. H. Muth is marked near the village of Mahanoy.[49] Also, when corroborating the physician's logs with names on the map, it is evident the logs record residents within about twenty miles of Muth's home.

Despite most of the surnames of his clients being of Germanic origin, Muth's journals are all written in English, showing that professionally, at least, he used the English language for his records. However, Muth did leave several clues that hint at his Pennsylvania Dutch roots. His 1861 journal includes a newspaper clipping announcing his marriage to Louisa Deppen. It also lists him as being from Rehrersburg. The clipping is in German and likely from a local German-language newspaper.[50] His 1862 journal contains his name inscribed in Germanic script on news paper. It is glued to one of the first pages.[51] Also interesting is his 1886 journal. It includes a Pennsylvania Dutch poem on newsprint that was clipped and glued to the back. The poem is "Ich Wot Ich Ware Ein Bauer."[52] This translates to "I Wish I Were a Farmer." Professor Abraham Reeser Horne published it in his pioneer volume of the Pennsylvania Dutch language.[53] These seemingly trivial details hint at Muth's knowledge of not only English but also German and Pennsylvania Dutch.

Muth's dealing with English, German, and Pennsylvania Dutch in his travels is not unique to him. Steven J. Peitzman wrote an article about Dr. Owen Wister of Germantown, Pennsylvania, a likely classmate of Dr. Muth's at the University of Pennsylvania. Peitzman provided an account of Wister seeing a patient, a mentally ill Dutch woman, who was ignorant of English. Wister fetched a local Pennsylvania Dutch parson to speak with her.[54] The incident illustrates the transition occurring in language use in a more urban area like Germantown at the time, which was gradually being overrun by Philadelphia. Muth, in his rural setting

---

49. *Map of Northumberland County, Pennsylvania: from Actual Surveys*, Montandon, PA: J. A. J. Cummings, 1874, accessed January 13, 2025, at https://www.loc.gov/item/2012592194/.

50. Reuben H. Muth, *Physician's Daybooks*, vol. 3, attached to inside cover (1858–1898, in possession of Lawrence Knorr, Mechanicsburg, Pennsylvania).

51. Ibid., vol. 4, attachment to inside cover.

52. Ibid., vol. 22, attachment to inside cover.

53. Walter E. Boyer, Albert F. Buffington, and Don Yoder, *Songs Along the Mahantongo: Pennsylvania Dutch Folksongs* (Hatboro, PA: Folklore Associates, 1951), 103.

54. Steven J. Peitzman, "The Fielding H. Garrison Lecture: 'I Am Their Physician': Dr. Owen J. Wister of Germantown and His Too Many Patients." *Bulletin of the History of Medicine* 83, no. 2 (2009): 254. https://doi:10.1353/bhm.0.0200.

in remote Northumberland County, likely encountered Dutch patients every day and would not have been able to rely on others for translation.

Reverend Isaac F. Stiely (1800 – 1869) was a generation older than Muth. Stiely, like Muth, was born and raised in western Berks County, near Wernersville, less than fifteen miles from Rehrersburg. As a young man, Stiely married Anna, the daughter of Peter Knorr, and purchased a plot of land from his father-in-law in Upper Mahantongo Township, Schuylkill County, close to the village of Rough and Ready. Stiely preached primarily at Salem Church in that village but also traveled to numerous churches in the area, perhaps crossing paths with the traveling doctor. The distance from Rough and Ready to Mahanoy (Red Cross) is only a dozen miles. According to his second-great-granddaughter, Marilyn Malick Herb, in the book *The Reverend Isaac Stiely: Minister of the Mahantongo Valley*, Stiely tended to many congregations in the area, adjusting his language from Pennsylvania Dutch to German and English, depending on what was needed.[55] Stiely was also famous for carving dozens of ornate tombstones, nearly all in German, and for inscribing fraktur for birth and marriage certificates in German.

Phoebe Gibbons wrote about regional cultural issues in the late 19th century. One of Ms. Gibbons' subjects was the Pennsylvania Dutch culture, which at that time was beginning to show signs of resisting contemporary technological advancements. She gained access to Amish and Mennonite events and observed Lutheran and Reformed German culture. One nugget from her book *Pennsylvania Dutch and Other Essays* relates how the Dutch locals resisted English speakers who knocked on the doors selling their goods. These salesmen resorted to trickery and charming the Dutch with stories to sell their wares.[56] Perhaps Dr. Muth and his peers used the Pennsylvania Dutch language when interacting with his rural patients to gain their confidence and trust.

Another contemporary, David Baer Hackman (1827 – 1896), lived most of his life in Manheim, Lancaster County, Pennsylvania. During the early 1850s, Hackman, also a Pennsylvania Dutchman, traveled west as part of the California Gold Rush. Hackman's letters and journals were

---

55. Lawrence Knorr, *The Relations of Isaac F. Stiely: Minister of the Mahantongo Valley* (Mechanicsburg, PA: Sunbury Press, 2010), 10.

56. Phoebe Earle Gibbons, *Pennsylvania Dutch and Other Essays* (Philadelphia: J. B. Lippincott & Co., 1872), 10.

incorporated into the book *A Pennsylvania Mennonite and the California Gold Rush*. Though Hackman was raised in the heart of Pennsylvania Dutch country, all his correspondence was recorded in English, including letters to his mother, brother, and sweetheart. However, though Hackman and his relatives back home were using English when writing to one another, he related a tale of prospecting with a family of fellow Pennsylvania Dutch who had also made the long journey. Said the eldest member of the family, "*Yah ich hab evva sella grassa stumba, noch net gafunna vu sell feala gold drunne stech un so long os ich sell net fin gana ich net is aim.*" (translation: "Yes, I have forever stumbled through the grass, not yet finding the great pile of gold I seek, but as long as I am able, it is my goal.")[57] Hackman thought enough of this conversation to include the Dutch verbatim in his letter. Obviously, Hackman understood the conversation as he framed the story in English. If so, this would align with the observations of Loudon and Gibbons regarding mixed language use among those in the region.

Clearly, Reuben H. Muth and many of his Pennsylvania Dutch contemporaries were multi-lingual during the mid to late 1800s. Economist Edward Paul Lazear wrote about the possible motivations for culture and language assimilation, comparing earlier German immigrants with contemporary Spanish-speaking immigrants.[58] According to Lazear, the degree to which immigrants will assimilate to the dominant language can be quantified based on the ratio of speakers of the language in the community. Immigrants tend to assimilate where they are overwhelmed by the dominant language or will otherwise collect where their native language and culture are more prevalent.[59] If Lazear is correct, the Pennsylvania Dutch were clinging to their language because there was a high concentration of Dutch speakers in the area. When Hackman was in California, amid a stew of languages, he used Pennsylvania Dutch only when speaking with others who preferred it. He appeared to use English in all other instances.

When comparing the experiences of Dr. Muth, Muth's elders, Hackman, and Stiely, it's apparent the older generation seemed more likely

57. Lawrence Knorr, *A Pennsylvania Mennonite and the California Gold Rush: The Journal and Letters of David Baer Hackman* (Mechanicsburg, PA: Sunbury Press, 2010), 69.

58. Edward P. Lazear, "Culture and Language." *Journal of Political Economy* 107, no. S6 (1999): S100–108, https://doi:10.1086/250105.

59. Lazear, S124–25.

to use German for significant events like births and deaths, while the younger generation, Dr. Muth and Hackman, only used Pennsylvania Dutch in conversation and left little evidence of using German. While Hackman was in California, he tended to associate with other Pennsylvania Dutch who had also made the journey, but like Muth, he resorted to using English in his correspondence and business transactions. Lazear's observations may not explain this apparent preference for English for written correspondence. Perhaps, given that Pennsylvania Dutch was primarily an oral language until the late 1800s, English was the logical choice given the surrounding English-speaking community.

Ultimately, unlike his parents' and grandparents' tombstones at Athalaha Cemetery in Rehrersburg, the monument marking the final resting place of Reuben H. Muth is carved in English rather than German.[60] There is no starker evidence of a change in language preference than what is etched in stone for the ages.

---

60. Reuben H. Muth tombstone, 1899. Inscription carving. Saint Peters Lutheran Church Cemetery, Red Cross, Pennsylvania. Viewed July 22, 2020.

17

Practice, Peers, and Patients

The medical practice of Reuben Harris Muth, M.D., lasted from his graduation from the University of Pennsylvania in 1855 until just before he died in 1899. From 1855 through 1857, Dr. Muth most likely worked in partnership or in the employment of Dr. Samuel K. Treichler, of Jonestown, Pennsylvania, with whom he attended the University of Pennsylvania through 1854 and whom he knew from his hometown of Rehrersburg, Berks County, Pennsylvania.

For the years 1858 through 1898, Dr. Muth practiced medicine independently, with a hiatus from the middle of January 1876 until the end of that year. From January 1858 through early 1860, Dr. Muth practiced in Fredericksburg, Pennsylvania, perhaps earning his independence from Dr. Treichler but in competition with Dr. Beaver, who was very prominent in the town at that time. Then, in early 1860, Dr. Muth relocated to Mahanoy, Northumberland County, where he lived for the rest of his life, perhaps a move recommended by Dr. Jacob Tryon of Rehrersburg.

The set of daybooks that were used to record his activities chronicled his patient interactions from 1858 through 1898, accounting for forty-one years of his career, totaling 28,135 visits and over $25,000 in fees.[1] All entries were transcribed into an Excel workbook with tabs for each year. Thus, every patient interaction was tabulated electronically to permit this accumulation. This work required hundreds of man-hours of effort over eighteen months of elapsed time and forms the quantitative foundation of this portion of the study.

---

1. See Appendix D: "Summary" for Dr. Muth's Career Earnings.

Regarding the daybooks themselves, they are pocket-sized leather registers with spaces to record patient visits according to the date and the requisite fees charged. The primary purpose of the daybooks, as utilized by Dr. Muth, was as a pocket calendar with his patient visitation schedule, as planned or recorded after the fact. He also used the books as an account ledger, transferring the charges at the end of the year into an open balance that he carried over to the following year. Dr. Muth also made numerous personal notations in his books, mostly about the weather and flora evident on his travels and later the activities on his farm. Dr. Muth was most likely a saddlebag doctor for the first few years of his career and then traveled via carriage. Later in his career, he appears to have seen patients in his home office. All notations from the daybooks were worked into the biographical narrative of Dr. Muth's life. All the appointment data was transcribed into the workbook.

The daybooks were produced by four major publishers, within which he switched eight times. From 1858 through 1866, Dr. Muth utilized *The Physicians Visiting List* produced by Lindsay and Blakiston of Philadelphia, Pennsylvania.[2] Dr. Muth then switched to *The Physicians Daily Pocket Record* published by Medical & Surgical Reporter of Philadelphia, Pennsylvania from 1867 through 1876. He returned to *The Physicians Visiting List* from 1877 through 1879 and then back to *The Physicians Daily Pocket Record* through 1884. From 1885 through 1887, Dr. Muth again utilized *The Physicians Visiting List*, but it was now produced by P. Blakiston and Son Company. Apparently, Linsday had retired. From 1888 through 1890, Dr. Muth was back with *The Physicians Daily Pocket Record*. For 1891 and 1892, Dr. Muth toggled back to *The Physicians Visiting List*. For the next three years, from 1893 through 1895, Dr. Muth introduced an entirely new published, Lea Brothers & Co. of Philadelphia, who manufactured *The Medical News Visiting List*. Finally, to close out his career, Dr. Muth returned to his favored *The Physicians Visiting List* by P. Blakiston and Son Company. Thus, he used *The Physicians Visiting List* eighteen times, doubling up on two of the years, to make twenty years of utilization. *The Physicians Daily Pocket Record* was the second most popular, acquired thirteen times and doubled up five times for a total of eighteen years of use. *The Medical News Visiting List* was

---

2. See Appendix A: "Journals" for an inventory of the daybooks by year and publisher.

only used for three years, making the total of daybook utilization forty-one years in thirty-four volumes.

The reason for switching between publishers may have more to do with promotions and journal subscriptions. These same publishers also produced popular medical journals and often promoted a discounted daybook as a bonus.

Dr. Muth's career arc did not follow a clear upward trend followed by a clear downward trend (see Table 1). Rather, his career, from a total fees perspective, fluctuated widely and was interrupted at age sixty during 1876 (year 19) when he took a hiatus. The initial build of his career corresponded with his start in Fredericksburg, Lebanon County, Pennsylvania, through year 3 (1860). Following the death of his wife and perhaps due to local competition, he moved to Mahanoy, Jackson Township, Northumberland County, Pennsylvania. He appears to struggle in the early years at the new location, as he married into the prosperous Deppen family. It was only by year 9 (1866) that he built momentum for a few years before a significant dip in year 12 (1869). He followed with a build-up to the peak of his career in year 18 (1875). It appears Dr. Muth's sabbatical, for whatever reason, did not severely damage his practice, as he returned to a strong position in year 20 (1877). However, rather than build his practice to new heights, Dr. Muth's career ebbed over a long downward tail. Perhaps he was simply not accepting new patients, or new patients were not selecting him. This move towards apparent retirement began in earnest at year 35 (1892) and lasted until the end of his career in 1898. Dr. Muth died in early 1899 after a brief illness.

All told, Dr. Muth earned $25,371.13 over the forty-one years detailed in the daybooks. This was an average of $618.81 per year, typically ranging between $500 and $800 per year, peaking at $1121.20 in 1875. This was right on target nationally, as the average physician rarely earned more than $600 a year, as compared to a factory worker at $360 or a farm laborer at under $200 per annum.[3]

Regarding Dr. Muth's patients versus visits, while they follow a similar pattern to his fees, there is an interesting relationship between the two data points. It appears Dr. Muth's weekly scheduled visits to his patients varied significantly over time, recognized by fluctuations in the gaps

---

3. R.G. Slawson, "Medical Training in the United States Prior to the Civil War," *Journal of Evidence-Based Complementary & Alternative Medicine.* 2012;17(1):18.

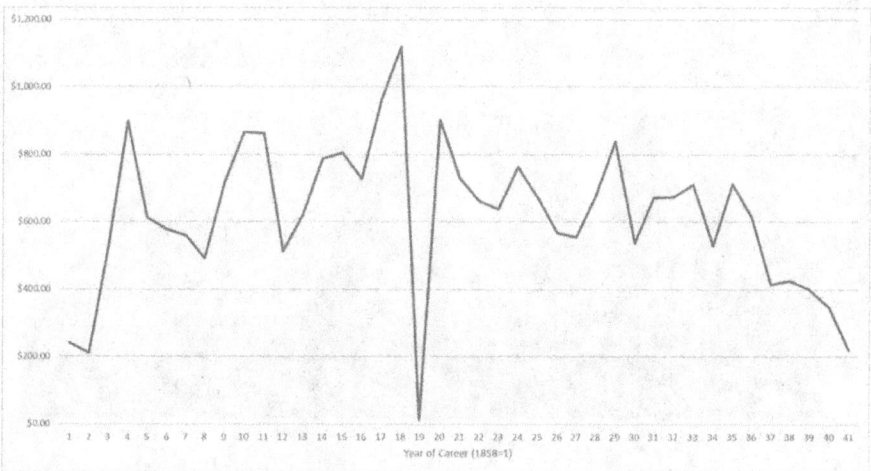

Table 1. Dr. Muth's Career Income by Year.
Source: Data from Appendix C: "Statistical Summary."

between the two trend lines. In other words, there are years when he sees patients more often in a week and years when he sees patients less often. Given the large sample size of data, the explanation of the difference is most likely behavioral on the part of the doctor and may represent shifts from when he was traveling about the countryside as a visiting doctor versus seeing patients in his home office. Alternately, he could have been seeing patients closer to home some years and then traveling more during other years, in effect being less interactive with his patients. Or, perhaps, his patients were requiring different treatments, maybe due to an aging population or increased use of new procedures and medications. Compared to Dr. Langstaff in the data collected by Jacalyn Duffin, Dr. Muth saw about one-third of the patients of the Canadian physician.[4]

When calculating the ratio of visits to patients each week over time, the behavioral fluctuation becomes more apparent. Table 3 (see page 156) illustrates these ratios on an annual basis, including a linear career trend line. Generally, it appears mid-career that Dr. Muth is seeing patients less frequently, whereas earlier and later in his career, the appointment intensity increases. Overall, the general trend is upward, meaning Dr. Muth, throughout his career, saw the same patient more often during a given week. A possible explanation is travel time. Considering travel time

---

4. Jacalyn Duffin, *Langstaff: A Nineteenth-Century Medical Life* (Toronto: University of Toronto Press, 1993), 94.

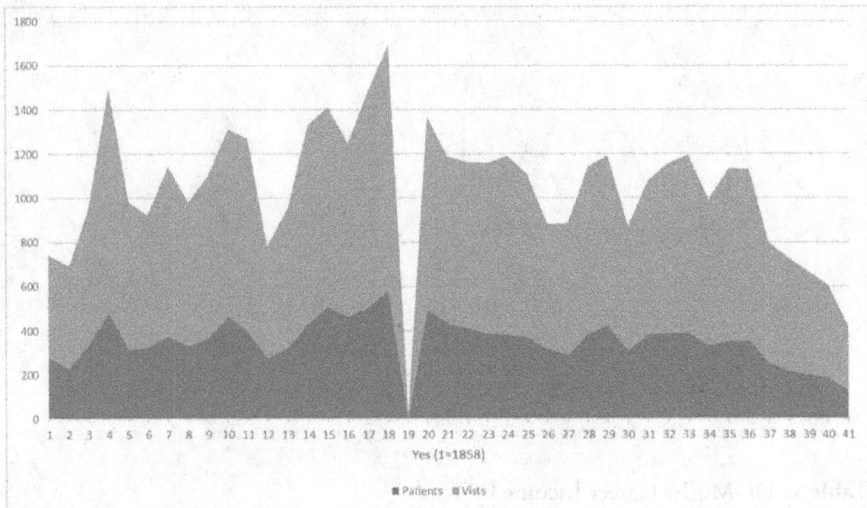

Table 2. Dr. Muth's Career Weekly Patients and Visits.
Source: Data from Appendix C: "Statistical Summary."

decreases the amount of time available for service, Dr. Muth may have accomplished more on traveling visits versus seeing patients in his office. In other words, instead of always scheduling a follow-up visit, perhaps he accomplished both tasks at the same time, when practicable. Thus, it is possible that mid-career Dr. Muth spent more time out and about.

Table 4 illustrates the fluctuation in the average fee charged per visit. Doctors' fees at this time varied based on whether or not the doctor traveled to the patient or the patient came to the doctor. The mileage to the patient was a significant cost factor. Women and children generally

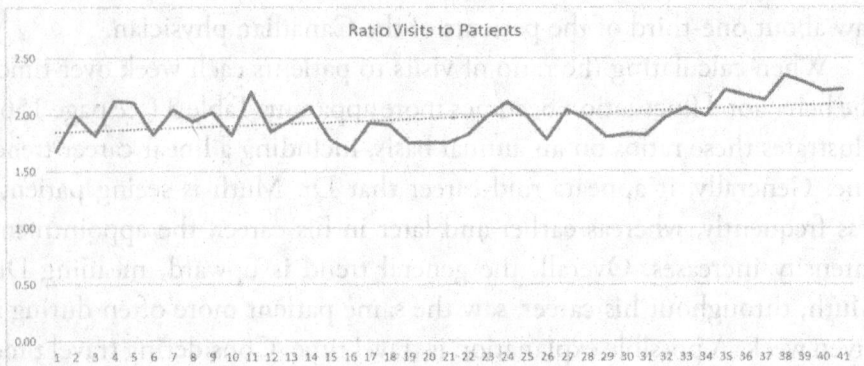

Table 3. Ratio of Weekly Visits to Patients Over Time.
Source: Data from Appendix C: "Statistical Summary."

Average Fees per Visit Over Time

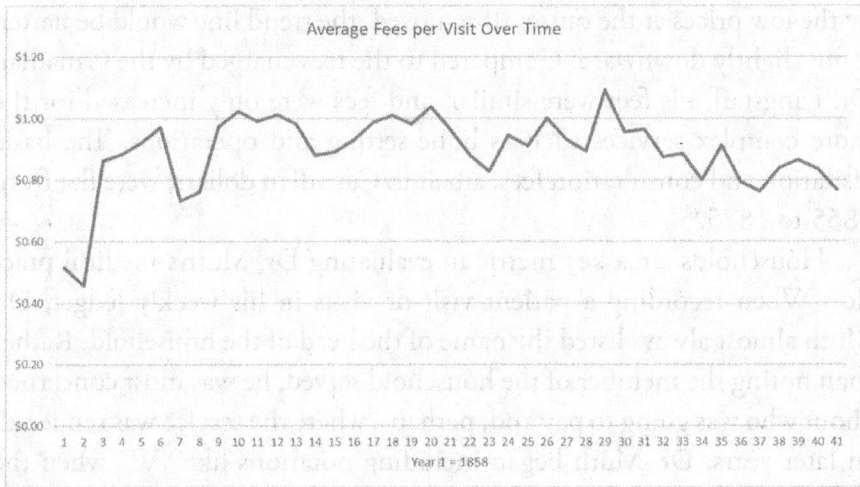

Table 4. Ratio of Fees per Visit Over Time.
Source: Data from Appendix C: "Statistical Summary."

generated lower fees than men. Likewise, procedures were a factor. For instance, obstetric appointments or the setting of broken bones were more expensive than the typical check-up. Lastly, medicinal doses were typically a quarter dollar or less.

The low fees early in Dr. Muth's career, while in Fredericksburg, probably represent him as in start-up mode, seeing patients in his office in town. From Year 3 (1860) onward, his fees generally remain in a range of eighty cents to one dollar per visit, with few exceptions. Fees tend to be higher during his mid-career period, aligning with the earlier supposition regarding visits per patient, that he was traveling about the countryside more. Later in his career, the fees bend lower, aligning with the possibility he saw more patients in his office during those years. Curiously, there is no evidence of significant price inflation regarding his fees throughout the forty-one years that are measured. According to Greenspan, the productivity gains of the expanding railroad network may have had a depressive impact on commodity prices as it was easier to move things farther and faster and at a lower cost.[5] This may have had the effect of taming the cost of living and suppressing service fees. While the linear trend line indicates a slight upward movement over the years, the difference is a less than five percent movement. Most of this can be explained

5. Alan Greenspan and Adrian Woolridge. *Capitalism in America: A History* (New York, N.Y.: Penguin Press, 2018), 97.

by the low prices at the outset. If removed, the trend line would be flatter, if not slightly downward. Compared to the fees charged by the Canadian Dr. Langstaff, his fees were similar, and fees were only increased for the more complex services such as bone-setting and operations. The basic visitation and consultation fees, albeit in Canadian dollars, were flat from 1855 to 1875.[6]

Households are a key metric in evaluating Dr. Muth's medical practice. When recording a patient visit or visits in his weekly ledger, Dr. Muth almost always listed the name of the head of the household. Rather than noting the member of the household served, he was most concerned about who was going to pay and, perhaps, where the service was rendered. In later years, Dr. Muth began including notations like "W" when the wife was the patient or "C" when a child was the patient, but he rarely mentioned them by name. Table 5 illustrates the number of households serviced by Dr. Muth throughout his career. In the early going, the move to Mahanoy during Year 3 (1860) was a boon. His marriage into the Deppen family resulted in the highest number of households serviced in Year 4 (1861). However, the practice generally faded from there, with a rally mid-career. The late-career drop-off also relates to the decline in visits noted earlier. It is very interesting that after being "new" to the community and marrying into a prominent family, Dr. Muth rapidly lost about one-third of the households. Was this a performance issue? Or was this about choice? His wife was pregnant circa Years 5 and 6 and lost a baby during the latter (1863). The couple's first child was then born during Year 9 (1866), so family concerns could have outweighed the doctor's ability to travel to the more remote households. Another explanation could be competition from other physicians. Dr. Muth competed with Dr. Haas within the Jackson Township community. Perhaps this was more collaborative rather than competitive since it seems Dr. Muth temporarily handed his practice to someone else during Year 19 (1876) and then recovered well the following year. Later in his career, Dr. Krebs moved into the Herndon area, perhaps shaving off opportunities in that riverside community for Dr. Muth. Again, Dr. Muth was known to collaborate with Dr. Krebs on a significant surgery, so if there was competition it was certainly gentlemanly. Overall, the linear trendline

6. Jacalyn Duffin, *Langstaff: A Nineteenth-Century Medical Life* (Toronto: University of Toronto Press, 1993), 47.

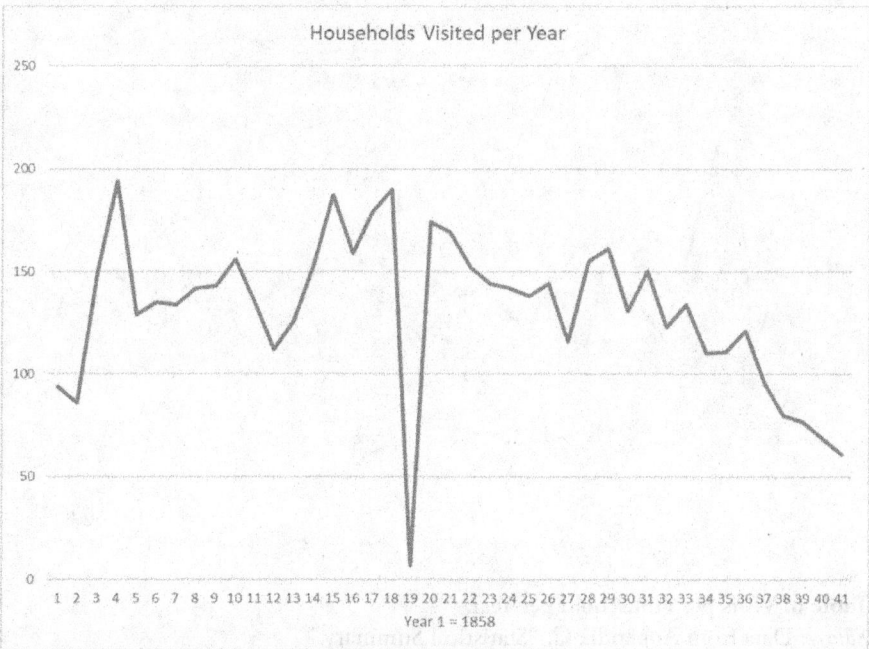

Table 5. Households Visited per Year.
Source: Data from Appendix C: "Statistical Summary."

throughout Dr. Muth's career was generally downward, from about 150 households to about 110. This could be due to Dr. Muth retaining patients he favored or who favored him. It also illustrates that, over time, he may have made less effort to attract new patients and preferred to stick with the households he had known for many years. Of course, the final tail downward indicates he may have deliberately refused to see new patients, servicing the patients who were willing to come to him at his home office as he aged and traveled the countryside less. Compared to Dr. Langstaff, the Canadian Dr. Muth visited about one-fourth of the households seen by Langstaff.[7]

Another interesting metric is the Visits per Household per Year, illustrated in Table 6 (see page 160). How often did the doctor visit with a household, whether at his office or their home? The chart indicates Dr. Muth saw individual households more often early and late in his career and generally less often mid-career. This again aligns with the supposition that he shifted from in-home visits to traveling visits and then back

7. Jacalyn Duffin, *Langstaff: A Nineteenth-Century Medical Life* (Toronto: University of Toronto Press, 1993), 94.

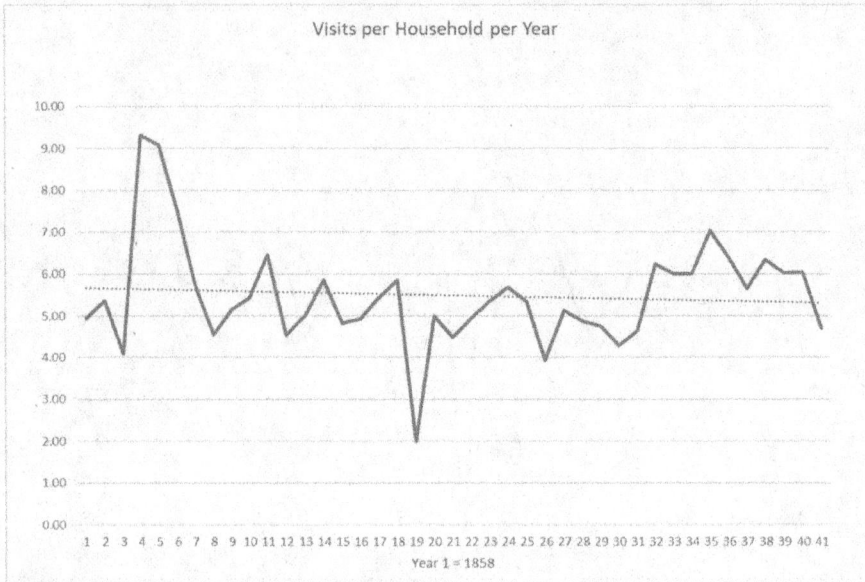

Table 6. Visits per Household per Year.
Source: Data from Appendix C: "Statistical Summary."

over his forty-one years. The low figure for Year 19 (1876) is anomalous because only a few weeks of data were recorded. Overall, while the linear trend line is generally downward, the slope is slight, indicating a fairly stable tendency to visit households between five to six times per year. This means the doctor typically visited the household about every other month. Another possibility, considering the average household size was roughly between five and six, is that the doctor saw each member of the household once per year on average. If all the patients were healthy all the time, then this would be akin to an annual wellness check. However, we know from the daybooks that the number of visits varied widely, as sickly patients in crisis warranted an intense period of multiple concentrated visits, and some households only appeared once in the ledger or not at all each year. Interestingly, the average visits per household were roughly the same when compared to Dr. Langstaff, ranging from five to six visits per year.[8]

How much did a typical household under Dr. Muth's care spend on doctor's fees? Table 7 illustrates this metric throughout Dr. Muth's career. As noted earlier, the number of households declined after peaking earlier

8. Jacalyn Duffin, *Langstaff: A Nineteenth-Century Medical Life* (Toronto: University of Toronto Press, 1993), 94.

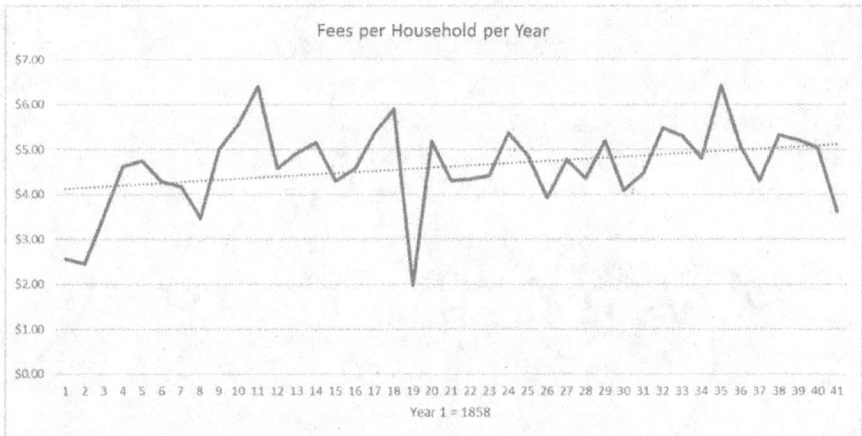

Table 7. Fees per Household per Year.
Source: Data from Appendix C: "Statistical Summary."

in his career. However, the number of visits per household increased over time at the end of his career. One way to earn more per household while losing households is to provide more service and to charge more. It appears from considering the other metrics along with the Fees per Household, Doctor Muth provided more services to the households later in his career. Thus, the typical annual fees paid to the doctor ranged between four and five dollars throughout most of his career. If the average laborer earned twenty dollars a week or about one thousand dollars a year, the cost of physician's care was only about one-half of one percent of annual income. This is significantly lower than the percentage of income spent on healthcare today by a typical family. Perhaps, rather than illustrating inflation, the gradual upwards linear trendline indicates an increase in services and therapies available to patients over time as technology changed. The trend could also be explained by the gradual aging of a patient population Dr. Muth was permitting to atrophy as his practice faded. Older patients often had intense palliative care near the end of their lives and had more instances of illness.

Another remarkable angle concerning the Fees per Household is to consider them versus the number of persons in a typical household. If there were five persons on average in a household of varying genders and ages, the average cost per person per year for the doctor was roughly one

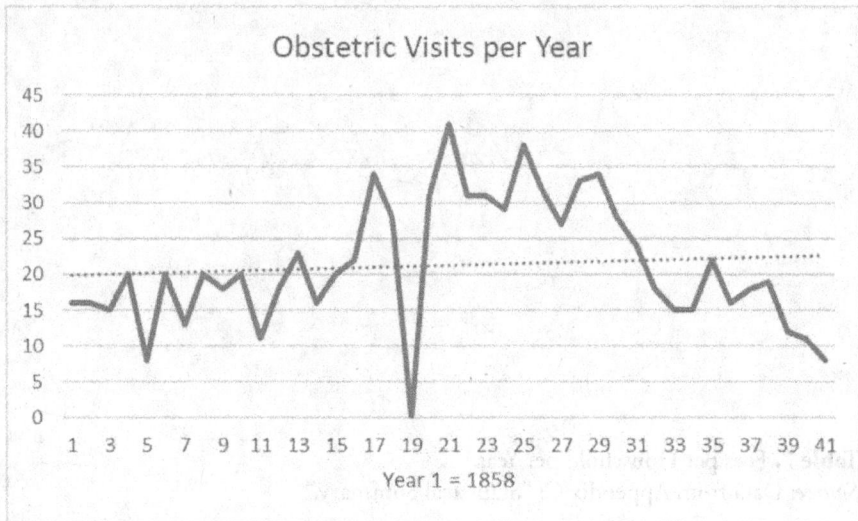

Table 8. Obstetric Appointments per Year.
Source: Data from Appendix C: "Statistical Summary."

dollar! Even considering the adjustment for inflation to our present time (2025), the typical annual expense per person for the doctor would be about thirty dollars. This is considerably less than what most households expend on healthcare today. Perhaps Dr. Muth wasn't the only healthcare provider utilized in these communities, or perhaps there was resistance to using trained physicians to treat day-to-day medical needs. How often was the pow-wow practitioner called to ward off sickness, or how often were home remedies from the garden used to alleviate symptoms? We cannot know. However the level of service utilized regarding Dr. Muth in this rural Pennsylvania Dutch community seems to indicate the doctor was called only under the most extreme circumstances.

Doctor Muth attended 871 births over his forty-one years recorded in his daybooks. This is an average of over twenty-one births per year, slightly less than two per month. The fees charged ranged from two to five dollars per obstetric appointment, not counting those done for free. Following his career, it appears Dr. Muth's peak for delivering babies occurred during the middle years of his career, corresponding with his apparent trend to spend more time out visiting versus in his office. Was the increase in births handled by Dr. Muth a result of a baby boom in the

Percent of Households with Obstetric Visits

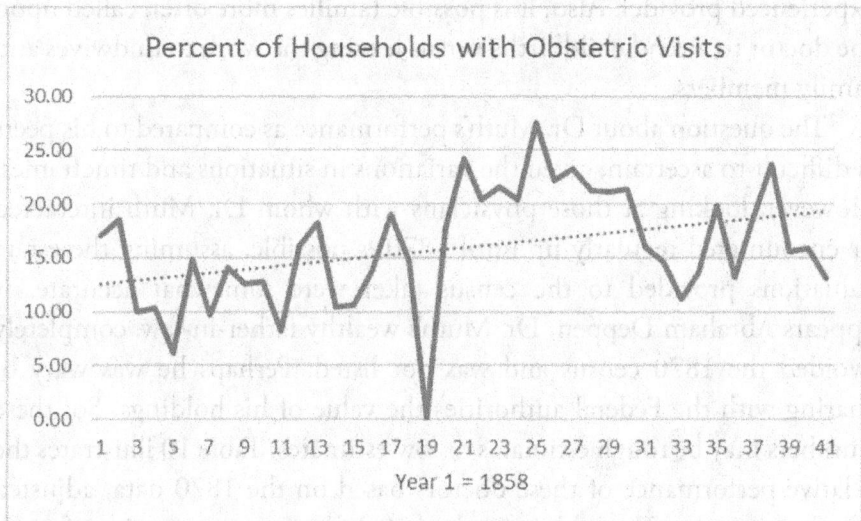

Table 9. Frequency of Obstetric Appointments per Household.
Source: Data from Appendix C: "Statistical Summary."

region? The births were low during the Civil War years when many men were away fighting. But from Year 13 (1870) through Year 28 (1885), Dr. Muth birthed the most children. This trend aligns with changes in the census from 1860 through 1880 in Jackson Township, Northumberland County, Pennsylvania. Dr. Langstaff assisted two to five times the number of births in his Canadian practice.[9] Obviously, he was working quite a bit more as a physician than Dr. Muth.

Given that Dr. Muth's career ebbed, it would likely be incorrect to assume the birth rate also decreased in his community. Rather, by comparing the number of births to the number of households serviced by Dr. Muth, Table 9 above illustrates the frequency of births among the families for which he provided care. This tells a very different story. It appears the birth rates were low, below fifteen percent of households before Year 11 (1868), and markedly higher after, nearing one-quarter of all households ten years later in 1878. The overall career trendline is significantly positive, indicating that even though Dr. Muth's overall practice was fading during the last decade or so, he answered the call for obstetric appointments at an increasing rate. This could mean that there simply were more births in these years, or Dr. Muth was a preferred,

9. Jacalyn Duffin, *Langstaff: A Nineteenth-Century Medical Life* (Toronto: University of Toronto Press, 1993), 181.

experienced provider. Also, it is possible families more often called upon the doctor to attend childbirths versus leaving the work to midwives and family members.

The question about Dr. Muth's performance as compared to his peers is difficult to ascertain, given the variations in situations and timeframes. However, looking at those physicians with whom Dr. Muth interacted or encountered regularly up until 1870 is possible, assuming the estate valuations provided to the census taker were somewhat accurate. It appears Abraham Deppen, Dr. Muth's wealthy father-in-law, completely avoided the 1870 census and was not listed. Perhaps he was wary of sharing with the Federal authorities the value of his holdings. So, these numbers may be rough estimates or low estimates. Table 10 illustrates the relative performance of these doctors based on the 1870 data, adjusted for their careers. The table records their lifespans, community of practice, graduation date from medical school, school attended, the years of their practice, length of practice, real estate valuation in 1870, personal estate valuation in 1870, number of years worked through 1870, and the growth in real estate and personal estate per year up until 1870. The annual growth figures were calculated by dividing the 1870 estate values by the number of years in practice up until that point. The result is the average increase in the valuation of their estates each year, assuming their estates were negligible when they started their careers.

Dr. Muth's first mentor, Dr. Jacob M. Tryon, was late in his career in 1870 and had accumulated $952 per year in estate value. Dr. Lewis Royer, Muth's preceptor and son-in-law of Dr. Tryon, was also very successful with $2363 in annual estate value. Dr. Daniel H. Beaver, whom Dr. Muth encountered as competition in Fredericksburg, was very wealthy, accumulating $2586 in annual estate value. These gentlemen had the benefit of starting earlier than Dr. Muth and had established themselves before the rapid increase in medical school graduates hit the marketplace. It is likely they also had time to invest in other assets and income opportunities. Dr. Tryon was known to teach medical students at his home. Dr. Royer and Dr. Beaver were involved in other enterprises.

Dr. Samuel K. Treichler, Percival Tryon, and Dr. Joseph Haas are better comparisons to Dr. Muth because they are within a few years of

Physician	Born	Died	Where Lived	Grad	Institution	Start	End	Years	1870 RE	1870 PE	1870 Yrs	RE/YR	PE/YR
Jacob M Tryon	1800	1887	Rehrersburg, PA	1820	Father	1820	1884	64	$26,600	$20,975	50	$532	$420
Lewis Royer	1822	1904	Trappe, PA	1843	Penn	1843	1904	61	$45,800	$18,000	27	$1,696	$667
Daniel H Beaver	1819	1884	Fredericksburg, PA	1846	Penn	1846	1884	38	$37,050	$25,000	24	$1,544	$1,042
Percival Tryon	1828	1881	Hamburg, PA	1851	Penn	1851	1881	30	$4,300	$800	19	$226	$42
Joseph Haas	1830	1905	Mahanoy, PA	1852	Jefferson	1852	1905	53	$8,000	$2,000	18	$444	$111
Samuel K Treichler	1831	1872	Jonestown, PA	1854	Penn	1854	1872	18	$4,500	$4,000	16	$281	$250
Reuben H Muth	1826	1899	Mahanoy, PA	1855	Penn	1855	1898	43	$2,000	$1,000	15	$133	$67
Andrew Jackson Kantz	1837	1899	Berrysburg, PA	1866	Iowa State	1866	1899	33	$1,500	$300	4	$375	$75

Table 10. Performance versus Peers.
Source: Data from Appendix C. "Statistical Summary" and US Census.

each other and started their careers around the same time. Dr. Muth, though older than them, started his career last. Haas and Treichler performed similarly, with Haas accumulating $555 in annual value while Dr. Treichler accumulated $531. Tryon, on the other hand, struggled, accumulating $266 per year. Dr. Muth trailed them all with an average estate increase of only $200 per year, way below nearly all of his peers.

Dr. Andrew Jackson Kantz is another interesting comparison because he was eleven years younger than Muth and started his career eleven years later. He only had four years in his career by 1870, at which time he had averaged accumulating $450 per year, similar to Haas and Treichler, though his total estate was still less than Muth's at $1800 in total.

According to Barnes Riznik in his article "The Professional Lives of Early Nineteenth-Century New England Doctors," struggles were not uncommon for young physicians noting "practitioners seldom received more than $500 a year in money and kind."[10] Riznik noted the cause as a surplus of doctors in many communities, forcing them to move[11] while others were deeply in debt.[12]

As seen early in his career, it appeared Dr. Muth worked for Dr. Treichler, indicating he may have been in debt to him. Thus Dr. Treichler probably started his career in better financial condition than Dr. Muth. Dr. Haas appears to have been in a similar situation to Dr. Treichler. Another factor was the movement of his practice. Dr. Muth started in Fredericksburg and then moved to Mahanoy. Dr. Treichler stayed put in Jonestown and Dr. Haas stayed in Mahanoy as well. Jacob Tryon and Beaver were pillars of their local communities and spent their lives there. So, the cost of moving could have been a factor, or perhaps the movement

10. Barnes Riznik, "The Professional Lives of Early Nineteenth-Century New England Doctors." *Journal of the History of Medicine and Allied Sciences* 19, no. 1 (January 1964): 6.
11. Ibid.
12. Ibid., 7.

was necessary because of the poor performance, similar to Riznik's findings in New England. Or, perhaps, as Dr. Grumbine said, Dr. Muth was not a very aggressive person.[13]

Of course, the other possibility is Dr. Muth fudged his numbers because, as a Peace Democrat during the Civil War, he did not trust the Federal government. Given his father-in-law's lack of participation, maybe Muth was encouraged to provide only a low-ball number. Given his interaction with the Draft Provost in 1863, when Muth gave an earlier birthdate for himself, it is possible he was evading Federal authorities.

Of course, later, Dr. Muth was reported as riding in a new carriage.[14] His journal, over the years, recorded purchases and activities, noting that he appeared to be thriving. Perhaps in our current era, Dr. Muth might have piqued the interest of the Internal Revenue Service!

Another clue about Dr. Muth's success and whether he was obscuring it can be discerned from his estate. According to the appraisal filed after his death, his estate was worth $3000. This is unchanged from his numbers in 1870. Thus, Dr. Muth appears to have spent nearly every cent he earned, likely enjoying the better life of living among his wealthy in-laws, the Deppens. Likewise, Dr. Percival Tryon appears to be benefitting from his father's success, sharing his practice with him in Rehrersburg.

Based on the patients serviced after his move to Mahanoy in 1860, Dr. Muth's range typically encompassed Jackson, Washington, and Jordan Townships in Northumberland County and occasionally into neighboring townships. Mahanoy, now Red Cross, is situated on the eastern edge of Jackson Township, close to the border with Washington Township. The east/west road between Mahanoy and Rebuck was a busy one for Dr. Muth. Given this was the likely center of his traveling practice, Table 11 tabulates the populations and number of households in this area. Based on the 1890 US Census Summary for Pennsylvania, these three townships had a stable population of over 2700 people. Assuming a typical household size of five persons, there were approximately 550 households in the area. Based on his summarized daybook entries, Dr. Muth typically served about 140 households per year. This leaves about 410 households that were serviced by someone else or were not serviced

---

13. Ezra Grumbine, *Stories of Old Stumpstown: A History of Interesting Events, Traditions, and Anecdotes of Early Fredericksburg* (Lebanon, PA: Lebanon County Historical Society, 1909), 98.

14. "From Mahanoy," *Northumberland County Democrat*, August 1, 1884, 4.

Township	1880	1890
Jackson	959	1046
Washington	811	788
Jordan	973	914
TOTAL	2743	2748
Households	548.6	549.6

Table 11. Township Populations.
Source: Data from US Census Summary 1890.

at all. As mentioned previously, Dr. Haas was the primary competition in this area. His estate, as of 1870, was growing at a rate of $555 per year versus Dr. Muth's figure of $200. This is a ratio of 2.775 to 1 in favor of Haas. Assuming Dr. Haas must have been better at filling his daybook and seeing more patients, if he saw a ratio of 2.775 to 1 more households, on average, his household count would be close to 390 per year. Combining Muth's 140 and Haas's estimated 390 sums to 530, just shy of the estimated number of households in these three townships. We do know that Dr. Krebs was already serving the Herndon area, along the Susquehanna River, in western Jackson Township, but he may have ranged along the river road, north-south, and not compete as much in the valley.

Pulling back to the county level, the population of Northumberland County, which was mainly in the center of the county near Sunbury, a different story comes into focus, unlike the lower townships home to Drs. Muth and Haas, the rest of the county was growing. However, based on the number of doctors who registered to practice between 1881 and 1891 versus the number of households in the county, Muth and Haas were much busier on average than the typical Northumberland County physician.

Based on the registry of physicians published in Bell's history of Northumberland County, there were 174 doctors by 1891. Given that Dr. Jacob S. Krebs began his practice in early 1881, we can be relatively sure that most, if not all, of the doctors on the list before Krebs were practicing at the time the registry was started. This would be about 116 doctors as of 1881. In other words, about 58 new doctors registered in

County	1880	1890
Northumberland	53123	74698
Households	10625	14940
Doctors	116	174
HH/Doc	91.59	85.86

Table 12. County Population.
Source: Data from US Census Summary 1890.

Northumberland County throughout the 1880s up until 1891, when the list was published. Of course, we do not account for those who moved away, retired, or passed away, so this approximation should be considered a low figure of average households per registered physician. Based on Table 12 above, circa 1880, the low estimate of households per physician is about 92. Ten years later, this dropped to 86, though, again, we do not know the attrition rate.

Given these numbers, it would appear there are too many doctors for Northumberland County. If Dr. Muth, at 140 households per year, were at the low end of his peers, there would be a lot of physicians in the more populated areas of Northumberland County who were doing worse. Likewise, Dr. Haas appears to be a star, far outshining the number of estimated households. Perhaps not all the physicians in Northumberland County circulated to households. Those involved in making or selling medicines might sell to the general public. Others could be teaching physicians and yet others could be working in hospitals in urban settings. It is also possible that people in urban settings utilized more services from physicians, seeing their doctors more frequently than people in rural communities.

Regarding those patients, several of Dr. Muth's are of particular interest, especially if viewed for the entire doctor/patient relationship. As mentioned previously, Benneville Lahr committed suicide on Thursday, May 2, 1872.[15] Dr. Muth had among his medical library books the first edition (1858) of Bucknill and Tuke's book on insanity. Regarding depression, also known as melancholia, the authors noted the difficulty in treatment, especially in the later stages.[16] We can imagine Dr. Muth

---

15. Reuben H. Muth, *Physician's Daybooks*, vol. 10, Daily Memoranda for April 28 to May 4, 1872 (1858–1898, in possession of Lawrence Knorr, Mechanicsburg, Pennsylvania).

16. John Charles Bucknill, M.D. and Daniel H. Tuke, M.D., *A Manual of Psychological Medicine* (Philadelphia, PA: Blanchard and Lea, 1858), 152–181.

referring to this tome at the time and being perplexed as to what to do. The tone of his notation in his daybook seemed to convey desperation after the suicide had occurred.

According to the 1860 Census for Jackson Township, Northumberland County, Pennsylvania, Benneville Lahr, 32, was a laborer with an estate of only $100, living between his father, George, a successful farmer, and brother, Lafayette.[17] He lived with his wife, Ann, 27, and daughters Harriet and Galen, ages six and two. By 1870, Beneville appears to be in a better situation, now living between Benjamin Clements and Catherine Lahr. Now a farmer, Benjamin's real estate was valued modestly at $1000 and his personal estate at $1800. Now 43, Benneville was living with Anna, 34; Harriet, 15; Galen, 13; and Hannah, 9.[18] He appears to be working his late father's farm. George had passed in 1866, leaving his widow, Catherine.[19]

Table 13 (see page 170) contains the entire doctor/household history of Benneville Lahr's family from the first day of service in 1861, not long after Dr. Muth moved to Northumberland County, until Benneville Lahr's suicide. Over the eleven years of service, Dr. Muth visited the Lahr homestead thirty-eight times, charging a total of $37 in fees. Three dollars were spent on December 9, 1861, to assist with the birth of Hannah Lahr, the youngest child. Unfortunately, we do not know who was assisted in the household on the other visits.

Curiously, of the eleven years Dr. Muth served the Lahr household, there were four years during which no visits were made: 1864, 1867, 1869, and 1870. This means the Lahr household would not have been counted in the total households served by Dr. Muth during those years. Eleven of the 38 visits occurred during November / December 1866. Perhaps someone in the household was seriously ill at that time. All told, 38 visits over eleven years for a sum of $37 is a relatively low level of healthcare, even adjusted for inflation. Given Lahr's estate of $2800, His cost of healthcare over the period is only a little more than one percent of the increase in his estate value. The percentage of his total income dedicated to healthcare is then likely less than one percent, assuming Lahr did not save every penny he earned from farming.

---

17. Census 1860, pg 61 hh 431.
18. Census 1870, pg 51 hh 37.
19. F-A-G https://www.findagrave.com/memorial/38943301/john_george_lahr.

Date	Day	Fee	Note
Oct 5, 1861	Saturday	$1.00	Visit
Oct 6, 1861	Sunday	$1.00	Visit
Oct 7, 1861	Monday	$1.00	Visit
Dec 9, 1861	Monday	$3.00	OB-Gyn - Birth of Hannah
Oct 12, 1862	Sunday	$1.00	Visit
Oct 13, 1862	Monay	$1.00	Visit
Oct 14, 1862	Tuesday	$1.00	Visit
Jan 8, 1863	Thursday	$1.00	Visit
Jan 9, 1863	Friday	$1.00	Visit
Jan 10, 1863	Saturday	$1.00	Visit
Jan 29, 1865	Sunday	$0.25	Medicine
Feb 20, 1865	Monday	$0.30	Medicine
Mar 6, 1865	Monday	$0.25	Medicine
Mar 31, 1865	Friday	$0.20	Visit
Nov 7, 1866	Wednesday	$1.00	Visit
Nov 9, 1866	Friday	$1.00	Visit
Nov 11, 1866	Sunday	$1.00	Visit
Nov 13, 1866	Tuesday	$1.00	Visit
Nov 17, 1866	Saturday	$1.00	Visit
Nov 20, 1866	Tuesday	$1.00	Visit
Nov 22, 1866	Thursday	$1.00	Visit
Nov 23, 1866	Friday	$2.00	Visited Twice
Nov 24, 1866	Saturday	$1.00	Visit
Nov 25, 1866	Sunday	$1.00	Visit
Nov 26, 1866	Monday	$1.00	Visit
Nov 27, 1866	Tuesday	$1.00	Visit
Nov 28, 1866	Wednesday	$1.00	Visit
Nov 30, 1866	Friday	$1.00	Visit
Dec 2, 1866	Sunday	$1.00	Visit
Nov 1, 1868	Sunday	$0.75	Visit
Nov 2, 1868	Monday	$0.75	Visit
Nov 3, 1868	Tuesday	$0.75	Visit
Nov 26, 1871	Sunday	$1.00	Visit
Nov 27, 1871	Monday	$1.00	Visit
Nov 28, 1871	Tuesday	$1.00	Visit
Nov 29, 1871	Wednesday	$1.00	Visit
Dec 1, 1871	Friday	$1.00	Visit
May 1, 1872	Wednesday	$0.75	Visit
38	TOTALS	$37.00	

Table 13. Benneville Lahr Household.
Source: Dr. Muth's Daybooks.

Sadly, the final visit for Dr. Muth was the day before the suicide. What was the purpose of this visit? What was discussed? Was someone else in the house ill, or did Benneville need attention for his melancholia? Finally, Benneville Lahr had registered for the military draft during the Pennsylvania emergency just before Gettysburg but did not serve. So, his depression was not connected to military service.

Washington Otto (1833–1897) and his household were long-time patients of Dr. Muth's, ranging from 1861 through 1893. Dr. Muth visited the Ottos 115 times over 32 years, tallying $95.86 in fees. During this span, there were seven years when no services were rendered, including the year Dr. Muth was off (1876). During this time, Dr. Muth delivered seven of the Ottos' nine children, missing only the firstborn, William, in 1863, and Edwin, born in 1876. Dr. Muth also set a fracture for someone in the household in 1879 and then assisted Washington with his horrendous injury when he was pinched between a wagon wheel and the loading dock at the train depot in 1889. His obituary mentioned he was ill and in pain for the remaining years of his life. The injury was blamed for his ultimate demise, though he survived nearly eight years. Many of the visits to the household in the latter years are most likely to treat Washington for the pain he was experiencing. Most of the children had grown by then and were out of the household. Ultimately, Washington Otto and his family spent only about four dollars per year on healthcare. Again, this is likely less than one percent of the earnings of this family.

Table 14 (see page 172) tabulates the fees charged to Washington Otto for healthcare provided by Dr. Muth.

In late February 1893, it appears a dispute arose between Dr. Muth and his brother-in-law, George Deppen. An accounting was created showing a balance due for services rendered at $14.25 for the period from 1889 through 1893. Why this accounting was done is unknown, but it is only a portion of the overall services rendered by Dr. Muth for this family. George and his wife also hosted George's father, Abraham Deppen, for a time, so the unpaid expenses may have been for Dr. Muth's father-in-law or perhaps to be paid by him.

Dr. Muth first assisted the George Deppen Household in 1870 with the birth of daughter Jane Deppen. Three of the next four years, Dr. Muth was called upon once to assist with the birth of a child: Laura,

Year	Visits	Fees	Notes
1861	1	$0.31	
1862	2	$2.00	
1864	4	$1.30	
1865	3	$4.50	Birth of Abraham Lincoln Otto
1866	1	$3.00	Birth of Agnes Otto
1867	1	$1.50	
1868	6	$11.00	Birth of George L Otto
1869	2	$4.25	Brith of Mary Otto
1871	8	$6.15	
1872	6	$4.00	
1873	3	$6.00	Birth of Lydia Mary Otto
1874	2	$4.75	Birth of John C Otto
1875	1	$0.75	
1878	2	$3.50	Set fracture
1879	3	$4.50	Birth of Cora Anna Otto
1881	1	$0.75	
1882	7	$3.50	
1883	3	$2.25	
1884	6	$2.30	
1885	7	$2.75	
1887	23	$12.00	
1888	1	$0.00	
1889	9	$8.00	Injury at depot
1891	4	$2.50	3 vists SYA
1892	8	$4.00	
1893	1	$0.30	
26	115	$95.86	TOTALS

Table 14. Washington Otto Household.
Source: Dr. Muth's Daybooks and US Census.

1871; George, 1873; and Harry, 1874. Clearly, the Deppens were using another physician for their other needs, and Dr. Muth was only called upon for childbirth. Then, after Dr. Muth returned from his hiatus from 1877 until 1894, he visited the George Deppen household on a regular basis, though another doctor may have handled the pregnancies at first. During this period, he made 175 visits for fees totaling $162.90. Thus, during those 18 years, Dr. Muth made nearly ten visits a year and charged about $9 per year. The George Deppen household was larger than most, with over ten children, so there was likely a greater need for services.

George Deppen was also involved in trading grain, like his father, and was beginning to accumulate some wealth. So, the extra cost of medical care was not a concern. In fact, the family's medical costs may also have been one percent of income or less per year.

Table 15 below summarizes the annual medical visits and fees related to Dr. Muth's services throughout the relationship. Most remarkable is the number of childbirths attributed to this family. Dr. Muth handled no less than eleven, though the last one may have been stillborn. That final birth, in 1892, occurred during the 45th year of the mother's, Mary Ann Mertz Deppen's, life.

After the dispute in 1893, Dr. Muth only visited this family a few more times in 1894, so the relationship appeared to be winding down at a time when Dr. Muth's practice was also in decline.

Year	Visits	Fees	Notes
1870	1	$4.00	Birth of Jane Deppen
1871	1	$4.00	Birth of Laura A Deppen
1873	1	$4.00	Birth of George Edward Deppen
1874	1	$4.00	Birth of Harry C Deppen
1877	19	$18.30	
1878	7	$5.70	
1879	9	$10.75	Birth of Carrie Louisa Deppen
1881	23	$24.25	Birth of John E Deppen
1882	9	$8.00	
1883	8	$9.50	Birth of Nettie I Deppen
1884	5	$2.25	
1885	11	$10.20	
1886	10	$13.00	Birth of Lawrence D Deppen
1887	3	$3.00	
1888	4	$7.00	Birth of A Earl Deppen
1889	10	$7.75	
1890	5	$7.00	Birth of Ruth A Deppen
1891	15	$14.95	
1892	24	$21.25	Birth of ?
1893	8	$7.25	
1894	5	$2.75	
21	179	$188.90	TOTALS

Table 15. George Deppen Household.
Source: Dr. Muth's Daybooks and US Census.

Based on these households, which were typical in the data, the doctor saw a particular patient less than once a year and charged, on average, less than one dollar per year per patient. Of course, when serious injury or illness occurred, the doctor visited more frequently, if not intensely. Thus, healthy patients rarely saw the doctor, even for preventative purposes such as vaccinations.

18

Summation of a Long Career

So what to make of this journey through 14,388 daybook entries recording 28,135 patient visits over forty-one years? The initial effort to transcribe and tabulate the daybooks of Dr. Reuben H. Muth's entire career was monumental. The amount of data available resulting from this effort cannot be consumed and processed in one monograph or for one purpose. Scholars from various disciplines and of varied purposes may find it useful for years to come. In this case, at this time, however, the resultant data has provided a framework for the biography of this otherwise unknown rural physician from Pennsylvania. It also provides clues as to the behavior and economic decisions made by a physician and his patients in the nineteenth century.

Regarding the biography of Dr. Muth, utilizing the suggestions of Clair Prechtel-Kluskens and others, connecting the threads of the schedules and interactions recorded in the daybooks with other available records from federal, state, and local sources, the full life of Reuben Harris Muth has been reconstructed forensically, without the aid of personal diaries and letters often used in such research. While this has provided a comprehensive timeline with key milestones, events, and people, it was difficult to locate the "soul" of Reuben Harris Muth. We were left with breadcrumbs of circumstantial evidence regarding his thoughts and beliefs and had to construct a "theory of his life" based mostly on the recordings of others. Dr. Muth, in his youth, appeared somewhat aimless as he navigated Marshall College in Mercersburg at an older age than most students. It appears he was only able to "get off the farm" due to an inheritance. He then, for some reason, did not finish. Evidence suggests he may have misbehaved with some of his classmates, perhaps indulging in drinking and other "un-Christian-like" behavior at a conservative German Reformed school. While some of his classmates were able to receive penitence, Dr. Muth was not. Was he the instigator?

We next track Dr. Muth to medical school, likely through the manipulation or encouragement of the local family who dominated the medical practice in the area. This family made a living from training young men for the medical profession, so it is not known whether Dr. Muth was lured into the profession or if he suddenly decided in his late twenties to pursue this career path. Perhaps the apparent friendship, short-lived as it may have been, with Samuel K. Treichler made the path to becoming a doctor easier. Treichler had started first, and then the two went to Philadelphia together. It appears Treichler may have helped Muth financially, and Muth may have been indebted to him, thus the period after graduation when Muth did not have his own practice but was working.

Dr. Muth's movement to Fredericksburg to start a practice in a town already dominated by Dr. Beaver is a curious phase. This appears to be a necessary step to pay back Dr. Treichler, who was practicing a few miles west in Jonestown. Also perplexing was Dr. Muth's marriage to a teenage girl with tuberculosis. Surely, he knew she was not well and would likely not live long. Why would he marry her? Was he truly in love?

Almost morbidly, Dr. Muth tracked every penny spent on his first wife's funeral and then attempted to build a practice for nearly two years in Fredericksburg. Given the competition and Dr. Muth's apparent mild-mannered nature, the practice did not grow, and he decided to relocate.

Why did Dr. Muth choose to go to Mahanoy in Northumberland County? We cannot know. Given the connections with the Trion family in Fredericksburg and Mahanoy and the connections of his mother's Schneider family to both locations, there are several possibilities. However, not soon after moving, Dr. Muth was able to build a more vibrant practice just before the start of the Civil War.

Next, he met his future wife, Louisa Deppen, as a patient. We do not know if they knew they were second or third cousins. We do not know how they felt about each other, but we do know Dr. Muth saw her as a patient and married her within a year. She also happened to be the daughter of the wealthiest man in the area, who was the patriarch of an influential family. Was this marriage for love or a social transaction? Was Dr. Muth impressed with the Deppen abode and decided to pursue the homely spinster daughter of the prosperous grain merchant? Or was he enamored with Louisa's beauty, charm, and wit, and the two were a natural couple? We cannot know for lack of correspondence and photographs.

This couple struggled to have children. The first was lost at birth, which must have been frustrating for the young physician. The only surviving child, Henry Deppen Muth, was then the focus of attention. Meanwhile, Dr. Muth plateaued with his practice as he began taking up farming activities and ran the local horse insurance company.

As his son matured, Dr. Muth became concerned with his whereabouts, especially when he was away for extended periods. Was Dr. Muth worried that young Henry would behave as he had at college? Dr. Muth also hinted at an interest in wayward women. Was this a charitable aspect of his Christian upbringing and his professionalism as a provider of obstetric services? Or was this a sexual interest, perhaps as a frustrated husband?

As Dr. Muth turned closer to the church, he became involved in the governance of the local Lutheran congregation. He noted attendance at camp meetings and the celebration of key holidays. Meanwhile, his son was hiding something from him, only revealing after the fact he had married a young woman he had made pregnant.

If Dr. Muth was upset about his son's big surprise, it seemed to be short-lived as he was the doctor who helped bring his grandchildren into the world. When the second grandchild was named for him, all seemed patched over.

Ultimately, Dr. Muth lived beyond his seventy-second birthday and was a respected member of his community. Based on his daybooks, he worked most days, rarely taking a break. He served his community, helping to bring 871 new human beings into the world. He also provided services for indigent patients and often did not charge for services around holidays or when something catastrophic had happened.

A key element to Dr. Muth's life was his belonging to the Pennsylvania Dutch culture. It is likely his stance as an apparent Peace Democrat, passively resisting participation in the Civil War and interactions with the Federal Government, had something to do with the culture's tradition to align with the South-dominated Democratic party championed by Andrew Jackson and, more recently, James Buchanan. It is also very likely Dr. Muth attracted patients and gained their trust based on his ability to speak the Pennsylvania Dutch tongue, as many of his patients were of that background. It is also clear Dr. Muth, as an educated member of the community, could function in the English world as well as the German world. However, he may have been competing against the inclination of his rural patients to engage with the local powwow doctor rather than a serious "regular" physician. According to Kriebel, the Pennsylvania Dutch physicians who made the most money were open to the traditional beliefs and practices of the powwowers, focusing on natural and herbal cures.[1] Given Dr. Muth's financial performance and the lack of any hints of anything unusual in his practice, he was probably a "regular" who could gain the confidence of his patience only with his use of the language and by his apparent heritage.

From the daybooks and other sources, we were able to construct information about Dr. Muth's practice, peers, and patients. Regarding his practice, the summarized daybooks illustrate a career arc very typical for someone building a profession and then phasing out near retirement. There appeared to be an upward limit to Dr. Muth's practice, perhaps caused by the presence of competition, the population density of the rural community, or both. There also appeared to be little inflation regarding the fees charged over the years. We do not know if this was due to national, regional, or local economic trends, the effects of competition, or the doctor's preference.

Comparing Dr. Muth to his immediate peers provided a stark contrast. Dr. Muth was not close to the most successful of the lot. In fact, he was last in accumulating a personal estate value. Was this due to financial mismanagement on his part? Or was this due to his financial circumstances at the outset of his career, perhaps being in debt and then needing to move? Another perspective would be the attachment to the wealthy

1. David W. Kriebel, *Powwowing Among the Pennsylvania Dutch: A Traditional Medical Practice in the Modern World* (University Park, PA: Penn State University Press, 2007), 77.

Deppen family meant he did not need to work as hard. Or perhaps he was understating his estate value to Federal authorities. Also impacting him was the number of doctors coming to Northumberland County. Dr. Muth may have been doing better than the majority of them, tucked away in his rural oasis.

The most important story might be the patients. As stated, Dr. Muth made over 28,000 patient visits in his career and was involved in nearly 900 births. Though just scratching the surface of thousands of cases, those reviewed showed Dr. Muth was effective in his practice. Unfortunately, he could not prevent the suicide of one of his patients due to depression, but mental illness was not well understood at the time. Rather, Dr. Muth appeared to be a respected surgeon, called to assist a fellow doctor in need and making the news when he performed his magic with his scalpel, needle, and stitches.

Perhaps the most perplexing discovery requiring further study was the typical frequency and cost of healthcare in the nineteenth century. Based on the cases in the daybooks and economic records from the census, a typical household spent roughly one percent of its annual income on healthcare. The average expenditure per patient member of the household was less than one dollar per year. Typically, households only called upon the doctor about three in every five years. Yes, there were times of frequent and urgent visits, but it appears most people steered clear of the doctor most of the time. Granted, the technology and services available at the time were minimal, but many people were living into their seventies, eighties, and nineties. Comparing then to now, it is clear that while the overall human lifespan has not been extended much, the number of people who survive childhood and live well into adulthood, if not old age, has been greatly expanded. An as yet unanswered question is whether the tremendous increase in healthcare expenditures provides commensurate value. Perhaps living in a clean, rural Pennsylvania Dutch community is a lot healthier than medicine.

Ultimately, Dr. Muth may not have been the most successful physician in his area. In fact, he may have been among the lower tier of his fellow University of Pennsylvania graduates. But there might be something deeper occurring here. When Dr. Muth pasted the passage from the song

"I Wish I Were a Farmer" into the back of one of his daybooks, perhaps he meant it. Perhaps as he was riding about the countryside, he was more concerned about his gardens and livestock than he was about growing a medical practice. Regardless, it is clear from the record that this professionally educated physician positively impacted his rural Pennsylvania Dutch community.

Bibliography

Archival Sources

Berks County Property Records, 1887, Book 174, Page 428, Berks County Recorder of Deeds, Reading, Pennsylvania.

Berks County Wills, 1883, 42., Berks County Registrar of Wills, Reading, Pennsylvania.

Catalogue of the Officers and Students of Marshall College for 1847 – '48. Mercersburg, PA: H. A. Mish, 1848.

Catalogue of the Officers and Students of Marshall College for 1848 – '49. Chambersburg, PA: The German Reformed Messenger Office, 1849.

Catalogue of the Trustees, Officers, and Students of the University of Pennsylvania, Session 1851 – 52. Philadelphia, PA: L. R. Bailey, Printer, 1852.

Catalogue of the Trustees, Officers, and Students of the University of Pennsylvania, Session 1852 – 53. Philadelphia, PA: T. K. and P. G. Collins, Printers, 1853.

Catalogue of the Trustees, Officers, and Students of the University of Pennsylvania, Session 1853 – 54. Philadelphia, PA: T. K. and P. G. Collins, Printers, 1853.

Catalogue of the Trustees, Officers, and Students of the University of Pennsylvania, Session 1854 – 55. Philadelphia, PA: T. K. and P. G. Collins, Printers, 1855.

Inscription Book of the University of Pennsylvania Medical Department, School of Medicine, Student Records, call number UPC 2.7 #16, entries for October 13, 1853. University of Pennsylvania Archives and Records Center, Philadelphia, Pennsylvania.

National Archives and Records Administration (NARA); Washington, D.C.; Consolidated Lists of Civil War Draft Registration Records (Provost Marshal General's Bureau; Consolidated Enrollment Lists, 1863–1865); Record Group: 110, Records of the Provost Marshal General's Bureau (Civil War); Collection Name: Consolidated Enrollment Lists, 1863–1865 (Civil War Union Draft Records); NAI: 4213514.

Northumberland County Marriage Dockets, v. 6–7, 1893–1896, number 4872, Northumberland County Courthouse, Sunbury, Pennsylvania.

Northumberland County Wills, 1834–1871, Nos. 4 and 5., Northumberland County Registrar of Wills, Sunbury, Pennsylvania.

Northumberland County, Pennsylvania, Will Book 9, Page 248, Northumberland County Registrar of Wills, Sunbury, Pennsylvania.

Record Book of St. Peters Lutheran Church, Red Cross, PA, starting 1841.

U.S., Civil War Draft Registrations Records, 1863–1865, Pennsylvania, 14th Class 1, A-K, Volume 1.

Primary: Unpublished

Manning, Henry. Daybook of Henry Manning, M.D. at Rose Melnick Medical Museum, Youngstown State University, Youngstown, Ohio. https://digital.maag.ysu.edu/xmlui/handle/1989/7310.

Muth, Frederick. Tombstone inscription at Altalaha Lutheran Cemetery, Rehrersburg, Berks County, Pennsylvania. 1846.

Muth, Frederick. Tombstone inscription at Altalaha Lutheran Cemetery, Rehrersburg, Berks County, Pennsylvania. 1883.

Muth, Reuben H., tombstone, 1899. Inscription carving. Saint Peters Lutheran Church Cemetery, Red Cross, Pennsylvania. Viewed July 22, 2020.

Muth, Reuben H. *Physician's Daybooks*. 34 vols. 1858–1898. In possession of Lawrence Knorr, Mechanicsburg, Pennsylvania.

Muth, Reuben H. and Henry L. Muth. *Papers and records*. 1876–1924. In possession of Lawrence Knorr, Mechanicsburg, Pennsylvania.

Trinity Tulpehocken Reformed Church, Lebanon County, Pennsylvania, Marriage Records, 1769–1844 (Philadelphia, PA: Genealogical Society of Pennsylvania, 2001), 9. Accessed January 13, 2025, https://genpa.org/wp-content/uploads/member-collections/Trinity_Tulpehocken_Reformed_Church_Marriages_pages_1-38.pdf

Primary: Published / Government

Fagan, L, and H. F Bridgens. *Township map of Berks County, Pennsylvania, from actual surveys*. Philadelphia: H.F. Bridgens, 1862. Map. https://www.loc.gov/item/2003625159/.

Franklin, Benjamin. *[The Papers]; The Papers of Benjamin Franklin. 4. July 1, 1750, through June 30, 1753*. New Haven: Yale University Press, 1961.

Hopkins, Griffith Morgan, Jr, J. A. J. Cummings, and Kimber Cleaver. *Map of Northumberland County, Pennsylvania: from actual surveys* by G.M. Hopkins, Jr., Civil Engineer. Chillisquaque, PA: J.A.J. Cummings, 1858. Map. https://www.loc.gov/item/2006629792/.

Hopkins, Griffith Morgan, Jr, Kimber Cleaver, R. A. Ammerman, J. A. J Cummings, and John L Smith. *Map of Northumberland County, Pennsylvania: from actual surveys*. Montandon, PA: J.A.J. Cummings, 1874. Map. https://www.loc.gov/item/2012592194/.

Map of Northumberland County, Pennsylvania: from Actual Surveys. Map. Montandon, PA: J. A. J. Cummings, 1874. https://www.loc.gov/item/2012592194/.

Pensyl, Jack L. and Charlotte D. Walter. *The Baptismal Records of Himmel's Union Church, Rebuck, Northumberland County, Pennsylvania, 1774–1846*. Sunbury, PA: Northumberland County Historical Society, 1996.

Township Map of Berks County, Pennsylvania, from Actual Surveys. Map. Philadelphia: H.F. Bridgens, 1862. https://www.loc.gov/item/2003625159/.

US Census Bureau. 1820 United States Federal Census. Census Place: Tulpehocken Township, Berks County, Pennsylvania.

————. 1830 United States Federal Census. Census Place: Tulpehocken Township, Berks County, Pennsylvania.

————. 1840 United States Federal Census. Census Place: Tulpehocken Township, Berks County, Pennsylvania.

————. 1850 United States Federal Census. Census Place: Tulpehocken Township, Berks County, Pennsylvania.

————. 1850 United States Federal Census. Census Place: Schuylkill Haven, Schuylkill County, Pennsylvania.

————. 1850 United States Federal Census. Census Place: Fredericksburg, Bethel Township, Lebanon County, Pennsylvania.

————. 1860 United States Federal Census. Census Place: Fredericksburg, Bethel Township, Lebanon County, Pennsylvania.

————. 1860 United States Federal Census. Census Place: Bethel Township, Lebanon County, Pennsylvania.

————. 1860 United States Federal Census. Census Place: Jackson Township, Northumberland County, Pennsylvania.

————. 1870 United States Federal Census. Census Place: Jackson, Northumberland, Pennsylvania.

————. 1870 United States Federal Census. Census Place: Fredericksburg, Bethel Township, Lebanon County, Pennsylvania.

————. 1880 United States Federal Census. Census Place: Jackson Township, Northumberland County, Pennsylvania.

————. 1880 United States Federal Census. Census Place: Chapman Township, Snyder County, Pennsylvania.

————. 1900 United States Federal Census. Census Place: Chapman Township, Snyder County, Pennsylvania.

University of Pennsylvania. Society of the Alumni. *Biographical catalogue of the matriculates of the college, together with lists of the members of the college faculty and the trustees, officers and recipients of honorary degrees, 1749–1893*. Philadelphia, PA: University of Pennsylvania, 1894.

Weiser, Frederick S. *Tulpehocken Church Records, 1730–1800: Christ (Little Tulpehocken) Church and Altalaha Church, Rehrersburg*. Breinigsville, PA: Pennsylvania German Society, 1982.

————. *Records of Pastoral Acts at Christ Lutheran Church, Stouchsburg, Pennsylvania*. Birdsboro, PA: The Pennsylvania German Society, 1990.

Secondary: Books

Adams, George Worthington. *Doctor's In Blue: The Medical History of the Union Army in the Civil War*. Baton Rouge, La.: Louisiana State University Press, 1996.

Appel, Rev. Theodore, D.D. *Recollections of College Life at Marshall College, Mercersburg, Pennsylvania, from 1839 to 1845*. Reading, PA: Daniel Miller, 1886.

Bell, Herbert C., *History of Northumberland County*. Chicago, IL: Brown, Runk, and Co., 1891.

Bowditch, Vincent Yardley, Henry I. Bowditch, and the Shapiro Bruce Rogers Collection (Library of Congress). *Life and Correspondence of Henry Ingersoll Bowditch*. Boston Cambridge Mass: Houghton Mifflin and Co., 1902.

Bowen, Stephanie. *Guide to the Frederick Weiser '57 papers*. Gettysburg: Gettysburg College, 2013.

Boyer, Walter E., Albert F. Buffington, and Don Yoder. *Songs Along the Mahantongo: Pennsylvania Dutch Folksongs*. Hatboro, PA: Folklore Associates, 1951.

Brinton, Daniel G. *The Lenâpé and Their Legends*. Philadelphia, PA: D.G. Brinton, 1885.

Bucknill, John Charles, M.D. and Daniel H. Tuke, M.D. *A Manual of Psychological Medicine*. Philadelphia, PA: Blanchard and Lea, 1858.

Carlyle, Thomas. "The Hero is Divinity" in On Heroes, *Hero-Worship, & the Heroic in History*. London: James Fraser, 1841.

Craig, Michel Williams. *General Edward Hand: Winter's Doctor*. Lancaster, PA: Rock Ford Foundation, 1984.

Deppen, E. E., M. L. Deppen, *Counting Kindred of Christian Deppen*. Myerstown, PA: Church Center Press, 1940.

Devine, Shauna. *Learning from the Wounded: The Civil War and the Rise of American Medical Science*. Chapel Hill, N.C.: University of North Carolina Press, 2014.

Dorson, Richard M. *Buying the Wind: Regional Folklore in the United States*. Chicago: University of Chicago Press, 1964.

Dubbs, Joseph Henry. *History of Franklin and Marshall College; Franklin College, 1787–1853*. Lancaster, PA: Franklin & Marshall College Alumni Association, 1903.

Duffin, Jacalyn. *Langstaff: A Nineteenth-Century Medical Life*. Toronto: University of Toronto Press, 1993.

Elliott, Ella Zerbey. *Old Schuylkill Tales*. Pottsville, PA: Ella Zerbey Elliott, 1906.

Flexner, James Thomas. *Doctors on Horseback: Pioneers of American Medicine*. New York, N.Y.: Dover, 1937.

Fried, Stephen. *Rush*. New York, N.Y.: Crown, 2018.

Gibbons, Phoebe Earle. *Pennsylvania Dutch and Other Essays*. Philadelphia: J. B. Lippincott & Co., 1872.

Gibson, James E. Dr. *Bodo Otto and the Medical Background of the American Revolution*. Springfield, Ill.: C.C. Thomas, 1937.

Greenspan, Alan and Adrian Woolridge. *Capitalism in America: A History*. New York, N.Y.: Penguin Press, 2018.

Griffith, Beatrice Fox. *Pennsylvania Doctor*. Harrisburg, PA: Stackpole, 1957.

Griffith, R. Eglesfeld, M.D., *Medical Botany: or Descriptions of the More Important Plants Used in Medicine, with Their History, Properties, and Mode of Administration*. Philadelphia, PA: Lea and Blanchard, 1847.

Grumbine, Ezra. *Stories of Old Stumpstown: A History of Interesting Events, Traditions, and Anecdotes of Early Fredericksburg Known for Many Years as Stumpstown*. Lebanon, PA: Lebanon County Historical Society, 1910.

Hein, George E. Jr. and Schuyler C. Brossman, *A History of Altalaha Evangelical Lutheran Church, Rehrersburg, Berks County, Pennsylvania*. Rehrersburg, PA: Altalaha Church Council, 1982.

Hill, Dolores, Sandra Kauffman, Barbara Loose, Carol Mehler, Barry Miller, and Jodie Ziegler. *History of Rehrersburg*. Rehrersburg, PA: Andulhea Heritage Center, 2019.

Hoffert, Sylvia D. *Private Matters: American Attitudes Toward Childbearing and Infant Nurture in the Urban North 1800–1860*. Urbana: University of Illinois Press, 1989.

Hohman, Johann Georg. *Der Lange Verborgene Freund*. Ephrata, PA: J.G. Hohman, 1828.

Johnson, Willis Fletcher. *History of the Johnstown Flood, Illustrated*. Philadelphia, PA: Edgewood Publishing Company, 1889.

Jordan, Mildred. *The Distelfink Country of the Pennsylvania Dutch*. New York.: Crown Publishers, 1978.

Klees, Fredric. *The Pennsylvania Dutch*. New York: Macmillan Publishing, 1950.

Knorr, Lawrence. *The Descendants of Hans Peter Knorr*. Mechanicsburg, PA: Sunbury Press, 2005.

———. *The Relations of Milton Snavely Hershey*. Mechanicsburg, PA: Sunbury Press, 2009.

———. *A Pennsylvania Mennonite and the California Gold Rush: The Journal and Letters of David Baer Hackman*. Mechanicsburg, PA: Sunbury Press, 2010.

———. *The Relations of Isaac F. Stiely: Minister of the Mahantongo Valley*. Mechanicsburg, PA: Sunbury Press, 2010.

Kriebel, David W. *Powwowing Among the Pennsylvania Dutch: A Traditional Medical Practice in the Modern World*. University Park, PA: Penn State University Press, 2007.

Loudon, Mark L. *Pennsylvania Dutch: The Story of an American Language*. Baltimore: Johns Hopkins University Press, 2016.

Martz, Richard J. *Dalmatia, Pennsylvania: The First Two Hundred Years: A Bicentennial History, 1798–1998*. Dalmatia, PA: Mahanoy and Mahantongo Historical & Preservation Society, Inc., 1998.

Meade L. T. and Clifford Halifax. *Stories from the Diary of a Doctor*. Philadelphia: J.P. Lippincott, 1895.

Meiser, George M. and Gloria Jean Meiser. *The Passing Scene Volume 10*. Reading, PA: The Historical Society of Berks County, 1997.

Millard, Candice. *Destiny of the Republic: A Tale of Madness, Medicine and the Murder of a President*. New York: Knopf Doubleday Publishing Group, 2011.

Norwood, William Frederick. *Medical Education in the United States Before the Civil War*. Philadelphia, PA: University of Pennsylvania Press, 1944.

Richman, Irwin Richman. *The Brightest Ornament: A Biography of Nathaniel Chapman, M.D.* Bellefonte, PA: Pennsylvania Heritage, 1967.

Rothstein, William G. *American Physicians in the Nineteenth Century*. Baltimore, MD: Johns Hopkins University Press, 1972.

———. *American Medical Schools and the Practice of Medicine: A History*. New York: Oxford University Press, 1987.

Rupp, I. Daniel. *History of the Counties of Berks and Lebanon*. Lancaster, PA: G. Hills, 1844.

Sack, Paul. *History of Higher Education in Pennsylvania*. Harrisburg, PA: Pennsylvania Historical and Museum Commission, 1963.

Shoemaker, Alfred L. *Christmas in Pennsylvania*. Mechanicsburg, PA: Stackpole, 1999.

Shryock, Richard Harrison. *Medicine and Society in America, 1660–1860*. New York, N.Y.: New York University Press, 1960.

Strassburger, Ralph B., and William J. Hinke. *Pennsylvania German Pioneers*. Camden, ME: Picton Press, 1992.

Stowe, Steven M. *Doctoring the South: Southern Physicians and Everyday Medicine in the Mid-Nineteenth Century*, Chapel Hill: The University of North Carolina Press, 2004.

Tellor, Lloyd V. *The Diseases of Live Stock and Their Most Efficient Remedies*. Philadelphia, PA: D.G. Brinton, 1879.

Tinkcom, Harry Marlin. *The Republicans and Federalists in Pennsylvania, 1790–1801*. Harrisburg, PA: Pennsylvania Historical and Museum Commission, 1950.

Warner John Harley. *The Therapeutic Perspective: Medical Practice Knowledge and Identity in America 1820–1885*. Cambridge Mass: Harvard University Press, 1986.

White, Richard. *The Republic for Which It Stands: The United States during Reconstruction and the Gilded Age 1865–1896*. New York, NY: Oxford University Press, 2017.

Williams William Henry. *America's First Hospital: The Pennsylvania Hospital 1751–1841*. Wayne, PA: Haverford House, 1976.

Woman's Club of Mercersburg, *Old Mercersburg*. New York, N.Y.; Journal of American History, 1913.

Wood, Ralph, et al. *The Pennsylvania Germans*. Princeton, NJ: Princeton University Press, 1942.

Young, Alfred F. *The Shoemaker and the Tea Party: Memory and the American Revolution*. Boston Mass: Beacon Press, 1999.

Secondary: Unpublished Dissertations

Dudley, Anu King. "What was in the Doctor's Bag: A Material Culture Study of the Performance of Medicine in Antebellum New England." PhD diss., The University of Maine, 2007. ProQuest Dissertations & Theses Global.

Gangstad, Erin Nicole. "Of Mountain Air and Mineral Baths: Space, Place, and Rhetorics of Health and Medicine in 19th and 20th Century American Climatic Cure." PhD diss., The University of Wisconsin - Madison, 2023. ProQuest Dissertations & Theses Global.

Gurstelle, Krystyna Herian. "Uneven Paths to Health and Healing: Medicine, Politics and Power in 19th Century America." PhD diss., Drew University, 2022. ProQuest Dissertations & Theses Global.

Muth, Reuben H. Thesis: "Poisoned Wounds, 1855," University of Pennsylvania Libraries Special Collections, call number 378.748 POM 1855.2.33 Pt. 2. Catalog ID 992878763503681.

Secondary: Articles / Newspapers / Exhibits

"A Firemens Parade at Shamokin," *Northumberland County Democrat*, July 13, 1888, 1.

"A Mystery," *The Fort Wayne Journal Gazette*, September 20, 1893, 4.

"Accidents," Northumberland County Democrat, September 3, 1875, 3.

"Administrator's Notice," *Northumberland County Democrat*, February 23, 1899, 2.

Alexander, Diane, "The Recent Rise in Health Care Inflation." *Chicago Fed Letter*, no. 407, 2018, accessed January 5, 2025, https://www.chicagofed.org/publications/chicago-fed-letter/2018/407.

Altick, Richard D. "Pranks and Punishment in an Old Pennsylvania College," *Pennsylvania History: A Journal of Mid-Atlantic Studies* 4, no. 4 (1937): 241.

"At the Stricken City," *The Sunbury American*, June 21, 1889, 1.

Baker, Holly Cutting. "Patent Medicine in Pennsylvania Before 1906." *Pennsylvania Folklife* 27, no. 2 (Winter 1977–78): 20–33.

"Brandon," *The Sunbury Gazette*, February 20, 1864, 2.

Brossman, Schuyler. "Surname File Genealogists' Boon." *Sunday-The Daily News*, March 22, 1981. https://www.newspapers.com/clip/55031899/sunday-the-daily-news/.

———. "Researcher tracing Muths from Lebanon, Berks counties." *The Daily News*, February 22, 1993. https://www.newspapers.com/clip/55030995/the-daily-news/.

Buklijas, Tatjana. "Cultures of Death and Politics of Corpse Supply: Anatomy in Vienna, 1848–1914." *Bulletin of the History of Medicine* 82, no. 3 (2008): 570–607. http://www.jstor.org/stable/44448613.

Burlakoff, Nikolai. "Richard Mercer Dorson (1916–1981): A Memorate." *Journal of American Folklore* 131, no. 519 (2018): 91+.

Butler, S. W. *The Medical and Surgical Reporter*, Vol. XXVIII, No. 3 (January 18, 1873).

———. *The Medical and Surgical Reporter*, Vol. XXIX, No. 26 (December 27, 1873).

———. *The Medical and Surgical Reporter*, Vol. XXX, No. 3 (January 17, 1874).

———. *The Medical and Surgical Reporter*, Vol. XXXI, No. 7 (August 15, 1874).

"Capture of Savannah," *Northumberland County Democrat*, December 30, 1864, 2.

"Capture of Savannah," *The Sunbury Gazette, and Northumberland County Republican*, December 31, 1864, 2.

"Cholera in the East," *The Sunbury Gazette*, Nov. 20, 1874, 4.

Colbert, Lisa. "Amish Attitudes and Treatment of Illness." *Pennsylvania Folklife* 30, no. 1 (Autumn 1980): 9–15.

Coombs, Jan Coombs. "Rural Medical Practice in the 1880s: A View from Central Wisconsin." *Bulletin of the History of Medicine* 64, no. 1 (1990): 35–62.

"Court," *Reading Times*, January 31, 1884, 4.

"Death of Abraham Deppen," *Northumberland County Democrat*, August 14, 1899, 1.

"Death of Dr. A. J. Kantz," *Lykens Register*, February 2, 1899, 1.

"Death of Dr. A. J. Kantz," *Lykens Register*, February 2, 1899, 1.

"Death of Dr. Haas," *The Sunbury American*, February 3, 1905, 2.

"Death of Lee L. Grumbine," *Lebanon Courier*, August 24, 1904.

"Declaration of Independence," *Lancaster Intelligencer Journal*, July 4, 1826, 2.

Densmore, Christopher, "Understanding and Using Early Nineteenth Century Account Books." *The Midwestern Archivist* 5, no. 1 (1980): 5–19. http://www.jstor.org/stable/41101497.

"Died," *Northumberland County Democrat*, May 2, 1879, 3.

"Died," *Snyder County Tribune*, May 25, 1882, 2.

Dine, Sarah Blank. "Diaries and Doctors: Elizabeth Drinker and Philadelphia Medical Practice, 1760–1810." *Pennsylvania History* 68, no. 4 (2001): 413–34.

"Dissolution of Partnership," *Sunbury Gazette*, May 5, 1882, 2.

"Dr. A. H. Smink Dies Suddenly at Residence," *Shamokin News-Dispatch*, January 17, 1941.

"Dr. Frederick Thayer," *The Fort Wayne Journal Gazette*, January 19, 1893, pg, 3.

"Dr. Grumbine Passed Away This Morning," *The Daily News* (Lebanon, Pennsylvania), February 16, 1923, 6.

"Dr. J. S. Krebs Dies at Home," *Shamokin News-Dispatch*, June 10, 1938, 2.

"Dr. Lewis Royer Dead," *The Philadelphia Inquirer*, October 28, 1904, 4.

"Dr. Norwood Fills Loma Linda School of Medicine Post," *The San Bernardino County Sun*, October 6, 1961, 16.

"Dr. Thayer," *The Fort Wayne Journal Gazette*, October 1, 1893, 8.

"Dr. Thayer's" advertisement, circa 1888, found in Reuben H. Muth, Physician's Daybooks, vol. 24 (1858–1898, in possession of Lawrence Knorr.)

"Dr. Traill Green Dead," *The Times Leader* (Wilkes-Barre, Pennsylvania), May 4, 1897, 3.

Donmoyer, Patrick. "Joseph H. Hageman: Doctor, Baucher, Legend in 'Hexe-Schteddel.' *The Historical Review of Berks County* 81, 1 (2015): 30.

Dudley, Anú King. "Moxa in Nineteenth-Century Medical Practice." *Journal of the History of Medicine and Allied Sciences* 65, no. 2 (2010): 187–206.

Duffin, Jacalyn. "Census versus Medical Daybooks: a Comparison of Two Sources on Mortality in Nineteenth-Century Ontario." *Continuity and Change* 12, no. 2 (1997): 199–219.

Dugan, Patrick James. "The Origin and Practition of Pow-Wow Among the Pennsylvania Germans." *The Historical Review of Berks County* 53, 3 (1988): 134.

"Elderly Resident of Red Cross Dies," *Shamokin News-Dispatch*, February 5, 1962, 3.

"Election Returns for Northumberland County - Official," *The Sunbury Gazette*, October 15, 1864, 2.

"Escape of General Lee," *The Sunbury Gazette and Northumberland County Republican*, July 18, 1863, 2.

Estep, Glenn R. "A Medical Doctor's Experiences with the Amish." *The Pennsylvania Dutchman* 2, no. 22 (1950): 2.

"Figures of the Great Bridge," *The Sunbury Weekly News*, June 8, 1883.

Finger, Simon. "An Indissoluble Union: How the American War for Independence Transformed Philadelphia's Medical Community and Created a Public Health Establishment." *Pennsylvania History* 77, no. 1 (2010): 37–72.

"Fire at Mahanoy," *Northumberland County Democrat*, May 10, 1878, 3.

"Fire," *The Sunbury Gazette*, March 16, 1861, 2.

"For President," *Northumberland County Democrat*, May 22, 1864, 2.

"Frederick Muth," Berks County Wills, 1847 TU, pg 21.

"From Jackson Township," *Northumberland County Democrat*, April 2, 1880, 3.

"From Mahanoy, Jackson twp.," *Northumberland County Democrat*, August 16, 1878, 2.

"From Mahanoy," *Northumberland County Democrat*, July 27, 1883.

"From Mahanoy," *Northumberland County Democrat*, August 31, 1883.

"From Mahanoy," *Northumberland County Democrat*, April 11, 1884, 4.

"From Mahanoy," *Northumberland County Democrat*, August 1, 1884, 4.

"From Mahanoy" *Northumberland County Democrat*, Apr 19, 1889, 4.

"From Mahanoy," *Northumberland County Democrat*, May 7, 1891, 4.

"From Mahanoy," *Northumberland County Democrat*, October 15, 1891, 4.

"From Mahanoy," *Northumberland County Democrat*, July 14, 1898, 4.

"From Mahanoy," *Northumberland County Democrat*, September 29, 1898, 4.

"From Mahanoy," *Northumberland County Democrat*, November 24, 1898, 4.

"From Mahanoy," *Northumberland County Democrat*, January 12, 1899, 4.

"From Mahanoy," *Northumberland County Democrat*, January 26, 1899, 4.

"From Mahanoy," *Sunbury Daily*, February 1, 1899, 6.

"From Mahanoy." *Northumberland County Democrat*, February 2, 1899, 4.

"From Mahanoy," *Northumberland County Democrat*, February 9, 1899, 4.

"From Mahanoy," *Northumberland County Democrat*, February 16, 1899, 4.

"From Mahanoy," *Northumberland County Democrat*, March 2, 1899, 4.

"From Mahanoy," *Northumberland County Democrat*, April 13, 1899, 4.

"From Mahanoy," *Northumberland County Democrat*, May 11, 1899, 4.

"From Mahanoy," *Northumberland County Democrat*, July 6, 1899, 4.

"From Mahanoy," *Northumberland County Democrat*, August 3, 1899, 4.

"From Mahanoy," *Northumberland County Democrat*, August 31, 1899, 4.

"From the Lower End," *Northumberland County Democrat*, June 13, 1873, 3.

"From the Lower End," *Sunbury Daily*, August 14, 1874, 1.

Gard, Richard, "In Memoriam: Joseph Francis Kett," *Virginia* 113, 23 (Summer 2024): 68.

"Garfield," *Northumberland County Democrat*, July 8, 1881, 1.

"Gave No Bonds," *Fort Wayne Daily News*, August 2, 1895, 1.

Gibson, James E. "John Augustus Otto." *The Historical Review of Berks County* 13, 1 (1947): 17.

"Goes To Jail," *Fort Wayne Daily News*, December 18, 1895, 1.

"Governor Hoyt's Biennial Message," *The Patriot-News*, January 5, 1881, 3.

"H.B. Smith," *The Daily Item* (Sunbury, Pennsylvania), August 3, 1897, 4.

"Hassler, Jacob," Genealogical Card File. Lancaster Mennonite Historical Society, Lancaster, Pennsylvania.

"He Denies It," *Fort Wayne Daily News*, December 17, 1895, 1.

Heindel, Ned D. & Natalie I. Foster. "The Allentown Academy: America's First German Medical School." *Pennsylvania Folklife* 30, no. 1 (Autumn 1980): 2–8.

"Herndon Happenings," *The Sunbury Gazette*, January 27, 1899, 14.

"Herndon, Dec, 11, 1869," *The Sunbury Gazette*, December 11, 1869, 3.

Higgins, James E. "'Under the Stimulus of Great Epidemics': Reformers, Epidemics, and the Rise of State Level Public Health in Pennsylvania, 1872–1905." *Pennsylvania History* 84, no. 2 (2017): 214–38.

"Improving," *The Sunbury Gazette and Northumberland County Republican*, January 17, 1863, 2.

"In a New Role," *The Fort Wayne News and Sentinel*, October 11, 1893, 1.

Jones, Claire L. "Instruments of Medical Information: The Rise of the Medical Trade Catalog in Britain, 1750–1914." *Technology and Culture* 54, no. 3 (2013): 563–99.

Jones, Jonathan S. "What Can (and Can't) We Learn From 19th Century Physicians' Account Books?" from *Fugitive Leaves: a blog from The Historical Medical Library of The College of Physicians of Philadelphia*, viewed at https://histmed.collegeofphysicians.org/19th-century-physicians-account-books/.

Kett, Joseph F. *The Formation of the American Medical Profession: The Role of Institutions, 1780–1860*. New Haven, Ct.: Yale University Press, 1968.

Korff, Emily Adams. "The Widow Was a Midwife." *The Historical Review of Berks County* 92, no. 1 (Winter 2025): 8–11.

"Latest News," *The Sunbury Gazette and Northumberland County Republican*, July 4, 1863, 2.

Lazear, Edward P. "Culture and Language." *Journal of Political Economy* 107, no. S6 (1999): S95–126.

Leavitt, Judith Walzer. "'A Worrying Profession': The Domestic Environment of Medical Practice in Mid-Nineteenth-Century America." *Bulletin of the History of Medicine* 69, no. 1 (1995): 1–29.

"Lewis Royer and Isabella Tryon, 27 July 1841," *Historical Society of Pennsylvania, Marriage Records, 1512–1989*. Historical Society of Pennsylvania, Philadelphia, Pennsylvania, accessed January 13, 2025, at https://www.familysearch.org/ark:/61903/1:1:6CYF-2HTZ.

Livingood, M.D., Louis J. "The Pioneer Doctor." *The Historical Review of Berks County* 1, 3 (1936): 75.

"Local Affairs," *The Miners' Journal*, March 22, 1851, 2.

"Local Affairs," *Reading Times*, Oct 16, 1872, 1.

"Local Shorts," *The Sunbury Weekly News*, December 4, 1885, pg 3.

Lockard, Priscilla Stevenson. "Our Good Old One-Room School Days." *Pennsylvania Folklife* 35, no. 1 (Fall 1985): 13.

"Mahanoy Correspondence," *Northumberland County Democrat*, October 9, 1868, 3.

"Mahanoy Matters," *The Daily Item* (Sunbury, Pennsylvania), August 30, 1894, 2.

"Mahanoy Matters," *The Daily Item* (Sunbury, Pennsylvania), October 3, 1894, 4.

"Mahanoy, Pennsylvania, Dec. 19, 1870," *Northumberland County Democrat*, August 12, 1870, 2.

"Mahanoy, Pennsylvania, July 19, 1870" *Northumberland County Democrat*, July 22, 1870, 3.

"Mahanoy," *Northumberland County Democrat*, July 25, 1873, 3.

"Mahanoy," *Northumberland County Democrat*, December 10, 1886, 4.

"Mahanoy," *Northumberland County Democrat*, May 20, 1887, 4.

"Mahanoy," *Northumberland County Democrat*, May 2, 1888, 4.

"Mahanoy," *Northumberland County Democrat*, May 18, 1888, 4.

"Mahanoy," *Northumberland County Democrat*, June 22, 1888, 4.

"Mahanoy," *Northumberland County Democrat*, December 6, 1889, 4.

"Maine Was Blown Up," *The Daily News* (Mt. Carmel, Pennsylvania), March 1, 1898, 1.

"Mandata," *Sunbury Daily*, February 1, 1899, 6.

"Marion, Sept. 27, 1859," *Reading Times*, September 29, 1859, 2.

"Marriages," *Sunbury Weekly News*, July 20, 1888, 3.

"Married." *Northumberland County Democrat*, June 21, 1861, page 3.

McGovern, Constance M. "The Community, the Hospital, and the Working-Class Patient: The Multiple Uses of Asylum in Nineteenth-Century America." *Pennsylvania History* 54, no. 1 (1987): 17–33.

"Michael Gordon Ruby," Sons of the American Revolution Membership Applications, 1889–1970.

"Middletown Matters," *The News* (Frederick, Maryland), April 20, 1889, 4.

"Mrs. E. Roberts," *Public Ledger* (Philadelphia), March 3, 1853, 2.

Mullin, Emily. "How Tuberculosis Shaped Victorian Fashion," *Smithsonian*, May 10, 2016, accessed November 28, 2024, https://www.smithsonianmag.com/science-nature/how-tuberculosis-shaped-victorian-fashion-180959029/.

"Muth Estate to Relatives, Friend," *The Daily Item*, February 20, 1962, 8.

"Muth, Frederick" Berks County Indentures, Book 53, Page 685.

"Muth: Infant Son," *List of Graves from St. Peters Church, Red Cross, Northumberland County, Pennsylvania*, compiled 1992 by Ralph E. French.

"National Prosperity for the New Year," *The Sunbury Gazette*, January 9, 1864, 1.

"Neighboring Notes," *Northumberland County Democrat*, July 23, 1886, 1.

"New Advertisements," *Northumberland County Democrat*, December 23, 1870, 3.

"New Subscribers," *Northumberland County Democrat*, May 22, 1864, 2.

"North'd County Medical Association," *Northumberland County Democrat*, July 16, 1869, 3.

Oda, Wilbur H. "An early Proponent of Medical Hypnosis in America." *The Pennsylvania Dutchman* 2, no. 1 (1950): 1.

"Oh! Doctor!" *Fort Wayne Weekly Journal*, October 5, 1893, 8.

"Old Tombstones in Cemetery of the Altalaha Evangelical Lutheran Church, Rehrersburg, Tulpehocken Twp. Berks County, Penna.," Genealogical Society of Pennsylvania, 7, no. 214, accessed December 30, 2024, https://genpa.org/wp-content/uploads/member-collections/fritz-berryman/OldTombstone_AltalahaEvangelical-Berks.pdf.

"Once More," *The Fort Wayne Journal Gazette*, October 12, 1893, 4.

Osborne, John B. "The Lancaster County Cholera Epidemic of 1854 and the Challenge to the Miasma Theory of Disease." *The Pennsylvania Magazine of History and Biography* 133, no. 1 (2009): 5–28.

"Other Items," *Northumberland County Democrat*, October 5, 1883.

"Our Herndon Letter," *The Sunbury Weekly News*, September 27, 1889, 2.

"Ourselves," *The Sunbury Gazette and Northumberland County Republican*, June 20, 1863, 2.

"Out on Bonds," *Fort Wayne Daily News*, August 9, 1895, 1.

"Overwhelmed," *The Sunbury American*, June 7, 1889, 1.

Peitzman, Steven J. "The Fielding H. Garrison Lecture: 'I Am Their Physician': Dr. Owen J. Wister of Germantown and His Too Many Patients." *Bulletin of the History of Medicine* 83, no. 2 (2009): 245–270. https://doi:10.1353/bhm.0.0200.

"Pennsylvania Invaded," *The Sunbury Gazette and Northumberland County Republican*, June 20, 1863, 2.

"Pennsylvania Superstitions," *Northumberland County Democrat*, August 1, 1890, 1.

"Personal Paragraphs," *The Daily Item* (Sunbury, Pennsylvania), February 6, 1899, 1.

"Personal Paragraphs," *The Daily Item* (Sunbury, Pennsylvania), June 24, 1898, 1.

"Personal," *Northumberland County Democrat*, December 25, 1890, 1.

Prechtel-Kluskens, Claire. "Researching the Career of a 19th-Century Physician." *Prologue Magazine* 36, no. 2 (Summer 2004). Accessed online at: https://www.archives.gov/publications/prologue/2004/summer/genea-doctor.html.

"Presidential Election Returns for Northumberland County," *The Sunbury Gazette*, November 12, 1864, 2.

"Public Sale of Estate of Lulu Muth," *The Daily Item*, June 22, 1962, 19.

"Public Sale of Real Estate," *Northumberland County Democrat*, October 15, 1880, 4.

"Puerperal Fever," *Fort Wayne Weekly Journal*, September 21, 1893, 5.

Rausch, David A. "Civil War Medicine: A Patient's Account." *Pennsylvania Folklife* 26, no. 5 (Summer 1977): 46–48.

"Red Cross Woman Dies At The Age of 93." *Shamokin News-Dispatch*, October 10, 1928, 1.

"Reminiscences of Sch. Haven And Vicinity By One Of Its Early Citizens." *The Call* (Schuylkill Haven, Pennsylvania), December 16, 1910, 1.

"Rev. Clement Z. Weiser Dead," *Lancaster Intelligencer Journal*, March 2, 1898, 4.

Riznik, Barnes. "The Professional Lives of Early Nineteenth-Century New England Doctors." *Journal of the History of Medicine and Allied Sciences* 19, no. 1 (January 1964): 1–16.

"Riznik Resigns At SSC, Takes Post At Museum," *Turlock Journal*, July 9, 1962, 2.

"Rothstein, William 'Bill' G.," *Baltimore Sun*, December 8, 2020, A8.

"Rural Man Found Dead in His Bed," *Shamokin News-Dispatch*, July 14, 1942, 3.

Sahli, Nancy. "A Stick to Break Our Heads With: Elizabeth Blackwell and Philadelphia Medicine." *Pennsylvania History*, vol. 44, no. 4, 1977, pp. 335–47.

"Sampson Has Taken Porto Rico," *The Daily News* (Mt. Carmel, Pennsylvania), May 13, 1898, 2.

Savitt, Todd L. "Physician Price Fixing in 19th Century Virginia" exhibit at The Claude Moore Health Sciences Library, University of Virginia, viewed at: http://blog.hsl.virginia.edu/feebill/credits/.

Schwalm, Leslie A. "A Body of 'Truly Scientific Work': The U.S. Sanitary Commission and the Elaboration of Race in the Civil War Era." *The Journal of the Civil War Era* 8, no. 4 (12, 2018): 647,676,739.

"Schuylkill Haven No. 4," *The Miners' Journal*, January 10, 1846, 2.

"Sent to Jail," *Fort Wayne Weekly Sentinel*, August 3, 1895, 1.

Severs, Susan R. & Abraham R. Horne. "Anglicizing the Pennsylvania Dutch: 1966 and 1875." *Pennsylvania Folklife* 16, no. 3 (Spring 1967): 46.

Shafer, Henry Burnell. "Medicine in Old Philadelphia." *Pennsylvania History* 4, no. 1 (1937): 21–31.

"Short Locals," *Juniata Sentinel and Republican*, June 2, 1886, 3.

"Shot Himself," *The Sunbury Gazette*, May 10, 1872, 3.

Shryock, Richard H. "A Century of Medical Progress in Philadelphia: 1750–1850." *Pennsylvania History* 8, no. 1 (1941): 7–28.

"Slavery to be Abolished" *The Sunbury Gazette*, February 4, 1865, 2.

Slawson, R.G. "Medical Training in the United States Prior to the Civil War." *Journal of Evidence-Based Complementary & Alternative Medicine.* 2012;17(1):11–27.

"South Fork Club Guilty," *Northumberland County Democrat*, July 12, 1889, 3.

"Spain Assents," *The Daily News* (Mt. Carmel, Pennsylvania), August 12, 1898, 1.

Starr, Paul. "Medicine, Economy and Society in Nineteenth-Century America." *Journal of Social History* 10, no. 4 (Jun 01, 1977): 588.

Stowe, Steven M. "Seeing Themselves at Work: Physicians and the Case Narrative in the Mid- Mid-Nineteenth-Century American South." *The American Historical Review* 101, no. 1 (1996): 41–79.

"Strikers and Deputies Battle Near Hazleton," *Mount Carmel Item* (Sunbury, Pennsylvania), September 11, 1897, 1.

"Sunbury Siftings," *Northumberland County Democrat*, August 20, 1886, 1.

Temkin, Owsei. "Richard Harrison Shryock: 1893–1972." *Journal of the History of Medicine and Allied Sciences* 27, no. 2 (1972): 131–32. http://www.jstor.org/stable/24622073.

"The Avon Park Fair," *Reading Times*, September 22, 1871.

"The Cholera Epidemic in Europe," *The Sunbury Gazette*, Feb. 6, 1874, 4.

"The Congressional vote of the 14th District," *The Sunbury Gazette*, October 22, 1864, 2.

"The Fair Full-Blown," *Public Press* (Northumberland, Pennsylvania), Mary 12, 1893, 1.

"The family of Daniel Schlegel," *Northumberland County Democrat*, May 13, 1887, 4.

"The Fruits of Copperhead Teaching – The Riots and Murders in the Coal Region," *The Sunbury Gazette*, November 28, 1863, 1.

"The Great Freshet" *The Sunbury Gazette*, March 25, 1865, 2.

"The Great Riots – The Draft," *The Sunbury Gazette*, August 1, 1863, 3.

"The Invasion," *The Sunbury Gazette and Northumberland County Republican*, June 27, 1863, 2.

"The late Frederick Muth," *Reading Times*, December 28, 1883, 1.

"The late panic," *Sunbury Gazette*, September 26, 1873, 2.

"The Maine Is Being Remembered," *The Daily Item* (Sunbury, Pennsylvania), May 2, 1898, 2.

"The National Calamity" *The Sunbury Gazette*, April 22, 1865, 2.

"The Physician's Register," *The Sunbury Weekly News*, Aug 26, 1881, 2.

"The Physician's Register," *The Sunbury Weekly News*, Aug 26, 1881, 2.

"The Physician's Register" *The Sunbury Weekly News*, Aug 26, 1881, 2.

"The Physicians of Northumberland County," *The Sunbury Gazette*, April 21, 1876, 3.

"The President Dead," *Northumberland County Democrat*, September 23, 1881, 2.

"The Raid," *The Sunbury Gazette*, August 7, 1864, 2.

"The Riots in New York," *The Sunbury Gazette and Northumberland County Republican*, July 18, 1863, 2.

"The Sun's Eclipse," *The Philadelphia Times*, August 30, 1886, 2.

"The Treaty and the People," *Northumberland County Democrat*, December 15, 1898, 2.

"To Be Arrested," *The Fort Wayne News and Sentinel*, April 20, 1893, 1.

Tomes, Nancy. "The Great American Medicine Show Revisited." *Bulletin of the History of Medicine* 79, no. 4 (2005): 627–663.

"Two New Laws," *The Patriot-News*, June 15, 1881, 1.

"Victory! Victory!" *The Sunbury Gazette*, April 15, 1865, 2.

"Was It Murder?" *The Fort Wayne News and Sentinel*, September 19, 1893, 1.

Weaver, Karol K. "'She Knew All the Old Remedies': Medical Caregiving and Neighborhood Women of the Anthracite Coal Region of Pennsylvania." *Pennsylvania History* 71, no. 4 (2004): 421–44.

Webster, Ian, "CPI Inflation Calculator" at www.in2013dollars.com.

"Went to Jail," *Fort Wayne Weekly Sentinel*, August 2, 1895, 1.

Wilson, Renate, and Woodrow J. Savacool. "The Theory and Practice of Pharmacy in Pennsylvania: Observations on Two Colonial Country Doctors." *Pennsylvania History* 68, no. 1 (2001): 31–65.

Secondary: Online Resources

"A Earl Deppen," Find a Grave, Memorial ID 46115501, accessed January 5, 2025, https://www.findagrave.com/memorial/46115501/a-earl-deppen.

"A Reference Handbook of the Medical Sciences," Civil War Medical Books, accessed December 31, 2024, http://www.civilwarmedicalbooks.com/Reference_Handbook_Medical_Sciences.html.

"Abraham Wentzell Schlegel" Find a Grave, Memorial ID 16065936, accessed January 5, 2025, https://www.findagrave.com/memorial/16065936/abraham-wentzell-schlegel.

"Albert Zartman Drumheller," Find a Grave, Memorial ID 38943627, accessed January 5, 2025, https://www.findagrave.com/memorial/38943627/albert-zartman-drumheller.

"Andrew Jackson 'A.J.' Kantz," Find a Grave, Memorial ID 30549467, accessed January 5, 2025, https://www.findagrave.com/memorial/30549467/andrew-jackson-kantz.

"Andrew L. Bucher," Find a Grave, Memorial ID 38916147, accessed January 5, 2025, https://www.findagrave.com/memorial/38916147/andrew-bucher.

"Anna Maria Schneider Muth," Find a Grave, Memorial ID 61620324, accessed January 5, 2025, https://www.findagrave.com/memorial/61620324/anna-maria-muth.

"Antique Visiting Country Doctor Pocket Ledger List Mahanoy PA 1858–1898 Old Book," eBay Listing for Item# 300781949802, accessed January 13, 2025 at https://www.ebay.com/itm/300781949802?ViewItem=&item=300781949802.

"Benjamin Franklin Latshaw," Find a Grave, Memorial ID 46471539, accessed January 5, 2025, https://www.findagrave.com/memorial/46471539/benjamin-franklin-latshaw.

"Benneville Lahr," Find a Grave, Memorial ID 39011245, accessed January 5, 2025, https://www.findagrave.com/memorial/39011245/benneville-lahr.

"Bertha A Treon Champion," Find a Grave, Memorial ID 185773999, accessed January 5, 2025, https://www.findagrave.com/memorial/185773999/bertha_a_champion.

"Caroline Rubendale Reed," Find a Grave, Memorial ID 46398816, accessed January 5, 2025, https://www.findagrave.com/memorial/46398816/caroline_reed.

"Casper Sowers," Find a Grave, Memorial ID 133848803, accessed December 30, 2024, https://www.findagrave.com/memorial/133848803/casper_sowers.

"Charles Clinton Wynn," Family Search, Record ID LHFV-GD8, accessed January 5, 2025, https://ancestors.familysearch.org/en/LHFV-GD8/charles-clinton-wynn -1863-1945.

"Charles Morris Brown," Find a Grave, Memorial ID 46116090, accessed January 5, 2025, https://www.findagrave.com/memorial/46116090/charles_morris_brown.

"Claude Clarance Reitz," Find a Grave, Memorial ID 39060508, accessed January 5, 2025, https://www.findagrave.com/memorial/39060508/claude_clarence_reitz.

"David Hottenstein," Find a Grave, Memorial ID 38976168, accessed January 5, 2025, https://www.findagrave.com/memorial/38976168/david-hottenstein.

"Dr Daniel Garrison Brinton," Find a Grave, Memorial ID 4201592, accessed January 5, 2025, https://www.findagrave.com/memorial/4201592/daniel-garrison-brinton.

"Dr Joseph Priestley," Find a Grave, Memorial ID 225692022, accessed January 12, 2025, https://www.findagrave.com/memorial/225692022/joseph-priestley.

"Dr. John Blair Deaver Sr." Find a Grave, Memorial ID 89336532, accessed January 5, 2025, https://www.findagrave.com/memorial/89336532/john-blair-deaver.

"Dr. Reuben H Muth" Find a Grave, Memorial ID 38942306, accessed January 5, 2025, https://www.findagrave.com/memorial/38942306/reuben-h-muth.

"Edmund J Muth," Find a Grave, Memorial ID 35875894, accessed January 5, 2025, https://www.findagrave.com/memorial/35875894/edmund-j-muth.

"Elias K Kobel," Find a Grave, Memorial ID 38975635, accessed January 5, 2025, https://www.findagrave.com/memorial/38975635/elias-k-kobel.

"Eve E Hoffman Deppen," Find a Grave, Memorial ID 38942353, accessed January 5, 2025, https://www.findagrave.com/memorial/38942353/eve-e-deppen.

"Franklyn T 'Frank' Wolf" Find a Grave, Memorial ID 38962465, accessed January 5, 2025, https://www.findagrave.com/memorial/38962465/franklyn-t-wolf.

"Friederick Muth," Find a Grave, Memorial ID 61620552, accessed December 30, 2024, https://www.findagrave.com/memorial/61620552/friederick-muth.

"George H. Malick," Find a Grave, Memorial ID 243247595, accessed January 5, 2025, https://www.findagrave.com/memorial/243247595/george_h_malick.

"George McClellan Lahr," Find a Grave, Memorial ID 39011455, accessed January 5, 2025, https://www.findagrave.com/memorial/39011455/george_mcclellan_lahr.

"George S Treon," Find a Grave, Memorial ID 34684226, accessed January 5, 2025, https://www.findagrave.com/memorial/34684226/george-samuel-treon.

"George Snyder," Find a Grave, Memorial ID 46318400, accessed January 5, 2025, https://www.findagrave.com/memorial/46318400/george-snyder.

"George Washington Malick," Find a Grave, Memorial ID 191046540, accessed January 5, 2025, https://www.findagrave.com/memorial/191046540/george_washington _malick.

"George Washington Ruby," Find a Grave, Memorial ID 207413571, accessed December 30, 2024, https://www.findagrave.com/memorial/207413571/george -washington-ruby.

"Godfrey Reitz," Find a Grave, Memorial ID 34697571, accessed January 5, 2025, https://www.findagrave.com/memorial/34697571/godfrey_reitz.

"Henry Adam Hilbush," Find a Grave, Memorial ID 39186213, accessed January 5, 2025, https://www.findagrave.com/memorial/39186213/henry_adam_hilbush.

"Henry Kurr," Find a Grave, Memorial ID 32409950, accessed January 5, 2025, https://www.findagrave.com/memorial/32409950/henry-kurr.

"Henry Peiffer," Find a Grave, Memorial ID 46497942, accessed January 5, 2025, https://www.findagrave.com/memorial/46497942/henry-peiffer.

"Henry T. Bowman," Find a Grave, Memorial ID 38620383, accessed January 5, 2025, https://www.findagrave.com/memorial/38620383/henry-t-bowman.

"Henry Z Drumheller," Find a Grave, Memorial ID 46467211, accessed January 5, 2025, https://www.findagrave.com/memorial/46467211/henry_z_drumheller.

"Herndon Camp Meeting, 1874–1983," accessed at https://www.lykensvalley.org/herndon-camp-meeting-1874-1983/.

"Isaac F Rebuck," Find a Grave, Memorial ID 34650004, accessed January 5, 2025, https://www.findagrave.com/memorial/34650004/isaac-f-rebuck.

"Israel Daniel Lahr," Find a Grave, Memorial ID 52309720, accessed January 5, 2025, https://www.findagrave.com/memorial/52309720/israel_daniel_lahr.

"Jacob Romberger Hilbush," Find a Grave, Memorial ID 38974922, accessed January 5, 2025, https://www.findagrave.com/memorial/38974922/jacob-romberger -hilbush.

"Jacob Samuel Wynn," Family Search, Record ID KLXF-D1B, accessed January 5, 2025, https://ancestors.familysearch.org/en/KLXF-D1B/jacob-samuel-wynn-1834 -1911.

"Jeremiah 'Jerry' Treon," Find a Grave, Memorial ID 51078484, accessed January 5, 2025, https://www.findagrave.com/memorial/51078484/jeremiah_treon.

"Joel Drumheller Heim," Find a Grave, Memorial ID 34482727, accessed January 5, 2025, https://www.findagrave.com/memorial/34482727/joel-drumheller-heim.

"Johann Jacob Schneider," Find a Grave, Memorial ID 34127162, accessed January 5, 2025, https://www.findagrave.com/memorial/34127162/johann_jacob_schneider.

"Johann Peter Schneider," Find a Grave, Memorial ID 34445042, accessed January 5, 2025, https://www.findagrave.com/memorial/34445042/johann_peter_schneider.

"John Bahner," Find a Grave, Memorial ID 51082257, accessed January 5, 2025, https://www.findagrave.com/memorial/51082257/john-banher.

"John Deppen," Find a Grave, Memorial ID 38942145, accessed January 5, 2025, https://www.findagrave.com/memorial/38942145/john-deppen.

"John George Lahr," Find a Grave, Memorial ID 38943301, accessed January 5, 2025, https://www.findagrave.com/memorial/38943301/john_george_lahr.

"John Muth," Find a Grave, Memorial ID 35875897, accessed December 30, 2024, https://www.findagrave.com/memorial/35875897/john-muth.

"John Muth," Find a Grave, Memorial ID 35875897, accessed January 5, 2025, https://www.findagrave.com/memorial/35875897/john-muth.

"John Oliver Ogle" Great Register Sonoma County (California), 107 no. 4264, accessed January 13, 2025 at: https://www.ancestry.com/search/collections/2221/records /4281632?tid=&pid=&queryId=3a0ab065-0d28-4b0b-9ab3-c6da8c286175&_ phsrc=GLB373&_phstart=successSource.

"Lawrence D Deppen," Find a Grave, Memorial ID 46318966, accessed January 5, 2025, https://www.findagrave.com/memorial/46318966/lawrence_d_deppen.

"Leah Deppen Bower," Find a Grave, Memorial ID 46466166, accessed January 5, 2025, https://www.findagrave.com/memorial/46466166/leah-bower.

"Lewis Royer," (Pennsylvania) Senate Library, Biography ID: 4358, accessed January 13, 2025, at https://www.library.pasen.gov/people/member-biography?id=4358.

"Lulu Herrold Muth," Find a Grave, Memorial ID 38972687, accessed January 5, 2025, https://www.findagrave.com/memorial/38972687/lulu-muth.

"Mary Ann Mertz Deppen," Find a Grave, Memorial ID 46318466, accessed January 5, 2025, https://www.findagrave.com/memorial/46318466/mary-ann-deppen.

"Mary Fisher Wolf Klick," Find a Grave, Memorial ID 26823234, accessed December 30, 2024, https://www.findagrave.com/memorial/26823234/mary_fisher_klick.

"Mary Louisa Muth," Find a Grave, Memorial ID 46387012, accessed January 5, 2025, at https://www.findagrave.com/memorial/46387012/mary_louisa_updegrove.

"Michael Bower," Find a Grave, Memorial ID 46466131, accessed January 5, 2025, https://www.findagrave.com/memorial/46466131/michael_bower.

"Milton Drumheller," Find a Grave, Memorial ID 34163405, accessed January 5, 2025, https://www.findagrave.com/memorial/34163405/milton-drumheller.

"Moses Merkel Wiest," Find a Grave, Memorial ID 28674352, accessed January 5, 2025, https://www.findagrave.com/memorial/28674352/moses-merkel-wiest.

"Nathan Charles Schlegel," Find a Grave, Memorial ID 102923475, accessed January 5, 2025, https://www.findagrave.com/memorial/102923475/nathan-charles-schlegel.

"Nettie I Deppen Rubendall," Find a Grave, Memorial ID 46415767, accessed January 5, 2025,https://www.findagrave.com/memorial/46415767/nettie_i_rubendall.

"Noah Klock," Find a Grave, Memorial ID 46378509, accessed January 5, 2025, https://www.findagrave.com/memorial/46378509/harvey_klock.

"Rachel Elizabeth Shipman," Family Search, Record ID KDMQ-W5D, accessed January 5, 2025, https://ancestors.familysearch.org/en/KDMQ-W5D/rachel-elizabeth-shipman-1805-1890.

"Rev John Gring," Find a Grave, Memorial ID 31313675, accessed December 30, 2024, https://www.findagrave.com/memorial/31313675/john-gring.

"Richard Muth," Find a Grave, Memorial ID 35875899, accessed January 5, 2025, https://www.findagrave.com/memorial/35875899/richard-muth.

"Samuel Gross Wagner," Find a Grave, Memorial ID 87369979, accessed December 30, 2024, https://www.findagrave.com/memorial/87369979/samuel-gross-wagner.

"Samuel Snyder," Find a Grave, Memorial ID 32416113, accessed January 5, 2025, https://www.findagrave.com/memorial/32416113/samuel-snyder.

"Samuel Treon," Find a Grave, Memorial ID 34693553, accessed January 5, 2025, https://www.findagrave.com/memorial/34693553/samuel_treon.

"Sarah Deppen Snyder," Find a Grave, Memorial ID 46318380, accessed January 5, 2025, https://www.findagrave.com/memorial/46318380/sarah-snyder.

"Sarah Shaffer Deppen," Find a Grave, Memorial ID 59854698, accessed January 5, 2025, https://www.findagrave.com/memorial/59854698/sarah-deppen.

"Saviry William Brown," Find a Grave, Memorial ID 46115831, accessed January 5, 2025, https://www.findagrave.com/memorial/46115831/saviry_william_brown.

"Solomon Tressler," Find a Grave, Memorial ID 38943167, accessed January 5, 2025, https://www.findagrave.com/memorial/38943167/solomon-tressler.

Webster, Ian, "CPI Inflation Calculator," accessed January 5, 2025, https://www.in2013dollars.com/us/inflation/1863?amount=1.

"William C Otto," Find a Grave, Memorial ID 46387783, accessed January 5, 2025, https://www.findagrave.com/memorial/46387783/william-c-otto.

"William Deppen," Find a Grave, Memorial ID 39931396, accessed January 5, 2025, https://www.findagrave.com/memorial/39931396/william-deppen.

"William Michael Zartman," Find a Grave, Memorial ID 52589518, accessed January 5, 2025, https://www.findagrave.com/memorial/52589518/william-michael-zartman.

"William Saviry Brown," Find a Grave, Memorial ID 208872330, accessed January 5, 2025, https://www.findagrave.com/memorial/208872330/william_saviry_brown.

"Wilson K Drumheller," Find a Grave, Memorial ID 46467258, accessed January 12, 2025, https://www.findagrave.com/memorial/46467258/wilson-k-drumheller.

Appendix A

Dr. Reuben H. Muth's Visiting Doctor's Journals

Volume	Period	Title	Publisher	City of Pub	Yr. Pub.	Notes
1	1858-1859	The Physicians Visiting List	Lindsay & Blakiston	Philadelphia	1858	Fredericksburg
2	1860	The Physicians Visiting List	Lindsay & Blakiston	Philadelphia	1860	Fredericksburg / Mahanoy
3	1861	The Physicians Visiting List	Lindsay & Blakiston	Philadelphia	1861	German news article in back mentioning his marriage to Louisa Deppen in German. "From Rehrersburg"
4	1862	The Physicians Visiting List	Lindsay & Blakiston	Philadelphia	1862	German script for name
5	1863	The Physicians Visiting List	Lindsay & Blakiston	Philadelphia	1863	
6	1864-1865	The Physicians Visiting List	Lindsay & Blakiston	Philadelphia	1864	
7	1866	The Physicians Visiting List	Lindsay & Blakiston	Philadelphia	1866	
8	1867-1868	The Physicians Daily Pocket Record	Medical & Surgical Reporter	Philadelphia	1867	
9	1869-1870	The Physicians Daily Pocket Record	Medical & Surgical Reporter	Philadelphia	1869	
10	1871-1872	The Physicians Daily Pocket Record	Medical & Surgical Reporter	Philadelphia	1871	
11	1873-1874	The Physicians Daily Pocket Record	Medical & Surgical Reporter	Philadelphia	1871	
12	1875 - Jan 1876	The Physicians Daily Pocket Record	Medical & Surgical Reporter	Philadelphia	1875	no entries for most of 1876
13	1877	The Physicians Visiting List	Lindsay & Blakiston	Philadelphia	1877	
14	1878	The Physicians Visiting List	Lindsay & Blakiston	Philadelphia	1878	
15	1879	The Physicians Visiting List	Lindsay & Blakiston	Philadelphia	1879	
16	1880	The Physicians Daily Pocket Record	Medical & Surgical Reporter	Philadelphia	1880	
17	1881	The Physicians Daily Pocket Record	Medical & Surgical Reporter	Philadelphia	1881	
18	1882	The Physicians Daily Pocket Record	Medical & Surgical Reporter	Philadelphia	1882	
19	1883	The Physicians Daily Pocket Record	Medical & Surgical Reporter	Philadelphia	1883	
20	1884	The Physicians Daily Pocket Record	Medical & Surgical Reporter	Philadelphia	1884	
21	1885	The Physicians Visiting List	P Blakiston & Son Company	Philadelphia	1885	
22	1886	The Physicians Visiting List	P Blakiston & Son Company	Philadelphia	1886	Dutch poem pasted in the back "I Wish I Was a Farmer"
23	1887	The Physicians Visiting List	P Blakiston & Son Company	Philadelphia	1887	
24	1888	The Physicians Daily Pocket Record	Medical & Surgical Reporter	Philadelphia	1888	
25	1889	The Physicians Daily Pocket Record	Medical & Surgical Reporter	Philadelphia	1889	
26	1890	The Physicians Daily Pocket Record	Medical & Surgical Reporter	Philadelphia	1890	
27	1891	The Physicians Visiting List	P Blakiston & Son Company	Philadelphia	1891	
28	1892	The Physicians Visiting List	UnK	UnK	UnK	Similar to 1891 - torn from binding
29	1893	The Medical News Visiting List	Lea Brothers & Co	Philadelphia	1892	
30	1894	The Medical News Visiting List	Lea Brothers & Co	Philadelphia	1893	
31	1895	The Medical News Visiting List	Lea Brothers & Co	Philadelphia	1894	
32	1896	The Physicians Visiting List	P Blakiston & Son Company	Philadelphia	1896	
33	1897	The Physicians Visiting List	P Blakiston & Son Company	Philadelphia	1897	
34	1898	The Physicians Visiting List	P Blakiston & Son Company	Philadelphia	1898	

Appendix B
List of Ephemera Items

Item	Date	Type	From	To	Description	Pub or Auth	Place	Note
1			S Lenker		Perscription with various roots and powders -- perhaps for an animal			
2		Note			Treatment for dysentary including opium			
3		Excuse			Owing to his feeble condition and to his physical inability to attend court			
4	6/17/1876	Ledger	J. P. Bohner	R. H. Muth	Church financial accounting of receivables and payables			
5	8/2/1876	Receipt	J. E. Kobel	R. H. Muth	$5 R.H. Muth Treasurer to pay Rev. A. R. Hottenstein			
6	8/7/1876	Receipt	D. Hill	R. H. Muth	$32 to the Treasurer of the Reformed Consistory of St. Peters Church at Mahanoy		Mahanoy	
7	10/26/1876	Receipt	J. R. Hilbush	R. H. Muth	$30 to the Treasurer of the Reformed Consistory of St. Peters Church at Mahanoy		Mahanoy	
8	1/16/1877	Receipt	D. Hill	R. H. Muth	$26.08 to the Treasurer of the Reformed Consistory of St. Peters Church at Mahanoy		Mahanoy	
9	2/24/1877	Receipt	J. E. Kobel	R. H. Muth	$125 to the Treasurer of the Reformed Consistory of St. Peters Church		Mahanoy	
10	8/29/1877	Promise	Abraham Ziegler	R. H. Muth	$6.15 for value received			
11	10/6/1877	Receipt	J. E. Kobel	R. H. Muth	$125 to the Treasurer of the Reformed Consistory of St. Peters Church		Mahanoy	
12	12/24/1879	Receipt	Mahanoy, Pa. Post Office	R. H. Muth	Registered mail receipt for letter sent to D.G. Brinton in Philadelphia		Mahanoy	
13	12/24/1883	Receipt	J. H. Muth	R. H. Muth	$5.97 possibly for auction items		Myerstown	
14	12/29/1885	Receipt	Mahanoy, Pa. Post Office	R. H. Muth	Registered mail receipt for letter sent to D.G. Brinton in Philadelphia		Mahanoy	
15	4/29/1886	Order	R.H. Muth	William Wood & Co.	2 Wood's Reference Hand-Book of the Medical Sciences		Lafayette Place	
16	9/1/1886	Order	R.H. Muth	William Wood & Co.	3 Wood's Reference Hand-Book of the Medical Sciences		Lafayette Place	
17	1888	Booklet			Avena Sativa: Preparations & Compounds	D.B. Keith & Co.	New York	
18		Invoice	A.B. Tressler & Co.		$5.92 in various dry goods		Mahanoy	
19	11/12/1888	Receipt	Isaac B. Tressler & Co.	R. H. Muth	$5.58 for ?		Northumberland Co.	
20	3/5/1890	Receipt	John Wyeth & Brother	R. H. Muth	$1.40 for hypodermics		Philadelphia	
21	12/27/1888	Invoice	The Philadelphia Record	R. H. Muth	Postcard invoice for $3.10 for 12 month subscription		Philadelphia	
22	1892	Booklet			Epilepsy	A G Selman, MD	Indianapolis	
23	1889-1892	Ledger			Tally of visits and medicine for a patient			
24	10/8/1892	Receipt	Isaac B. Tressler & Co.	R. H. Muth	$7.20 for one Holstine steer		Northumberland Co.	

List of Ephemera Items

Item	Date	Type	From	To	Description	Pub or Auth	Place	Note
25	10/2/1893	Invoice	Medical Department of the University of Pennsylvania		Dues invoice for membership		Philadelphia	
26	2/9/1895	Note	M. F. Middleton, M.D.		Instructions for treatment of neuralgia		Camden, NJ	
27	8/10/1896	Receipt	U.S. EX. CO.	R. H. Muth	$3.00 money order sent to Empire, NY			
28	Dec 1896	Invoice	Daniel Hetrich	R. H. Muth	$26 for professional service and med.		Mahanoy	
29			Alumni Society of the Medical Department of the University of Pennsylvania		Alumni Notes -- call for information		Philadelphia	
30	3/12/1923	Invoice	John O Kehres	Henry Muth	Invoice for a straw hat and repairs		Dornsife	Son of R.H. Muth
31	4/5/1923	Invoice	Edw. J. Otto	Henry Muth	$7.85 for 157 lb of oak planks		Herndon	Son of R.H. Muth
32	9/7/1923	Receipt	Lykens Valley Mutual Fire Insurance Company	H. D. Muth	Receipt for $2.41			Son of R.H. Muth
33	1/5/1924	Receipt	Herndon News	H. D. Muth	$1.50 for one month of news			Son of R.H. Muth
34	12/5/1924	Letter	John O Kehres	Henry Muth	Letter with invoice		Red Cross	Son of R.H. Muth

Appendix C
Statistical Summary

Volume	Year	Patients	Vists	Income	$/Vis	HH	V/HH	$/HH	OB:TOT	OB/HH
1	1858	277	465	$240.18	$0.52	94	4.95	$2.56	16	0.170
1	1859	231	461	$210.73	$0.46	86	5.36	$2.45	16	0.186
2	1860	338	613	$528.53	$0.86	150	4.09	$3.52	15	0.100
3	1861	479	1015	$897.85	$0.88	194	9.32	$4.62	20	0.103
4	1862	315	664	$612.08	$0.92	129	9.08	$4.74	8	0.062
5	1863	326	595	$577.26	$0.97	135	7.50	$4.28	20	0.148
6	1864	374	766	$559.50	$0.73	134	5.72	$4.18	13	0.097
6	1865	333	647	$492.10	$0.76	142	4.56	$3.47	20	0.141
7	1866	363	735	$715.09	$0.97	143	5.14	$5.00	18	0.126
8	1867	465	847	$865.82	$1.02	156	5.43	$5.55	20	0.128
8	1868	396	872	$863.65	$0.99	135	6.46	$6.40	11	0.081
9	1869	274	508	$513.50	$1.01	112	4.54	$4.58	18	0.161
9	1870	323	631	$619.70	$0.98	126	5.01	$4.92	23	0.183
10	1871	433	896	$788.45	$0.88	153	5.86	$5.15	16	0.105
10	1872	508	903	$804.60	$0.89	187	4.83	$4.30	20	0.107
11	1873	464	783	$728.69	$0.93	159	4.92	$4.58	22	0.138
11	1874	505	973	$961.75	$0.99	179	5.44	$5.37	34	0.190
12	1875	581	1110	$1,121.20	$1.01	190	5.84	$5.90	28	0.147
12	1876	8	14	$13.75	$0.98	7	2.00	$1.96	0	0.000
13	1877	497	869	$902.66	$1.04	174	4.99	$5.19	31	0.178
14	1878	433	757	$729.98	$0.96	169	4.48	$4.32	41	0.243
15	1879	411	751	$660.55	$0.88	152	4.94	$4.35	31	0.204
16	1880	388	770	$637.60	$0.83	144	5.35	$4.43	31	0.215
17	1881	382	808	$762.96	$0.94	142	5.69	$5.37	29	0.204
18	1882	370	738	$672.50	$0.91	138	5.35	$4.87	38	0.275
19	1883	317	566	$566.15	$1.00	144	3.93	$3.93	32	0.222
20	1884	291	595	$554.14	$0.93	116	5.13	$4.78	27	0.233
21	1885	386	756	$675.10	$0.89	155	4.88	$4.36	33	0.213
22	1886	425	767	$837.90	$1.09	161	4.76	$5.20	34	0.211
23	1887	307	562	$536.90	$0.96	131	4.29	$4.10	28	0.214
24	1888	382	696	$671.47	$0.96	150	4.64	$4.48	24	0.160
25	1889	387	768	$673.30	$0.88	123	6.24	$5.47	18	0.146
26	1890	390	804	$711.20	$0.88	134	6.00	$5.31	15	0.112
27	1891	332	661	$528.67	$0.80	110	6.01	$4.81	15	0.136
28	1892	352	781	$712.57	$0.91	111	7.04	$6.42	22	0.198
29	1893	356	773	$613.60	$0.79	121	6.39	$5.07	16	0.132
30	1894	254	542	$414.35	$0.76	96	5.65	$4.32	18	0.188
31	1895	216	507	$425.90	$0.84	80	6.34	$5.32	19	0.238
32	1896	202	463	$401.00	$0.87	77	6.01	$5.21	12	0.156
33	1897	188	416	$347.70	$0.84	69	6.03	$5.04	11	0.159
34	1898	129	287	$220.50	$0.77	61	4.70	$3.61	8	0.131
	TOT	14,388	28,135	$25,371.13	$0.90	5369	5.24	$4.73	871	0.162
	AVG	350.93	686.22	$618.81	$0.89	130.95	5.24	$4.73	21.24	0.162

www.ingramcontent.com/pod-product-compliance
Lightning Source LLC
Chambersburg PA
CBHW021319110426
42740CB00053B/3392